T0274796

WANT YOUR SELF

WANT YOUR SELF

Shift Your Self-Talk and Unearth the Strength in Who You Were All Along

KATIE HORWITCH

Sounds True
Boulder, CO 80306

Published 2023

Book design by Charli Barnes

Printed in Canada

BK06648

Library of Congress Cataloging-in-Publication Data
Names: Horwitch, Katie, author.
Title: Want your self : shift your self-talk and unearth the strength in who you were all along / by Katie Horwitch.
Description: Boulder, CO : Sounds True, 2023. | Includes bibliographical references. | Summary: "A book on women's empowerment through cultivating positive self-talk"-- Provided by publisher.
Identifiers: LCCN 2022058821 (print) | LCCN 2022058822 (ebook) | ISBN 9781649630742 (hardback) | ISBN 9781649630759 (ebook)
Subjects: LCSH: Self-talk. | Negativism. | Success. | Self-esteem in women.
Classification: LCC BF697.5.S47 H67 2023 (print) | LCC BF697.5.S47 (ebook) | DDC 158.1--dc23/eng/20230104
LC record available at https://lccn.loc.gov/2022058821
LC ebook record available at https://lccn.loc.gov/2022058822

10 9 8 7 6 5 4 3 2 1

For anyone who has ever felt that tiny flicker of an inkling inside that maybe, just maybe, they were enough all along.

And of course, for Dione.

CONTENTS

Prologue

THE NAVIGATION

We all do it.
I'm not good enough.

Not smart enough.

Not talented enough.

Not attractive enough.

I'm too sensitive.

Too awkward.

Too **much**.

Too much of **everything**.

The callous comments can come in crashing tidal waves or barely noticeable surface ripples. Belittling who we are, what we do, what we stand for, sometimes without even realizing it.

No big deal, you might think. *I'll get over it.*

But what if our thoughts, words, and feelings are all we are?

That's a pretty big deal.

And we won't "just get over it" . . .

We'll *become* it.

~

As I sit down to write this book, I know it can become one of two things: a *how-to* book, or a *you-already-know-how-to* book.

I choose the latter.

You've probably heard the stats somewhere. The average person has over 6,000 thoughts per day about themselves and the world around them.[1] We see up to 10,000 ads per day that bank on our desire to change who we are so we'll buy a given product or service.[2] And you don't need a fancy degree or extensive research to know those stats to be true: you only need to be a human walking through the world to notice how surrounded we are 24/7 by tasks, tropes, and taglines that reinforce that we're *broken beings* that *need to be fixed.*

There's no one singular entity to blame. We live in a culture that's largely engineered, both consciously and subconsciously, by conversations and campaigns and what's conceded as par for the course, to discourage us from being the person we *know* we're meant to be—the person we were put on earth to be but forgot to tend to along our journey. That paradigm prefers we stay disempowered and distant, angry and alone, fearful and fickle, so it can continue to sell us the solutions it's peddling. We're convinced we need to hide our lows, and we're coerced into hitting such highs that crashing becomes inevitable. We're given Band-Aids and bruises in a vicious cycle and then we're left wondering why it all hurts so much.

Cover up your quirks. Anti-age your wisdom. Swipe left, left, left.

And then we're told the kicker: it's Just How Things Are.

Is it any surprise, then, that our default M.O. is to focus on the extremes—high-highs and low-lows—swinging back and forth until we become dizzy?

It all feels like too much. But we don't have adequate words to describe our emotions or tools to deal with our self-diminishing inner demons . . .

. . . so we become fluent in a language we never intended to learn: negative self-talk.

Self-talk is the story we tell ourselves, about ourselves, as we walk through the world. *Negative* self-talk is when the story becomes dark: a story we tell that belittles who we are or what we do.

This story, you might say, feels *bad.*

And so this feeling, you might think, can be solved by replacing *bad* with *good.*

Let me tell you—if it was that straightforward, we wouldn't be here together right now.

This is not a book about badness or goodness. I've spent fifteen years writing about, speaking about, interviewing about, studying, questioning, and generally obsessing over the intricacies of self-talk and so-called positivity. I wrote this book because there was so much that I rarely heard people talking about, let alone practicing. I noticed patterns in the words and tactics being used over and over again in the name of self-love and positivity—meditations, mantras, looking on the bright side, talking yourself up as you look in the mirror—the list goes on. Good and well-intended tactics that worked, for some people, sometimes. We'll even talk about a few of them later.

But the deeper I dug over the years, the more I noticed that people would say those feel-good moments were often fleeting. They ultimately seemed to lead people right back to where they started, wanting to be another way and another Self than the one they were. What's worse, they'd feel like there was something wrong with *them.* Yes, these fleeting feel-good moments would often lead people into something longer lasting, but not exactly what they intended: a lingering sense of self-doubt, or worse, self-loathing.

If you keep heading down the same path and keep getting where you don't intend to be, that doesn't mean you're doing anything wrong. It means there are other roads you're yet to navigate, and other tools to help you get there. Somewhere, there's another road, taking you down another path, leading you to the place you *know* is there in the distance. Because of course you know it is. If you didn't, you wouldn't feel it in your bones and keep trying to get there.

The Process

Shifting your self-talk is a two-part process: shifting your *self*, and shifting your *talk*. Whether it's affirmations, the proverbial talk-to-yourself-like-you-would-your-best-friend, or some other words-based strategy, you're usually encouraged to jump to the *talk* part—especially if you're struggling with negative self-talk.

Two problems with that advice:

1. **Not everyone's self-talk shows up as words.** Some people don't have an inner monologue, and their "self-talk" doesn't show up as "talk" at all. Instead, they experience their self-told story through abstract visuals or feelings. Some people even say it plays out like a movie in their mind. If you're one of these people, and you're being told to start shifting your self-talk by replacing one word or phrase with another word or phrase, you'll likely feel lost, defeated, or just plain *nothing*, because you weren't starting with words and phrases to begin with.
2. **"Positive self-talk," as we commonly think of it, can do more harm than good depending on your state of mind.** There's a study out of the University of Waterloo that I'm fascinated by: First, they surveyed a group of people with either low or high self-esteem who regularly used "positive self-statements" to pump themselves up, believing they worked wonders. Next, they had those subjects repeat similar "positive self-statements" to themselves. The results were . . . a little different. People with low self-esteem felt *worse* after saying these positive statements than before they said them—but the people with preexisting high self-esteem were more likely to feel *better*. This form of "positive self-talk" was helpful to the people who needed it least and hurtful to the people who needed it most.[3]

No, you can't skip straight to the *talk* part. In order to make real, lasting changes, you must start with what's at the heart of your self-talk story: the *self* part.

And then there's the urgency of it all. I believe that shifting your self-talk is so much more than simply a subject that belongs in the self-help section of search engines and bookshelves (even though, let's call it like it is, you probably found this book in the self-help section of wherever you bought it). I believe in the urgency of the shift, not just the logistics: The story we tell ourselves *about ourselves* both directly and indirectly informs how we walk through the world. And how we walk through the world sets the stage for how others do the same. I believe that shifting your self-talk is the missing puzzle piece that we're *still* not talking about when it comes to putting out our global fire and unbreaking our collective heart.

As a forever front-row kind of student (apologies to all my classmates for all the times I asked our teacher "Do we have any homework tonight?" when there clearly was none intended until I asked), I'd love to think we learn best from lesson plans and classrooms—but it's not true.

We learn best from *each other*.

We learn how to Be in large part from the way we each walk through the world and the conversations we have about it. Including the conversations we have with our Selves, about ourselves, which inevitably trickle out into the world, creating a ripple effect.

You've come to the right place to get a new conversation—and ripple—started.

Want Your Self

A disclaimer: This book isn't meant to "fix" you. It's meant to *unearth* you. There are no stories, tools, or exercises in here that require you to access anyone other than the person you've been all along. *Because that's the exact person this world needs.*

Even if your surroundings suggest otherwise, please know that the world wants you to be your fullest, truest self. Heck, it's the reason you're here—to be fully and unquestionably YOU. It doesn't need another so-and-so. It doesn't need an army of carbon copies thinking the same things and feeling the same feels. It needs YOU. There's a reason the world gives you opportunities to be the You *you know* you're meant to be, every single day. Nothing about who you are is anything less than on purpose.

The stories you'll read in here are mine, but hopefully, they're yours too. I've been told that my journey is "all over the place." Do I believe this? Not really—or at least not in the way it's meant. I've had careers as an actor, writer, editor, fitness instructor, mindset coach, podcast host, and more—many of them at the same time. If I truly am "all over the place," I see it as a strength. The more places I go, the more I see. The more I notice, the more I learn. The more tools I gather, the more chances I get to use them. The more patterns I notice in the systems we've subscribed to, the more opportunities I notice to do things differently. My path—and yours too—is so many steps sewn together. Each micro-moment matters and helps shape our self-told story. I don't see that as "all over the place." I see it as open eyes and a story spread wide.

I'm not a doctor or clinical psychologist. What I am, though, is a Professional Noticer. My expertise lies not in knowing all the answers, but taking in and processing the world around me, and communicating it in a way that hopefully helps you ask better questions. It's point-zero-percent of a surprise to me that even as a proud introverted personality type, I've spent my professional life showing up in places and spaces where so many strive to be seen: from fitness studios and theatre stages to workshops and coaching sessions, the quest to figure out who we really are has always drawn me in.

What I've noticed is that when people show up seeking some sort of change—whether that's a major revelation, a small shift in the way they feel that day, or just a second of connection—they're usually met with generalizations and clichés about how all of us *are* or *aren't* all the time. Phrases like "We all have the same 24 hours in a day," "How you do anything is how you do everything," or even "If it was easy, everyone would do it" might resonate in the moment, but there's not a whole lot of personalization or nuance to them. There are many things I personally don't do that would probably be very easy to do if I chose to do them, many things that come easily to me that don't come easily to others, and many things others find super easy that I consider a massive struggle. Vague universal quantifiers like these can create a goodness hierarchy and leave us wondering: *What does this say about me?* And when left to fill in blanks on information we've yet to fully grasp, our best guess isn't always our best bet.

So we keep on guessing.

But your Self is not meant to feel so fleeting.

What my experience has shown me, over and over, is that there's a better way to make shift happen in your life—one that goes beyond self-improvement blanket statements. Not everything needs to be as catchy as a social media post. I'd even argue that the more nuanced and dialed-in a shift is, the more durable it will be.

~

This isn't a book of feel-good mantras or quick fixes. It's a call to action for your Self and a remembering of who you truly are. It will ask you to rethink the way you define and strive for self-love and confidence and positivity, not so that you can flip a switch and make it *all better forever and ever,* but so you can know what you're fighting for. What WE are fighting for. Together, we can start to speak a language that moves us forward through the Just How Things Ares of life, and usher in a new conversation about the conversations we have.

As you move through this book, you'll notice there are questions to ask yourself and exercises to work through. If you'd prefer to soak it all in, process the journey as a whole, and revisit them individually later, I've included an appendix at the end so you can easily find and come back to them. If they speak to you in the moment and you can't wait to dive in, feel free to go for it. The "right" way to read this is the way that's right for you.

Some new information in here might drop your jaw or jab your heart, but I truly believe that the best work and the best art uncovers what we already know but somehow forgot along the way. You're recognizing pieces of yourself, even if you can't pinpoint what exactly those pieces are.

And so, as you read through these pages, as you feel things deeply and fully and maybe your heart starts to pull a little, please know it's because you're coming face-to-face with the fullest, truest version of YOU. The one who knows things in your gut before you know them in your head and heart. The one who sees the light and the dark and chooses to examine not only both, but also everything in between. You don't need to look the other way, or be someone you're not. You never did.

When you start to feel something stir—stop and notice it. That's *you.*

Acknowledge the person who's emerging from hiding.

It's your Self.

It was there all along.

And your Self is worth not just finding, being, and staying. . . .

Your Self is so very—*very*—worth wanting.

Part One

YOU NEED A SELF

FIND YOUR SELF

BE YOUR SELF

STAY YOUR SELF

WANT YOUR SELF

Chapter One

THE MISINTERPRETATION

Isn't it funny—not *ha-ha* funny, more like *hmmm* funny—how our very first memories hold little pieces of buried treasure, often telling our story before we've begun?

It's 1991: I'm four years old and I'm standing in the center of my preschool classroom. I'm looking up at the newly created corkboard of student art that's just been unveiled before outdoor playtime. My arms are bare. My hair is tied half-up-half-down. My thick bangs skim my eyebrows. And I'm obsessed with all things Ariel.

The Little Mermaid is a cornerstone piece of cultural content for any baby-of-the-'80s, child-of-the-'90s. A seminal piece of work. A pièce de résistance, if you will. And I'm definitely not talking about the terrifying 1837 Hans Christian Andersen version that your great-great-grandmother read. You know, the one where—spoiler alert—the mermaid dies of a broken heart, dissolves into sea foam, and turns into literal air until she does good deeds for 300 years and can go to heaven. Do three centuries' worth of selfless acts or die and blow away forever. A fun bedtime story about blackmail for the kiddos of yore.

Nope—I'm talking about the G-rated Disney version, where the mermaid is named Ariel, and she's got a talking fish named Flounder as a BFF, and there's a worrywart crab named Sebastian who doubles as a glorified babysitter. In this more uplifting, more hopeful 1989 tale, Ariel gets her prince, gets her legs, and has a killer singing voice to boot. She sings of longing for more, and then she gets it. The walking, the running, the play-all-day-in-the-sunning. Ariel wants it all. And Ariel gets it all.

Just like almost every other stereotypical little girl in 1991, *The Little Mermaid* is my obsession. And Ariel, the one who gets it all, is my *icon*.

~

You know how people talk about getting back to who you were "before the world told you who to be"? That time during childhood when you felt wild and free and unaffected by society?

I never experienced that. I have no recollection of being wild and free, and none of being unaffected by society. I never really cried as a baby, or so I'm told. I don't think it was because nothing affected me. It was more like *everything* affected me. I was too busy observing and soaking in every little detail of the world to waste time on tears. My childhood wasn't notably traumatic or burdensome—I was just born with a head and heart that cared intensely from Day One. If my default was ever wild and free, I certainly don't remember it.

I was also born with what a yoga teacher once told me is called *high proprioception*, which means that I can literally feel my body in space. I can *feel* my skin on my muscles on my bones. I can *feel* how much space I take up just by standing still. I don't need to gaze into a mirror to know how I look, and I notice sensations in my body before any signs or symptoms bubble up. Psychologist Elaine Aron calls this being a *Highly Sensitive Person*, which essentially means I see things others can't and feel things others don't.[1] I can feel your emotions without hearing a word. What kind of day has it been? I'll know before you even say hello. Bright lights send my nervous system into overdrive, and a motorcycle revving its engine outside my window leaves me rattled for a good ten minutes. Crowded subway cars aren't just annoying; they're aggressive to every single one of my senses. I notice how the world affects me before I have words to describe what's happening. I am, essentially, a Professional Noticer. Always have been. Always will be.

My main outlet to interpret all my noticing as a child was art. I started drawing full faces and figures before most kids learned that crayons are for holding, not chewing. Grown-ups were in awe, marveling at my "creativity" and "talent." They often asked me questions like:

> How did you know to draw her arm around him like that?
>
> How did you know to draw her hand resting on his shoulder in that way?
>
> How did you know to make them look at each other with that specific look?

I didn't understand what the big deal was. It all felt so obvious . . .

> *I **notice** how your hugs linger with me way after you've left,* I thought.
>
> *I **sense** how your arms wrap around me tightly and how that makes me feel inside.*
>
> *I **see** how you look at each other, and at me, and at the world, and I know what it all means, whether you say it or not.*
>
> *I'm not being creative.*
>
> *I'm being truthful.*

~

Cut back to my preschool classroom in 1991. My teachers have been admiring my artwork for the entire year and have bestowed upon me the highest honor: the duty of creating the *Classroom Art Corkboard.*

For those of you not familiar with the deeply revered Classroom Art Corkboard: In most classrooms from preschool to sixth grade or so, there's an oversized corkboard hung on the wall displaying students' work. When you're almost a teen, it showcases book reports and math equations. When you're old enough to put writing to your daydreams, it's poems and imagined landscapes from prompts given to the whole class. And when you're in your first few years of life, it's doodles and drawings all set to a theme.

No matter the age or stage, teachers take great care to decorate each corkboard with colors and cutouts to represent whatever's being featured. The Classroom Art Corkboard doesn't always display art per se, but is always a piece of art itself—a shape-shifter, changing by the month, if not the week—and a well-executed corkboard can signal to both students and parents that *this* is the class to be in. This class is *special.*

Our art project's theme for this particular week in 1991 is "Under the Sea." My class will be creating an oceanscape together by drawing, splattering, and finger-painting our way to a crowd-sourced Pacific Ocean. And, as both my class's top artist and biggest Ariel fangirl, my teacher has asked if I'd be interested in creating the official themed adornment to decorate the corkboard. She would love some sea creatures to be floating around in the ocean, she says. Would I like to draw the characters from *The Little Mermaid*?

Would I ever!!!

This is a four-year-old artist's equivalent to being offered a residency at The Met or the Louvre. This is my *moment.*

I sketch, I color, and once I'm done, my teacher whisks away the oversized piece of butcher paper I've been using as my canvas to cut out each individual figure from the sheet, making sure not to lop off an arm or a fin or a meticulously drawn finger.

A few days later, I find myself looking up at the newly created "Under the Sea" corkboard that's just been revealed before recess. My arms are bare, free of the long sleeves that make me squirm because I can feel wisps of my arm fuzz get tangled each time they're shoved into a fabric prison. My hair is tied half-up-half-down, accented by a purple scrunchie I love because it's 1991 and of course I do. My thick bangs skim my eyebrows, blocking my upper periphery vision, so all I can see is what's ahead and below.

And so I cock my head up, and I see it. Two feet above lives my work: a life-sized-to-me Ariel, Flounder, and Sebastian alongside a seahorse and a turtle, plus a smattering of orange cardboard fish and tissue-paper seaweed strands the teacher has added for ambience. The class-made ocean flows below my hand-drawn creatures. A cacophony of finger smudges and scribbles and glitter glue stand in as sand. My teacher has written "Under The Sea" in brown Crayola marker in the corner.

I walk slowly toward the corkboard. The water is so beautiful. And I can't help but notice if it wasn't for the seaweed, and if it wasn't for Ariel and Sebastian and their marine-life friends, it might just look like a page of blue-green glitter scribbles. But all together, it creates an ocean.

I feel pride in my work, awe that I was "chosen," and a sense of purpose that I helped it all come together.

"KATIE."

Snap. My trance is broken. The teaching assistant is standing over me sternly.

"We're leaving. GET BACK IN LINE."

~

We're told the big, sweeping moments are the ones that will define our lives: the school we attend, the subject we major in, the person we marry (or don't), how many kids we have (or don't). We're told there's a dream plan with dream boxes to check off, and that those dream boxes all checked off are what make a dream life.

But I don't believe in a life made up of checkboxes. I don't believe it's the big things that tell our story. I believe it's the small, everyday occurrences that make us who we are. In the tiny micro-moments, we're presented with our biggest life choices. And in our interpretation of them, we decide not only who we are, but who we'll be.

The teaching assistant's four-second scolding in that early memory rattled me like a motorcycle crashing through my consciousness. I could have told someone and smashed that shame right away, but this was my first experience with shame, and I didn't yet know that shame cannot survive being spoken (I would learn that about three decades later from Brené Brown and her book *Daring Greatly*).[2]

And so I stayed silent. Those four seconds would lodge their way into my head and heart, revving over and over again on loop. The reverberation would last a lifetime.

Here is what I remember: I remember shrinking back and scurrying toward the door, holding back tears. I remember wanting to cry but not wanting to look like a whiner (no one likes whining). I remember feeling foolish. Because in my moment of awe and self-appreciation, I hadn't realized the class was filing into a neat and tidy line to go out onto the playground. I remember noticing the teaching assistant's energy—exasperated, angry, sharp like a knife—and the way she talked *at* me, not *to* me. I remember feeling deep shame for looking as if I'd intentionally ignored authority. ME! I, Katie Horwitch, a cautious and considerate over-feeler, hyper-noticer, and rule-follower, was scolded for getting swept off my feet by my own art, for not noticing that my class was leaving without me, and for being very, very bad at following the rules.

On that day, in that micro-moment, I decided my talents and strengths were for others to enjoy and benefit from, not for me. I decided it was wrong to take pride in myself and my strengths, and that doing so would get me in trouble. I needed to create, create, create, but only for others. Never for myself. My currency was my extraordinary-ness, I deduced—and just like Ariel would sell her voice to the sea witch for a chance to have it all, I would need to give my gifts in order to be loved. I needed to stay in line and move from one success to another, leaving them in a trail like breadcrumbs for others to follow in case they wanted more from me. And, of course, I needed to always follow the rules, so I'd never get left behind.

I didn't lose my confidence in that moment, but the lens I viewed that confidence through became scratched and dusty. Looking through that blurry lens, my self-image began to form. My highly sensitive Professional-Noticer-In-The-Making began to see proof around me that reinforced my new thesis: that confidence was synonymous with vanity, that power was synonymous with pettiness, and a potential mistake was always around the corner. I saw it in the TV shows I watched, the magazines I stole from my mom's monthly subscription stash, and most of all, the conversations I eavesdropped on between family members, friends, and total strangers.

Things like:

- Hearing the word "selfless" used as a compliment to describe women who sacrificed who they were for the sake of other people's comfort and success—women who were less of their Self so someone else could be more of theirs.
- Overhearing people gossip about powerful women in the media, referring to them as "bitches" or "full of themselves."
- Glancing down at a neon, seemingly progressive-for-the-90s magazine sitting in the waiting area at my mom's hair salon that made the bold move of using the word "ambitious" on its cover. A small mention buried by inches of talk about fixing trouble spots, making good impressions, and formulating yourself into someone who was meant to please men. (Confidence was fine, as long as it was a means to pleasing someone else.)
- Hearing so, so many iterations of "I'm sorry" scattered throughout my day as I racked my brain trying to figure out what exactly had been done by the sorry-sayers to warrant an apology.

These were not just one-off occurrences, I realized. This was a way of life.

The story I wrote for myself starting at four years old was that I had to be the most talented, the most beautiful, the most extraordinary, and the most perfect—but could never stop to smell the proverbial roses in my own garden. I became humble out of fear of being wrong, not out of faith in the fact that I was right all along just by being Me.

I would continue to build that story, sentence by sentence, moment by moment, by my own internal narrative: my self-talk.

Self-Talk

Self-talk is how we tell our story.

It's the narrative we've got on loop 24/7 that tells us who we are and who we should be. Think of each thought, each epiphany, each question and conclusion like rules of linguistics. When used over and over, they form patterns that shape our communication. Our self-talk patterns are like mental muscles that are constantly being strengthened by each aspiration and each inspiration. Together, those muscles form a language in which we are constantly becoming ever more fluent.

Negative self-talk is where the story takes a dangerous turn: our self-narrated autobiographies become a stream of chapters telling us we're not good enough, smart enough, kind enough, or *enough* enough to be ourselves out in the world. Negative self-talk is the story we tell ourselves, and tell others *about* ourselves, that belittles who we are or what we do. The scariest thing is that talking negatively about ourselves has become so common and such a standby for many of us that, many times, we don't even realize we're doing it.

The repercussions of a language built on negative self-talk are harsh and long-lasting, although sneaky and barely noticeable in the moment. It's a cultural virus that spreads under the radar and affects everything we do: we limit ourselves, our relationships, our bodies, and our worth by latching onto these default phrases that leech their way into and onto our minds—a vernacular that keeps us in a safe zone of stagnation. It sneaks up and distracts us, convincing us we're doing something to activate positive and permanent change in our lives.

Dwelling on our self-perceived flaws, shortcomings, and everything that's "holding us back" feels like a safe-enough step to take toward living the life we envision. We're thinking about it, so that counts for something—right?

The problem is that *thinking about* doing something is very different from *literally* doing something. Getting caught up in the drama of it all requires a finite amount of investment, without requiring us to do anything differently at all.

And so we *don't* change. **We get addicted to the problems instead of freed by the solutions.**

It's not like we mean to be so mean to ourselves. But it's become easy. It's become normalized. And hey, *everyone else does it.* We've created a norm where sharing our negative stories is how we bond. It's how we connect. Over our problems. Over our limitations.

What if, though, negative self-talk isn't all that we perceive it to be?

What if self-talk isn't even inherently good or bad?

What if it's all simply . . . information?

And what if noticing and deciphering that information holds the key to not only finding, being, and staying yourself . . . but also actually *wanting* the Self you've been granted in this lifetime, instead of constantly striving to be someone else?

What if all this time, we've been misinterpreting the language of the land?

~

We are who we believe ourselves to be. That belief system is based in and around our internally told story. My theory is that self-talk is what we make of it; we're just taught to make it something that ultimately doesn't serve us.

I have spent so very long in a battle between beliefs. All you need to be is a human in the world to know what it means to walk through that battle every day. You collect your armor, you study your strategies, and if you fail to plan, you plan to fail. All the while, the reverb keeps buzzing in your head and heart like a passing motorcycle. The TV shows. The social media feeds. The whispered or yelled conversations. Threatening to steal your power and your purpose word by word, because the world would prefer you to stay small and silent.

Sometimes the voices and the pages and the screens that shrink and scapegoat you win. Sometimes they control your belief-du-jour. Sometimes you might feel yourself turning into evaporated sea foam, disappearing into the air, bound to lifetimes of serving others as you remain invisible.

But through it all, you can feel a tug.

There is a voice inside you that knows who you are.

We all have that voice.

I am a product of the women who came before me, the women who walk around me, and the woman the universe designed me to be.

I am my mother—my first physical link to the world—and my two grandmothers, the links tying me to my lineage. I am my college professors, I am the cool girls who sat at the back of the middle school bus, I'm the bullied girls who cried their way home. I am my preschool teaching assistant telling me to get back in line. I am each friend, each colleague, each client, and each coach. I am the amalgam of so many who have come before me and sat beside me. And you are too. We are all not just one, but so many in disguise.

Yet with all the misinterpretation—all the noise, all the voices, all the people you've met and people you didn't even know left their mark—there is a voice inside that *knows.* And that knowing is not who you were before the world told you who to be (because even *that* interpretation assumes you're some kind of before-and-after project). That voice, that knowing, is the You *you* know you're meant to be, right now and always.

You must be brave enough to do the work that lets your Self live out loud.

Chapter Two

FROZEN IN TIME

It's not enough to just have a Self. You need a *sense* of Self. A strong one.

Why? Because if you're not intentional about creating one on your own, the world around you will swoop in and create one for you, on its own timeline, following its own rules. When it does, the actions you take and the language you speak will be a reflection of this fabricated self, this person who's been conjured up with a singular goal: fitting in.

If you're not clear on who you are, the world will sure as hell seize the opportunity to tell you who to be.

Here's the thing about your Self: She's malleable, yet ever-present. Fluid, but steadfast. Your Self is strengthened and sculpted in the micro-moments of life—but the macro vision of who you are and what you stand for is already deep inside you. Those tiny details can either help set your Self free, or keep it locked away.

You don't have a choice as to *every* micro-moment that plays out on the stage of your life, but you do have a choice as to whether or not you examine them. Whether or not you ask questions about the Self this world is trying to craft for you, or if instead you tell yourself it's Just The Way Things Are.

If those tiny-but-mighty unexamined micro-moments start to build up in your head and in your heart, you might begin to believe you're not capable of *making shift happen* in your life. And moreover, you might become convinced that if you *are* going to shift something—anything at all—it's got to be dictated by someone else.

Clay

I'm eight years old, and my parents have found an after-school art class for me to attend called The Art Experience. Every Tuesday and Thursday, I walk through a gate somewhere deep in the Valley of Los Angeles into an ivy-lined backyard and through the door of a mudroom that's been converted into a classroom for kids aged five to twelve. Sometimes we use Mod Podge to decoupage frames or boxes. Sometimes we all sit silently and analyze seashells, transferring our noticing to the page with our charcoal pencils. Sometimes we even sketch portraits of each other, and sometimes I get lucky and get paired with my art-class crush, who looks exactly like Andrew Keegan in *Camp Nowhere*, which I definitely haven't seen but like to pretend I have to seem cooler than I am. I don't even know if I think Andrew Keegan is cute or not, but he's plastered on all the *Tiger Beat* magazines I pretend to like when I have playdates with the Cool Girls in my class, so anyone who looks like him seems like a good idea for a crush, if "a crush" is the thing you're supposed to have to be cool. I've already been pretending for a while, so pretending to have crushes is a walk in the park. The pretending women do starts early.

Once a month, the art teacher covers a plastic picnic table with a tarp and brings out block upon block of wet, gray clay. I *love* Clay Day. I love everything about the clay. I love how it smells: like the hills behind my house the morning after it's rained. I love the color: a cool asphalt that morphs to a matte off-white as it cakes on my fingers and dries on my bare arms. I love how mysterious it is: a mish-mosh of unidentifiable minerals, harder to see than sand but large enough to identify.

We're encouraged to wear smocks and gloves on Clay Day, but I prefer to dig in full force—one of the *only* times I actually delight in getting messy.

Something that's vital to know about clay: when you're sculpting with a clump of raw material, you're instructed to "score" the bottoms and sides of pieces that you want to meld together. A handle to a cup. A head to a body. An arm to a menorah. Taking an oversized needle, you whisk short lines across the clay's different parts—the idea being that once the scored pieces meet, they're more likely to stay together than if the surfaces were smooth. The tiny peaks and valleys fuse, grabbing onto each other and merging their jagged edges to their deep crevices. If you try and mold one flat surface to another, as beautiful and perfect as the flat planes of clay might look, they'll fall apart instantly. The roughness is key for connection. It's in the roughness that the piece transforms.

Another thing that's vital to know: as you score, it's essential to always have a dish of water nearby. You keep your hands damp as you sculpt and you score to make sure the clay doesn't dry out. Because only wet clay that's been scored can fuse together to create strength. A big gray block of clay doesn't dry quickly per se, but it also doesn't dry as slowly as you think it would. Wait too long to score the ends, and you'll end up with flakes and cracks instead of ridges and dips.

Dried clay isn't moldable anymore—it's frozen in time.

Dione

Art has always been important to my family. Not just the appreciation of art, but the act of creating it. I got my artistic skills from my grandmother, my Gammy, Dione.

Dione was a true artist. And not like a *she-made-cute-cards-for-us-on-our-birthdays* kind of artist or *she-decorated-the-Christmas-tree-the-best-which-is-a-feat-for-anyone-but-especially-for-someone-who-is-fully-Jewish* kind of artist. A legit, canvas-painting artist. The quality of artist you read about in school or see in museums. Dione never sold her paintings, and I don't think she ever even tried. Creating art was for her own enjoyment. The halls of the big, beautiful house she and my grandfather shared were covered in her artwork, alongside David Hockney prints and professional family portraits. A Dione Original was just as valuable in my family as any pricey piece sold abroad or at auction. Embedded in the layers of each painting, there was also a little bit of her.

Dione loved me fiercely. She loved to tell the story of how, when I was a baby, she couldn't walk out of the room without me wailing for her. "You wouldn't even let me use the toilet!" she'd laugh. Such vast contrast to everything else I hear about how I was and how I've always been: A highly sensitive sponge who thrives on her own. A quiet, calm introvert who prefers playing by herself in silence for hours. Cuddly on the borderline of clingy, but rarely ever needy. Hugs are my Love Language, but I've never demanded another's presence to keep me entertained. Solitude was always how I gained my strength—the less time I had alone, the less stable I felt around others.

Apparently, though, Gammy leaving was just too much for me to handle. We all have our tipping points.

Clay doesn't just *happen*. There's usually water, air, or steam involved—something to keep the mineral deposits moving and morphing. And time. Always time. Something to erode and transform the rocks and soil from what they once were into what they will be. A volcano. A river. Unrelenting elements, merging together particles of the past and present to create something at once entirely different and completely the same. Smooth rocks, broken into shards, pulverized into bits, and delivered to us as a whole new package. Under a microscope, it's all still there. It's kind of mind-blowing that, under such specific conditions on loop, something can be so many things all at once.

My grandmother cared so very deeply. She expressed her care through her artwork, her gifts, her loving touch, her wide smiles—and also through her words, both praise and critique alike. Dione's softness and toughness weren't mutually exclusive. She had high standards for herself and for others. And while her softness often came out in her actions and the way she showed up for others with enthusiasm, her toughness usually came out in words that could feel abrasive, judgmental, or simply defeatist. She was deeply invested in appearances; her desire to feel a sense of belonging would reverberate in her offhand remarks about body size, manners, looks, and social standing. Sure, high-end brands and calendar invites counted, but even more than that, so did your everyday decorum and behavior. From standing posed for a photo one foot slightly in front of the other (hitting a neat 45-degree angle, heel-to-arch) to being able to carry an engaging conversation with your peers, I can only imagine that, to her, the way you presented yourself on the outside was a direct reflection of who you were on the inside. And if you didn't hit the proper marks, it wasn't the proper way to Be. Especially if you were a member of her family. *Especially* if she was applying those standards to herself.

I doubt this experience is anything less than universal: we often reserve our strongest opinions for those closest to us not only because we love them the most, but because we also see ourselves reflected in them. Call it criticism confused for care. "Worrying about" loved ones or sizing them up to others—their career, their relationships, their appearance, their choices—is the hallmark of so many relationships. Including the one we have with ourselves.

If it's true that we're the most critical of those closest to us, it makes perfect sense that the one who ends up bearing the brunt of our opinions is our Self. After all, who could be closer to you than *you*?

If I criticize myself, over and over, it must mean I care enough about myself to notice.

Because my grandmother was such a part of who I was, the river and rock that flowed before me, parts of me became like parts of her. As close as we were, as tied to her as I was—I picked up on everything. Without intending to, I picked up on the language she spoke—the same language so many other women around me spoke—and took it on as my own. I questioned how presentable I was: how mature, how attractive, how good, how worthwhile. I noticed the comparisons she'd make between people, women especially, and over time began to insert myself into the mix to try and get ahead of ending up on the lesser end of that comparison:

Am I pretty enough?

Smart enough?

Impressive enough?

Am I likable, or am I too much to handle?

If I don't give 110 percent every moment of every day, will I fade away?

I got what I later understood to be her self-questioning—but I put my own spin on it. While she veiled her self-questioning in judgment and criticism (of others and herself), my self-questioning showed up in the form of scarcity. If I didn't hit all my marks exactly so, I worried I'd somehow get demoted in the game of life.

To be clear, I also got my grandmother's love of beauty, culture, elegance, and family. Her dedication and devotion and deep way of loving. How easily she delighted. The emphasis she placed on showing up. Her giggle that bubbled over like champagne poured too quickly. And, of course, her artistic spirit. They don't all live in separate universes, the praise-worthy and the piercing. We can't always choose which traits we pick up from which people—and sometimes when we're close enough, we end up taking on them all.

~

"Gammy's really bad." A call from my mother and three missed calls from my brother made it clear. Within hours, I was flying across the country to sit by her side, singing her jazz standards while we were alone and "socializing," as much as socializing was possible, while family was with us in the room. An all-day event.

At one point my younger cousin Jenny and I broke away from the pack, choosing instead to squeeze ourselves together on one chair way too small for two humans (as we've done since she basically came out of the womb). We surveyed the room and looked at each other with wide eyes. There was my older cousin's newborn, rolling and giggling on the bed. My mom and aunt and other cousins (I have a lot of cousins) talking at decibels-too-loud-but-just-right-for-us levels and howling with laughter. My grandmother, in the center of it all.

"How *bizarre*," Jenny whispered.

It felt almost normal. Meant to be, even.

A room full of life—just with death looming.

My Gammy died four years ago. Four years that feel both like an eternity and just the other day. Ever since my grandfather Bill had passed a few years before that, she'd been a shell of herself, slowly collapsing inward into the vacant Billy-sized chasm left in her soul. No imminent health problems, no suffering through painful procedures to try and keep her alive. After four years without him, she was simply . . . done. As her granddaughter, with so much of her in so much of me, watching this decline felt like witnessing—and falling into—a deep state of melancholy.

And yet those last twenty-four hours will be seared in my memory for my entire life as sacred: a day of togetherness, laughter, song. Above all, joy. It was her middle name, after all. Joy. Same as mine. What I imagine might have been her one truest wish, granted—the core of her Self, coming alive and dancing in the air. She hadn't held a paintbrush in decades.

It's not my job to tell anyone else's story, and it's certainly not my job to make assumptions about them either. (My dad always says that to assume is to make an "ass" out of "u" and "me," which I've always thought of as one of the more delightfully groan-worthy Dad Jokes out there.) Early on, as I began my career as a writer, typing essays on Facebook and long posts on my blogs, I made a deal with myself to never tell a story that wasn't mine to tell. I don't know how to write well without writing personally, and as my personal writing transitioned into a more professional and therefore more public sphere, I realized that it wasn't only unkind to tell another's story—it was assuming a narrative I couldn't claim as truth. Nor did I want to.

That said, I feel a sense of obligation to my grandmother and to myself to do the deep, hard work of figuring out what it takes to reconfigure the stories and soul-language inside us all—the complex web of head and heart patterns that we've become fluent in without even knowing.

Emotional DNA

Emotional DNA, as performance coach Judy Wilkins-Smith says, is "a blueprint created by your ancestors, a set of decisions and events leading to patterns and outcomes. As your life unfolds, you end up repeating versions of these patterns that may have been created generations ago."[1] It's unconscious, repeated, and created by those who came before you and those who are all around you in this moment.

My Emotional DNA was molded like clay by the women around me—*all* of the women around me. I like to think of myself as a *femme*-molded team effort. As much of an impact as my father, grandfathers, and the many incredible men in my life have had on me, it was the women in my life, family and friends and teachers and more, who molded and shaped my womanhood like clay on a tarped picnic table, showing me what it means to be female in the world.

I learned how to be a leader. A nurturer. A friend. And I learned that you certainly don't give in and give up when challenged or questioned. If anything, you just pretend, when you need to, to get by.

I noticed that there was a lot of that. *Pretending* among women. Opinions stifled. Personalities muted. Strengths dimmed. I overheard it in conversations and saw it in movies. Pretending to be uncertain, submissive, selfless (which really means you've got *less Self*), and small. I gathered proof that confidence was *not* a socially desirable trait for women to have, and that I was supposed to be at the mercy of everyone else around me. It wasn't hard to collect that proof either. It was all around me, in swift asides and catchy headlines and the looks I'd notice from across the room. Each micro-moment reinforcing the next.

But that little voice inside me, that voice that knows (and *always* knows), told me that *nothing* was worth parting ways with my confidence over.

And so I carried my confidence with me like my own little secret, both ashamed of it and unwilling to let it go. The world was asking me to give in and give up that core essence of who I was, and I refused, even though I knew it would probably make my life easier to just follow along.

I became an expert at feigning humility, selflessness, modesty, and I-don't-matter-ness. But I knew in my bones that I mattered a great deal. I just needed to hide that part of myself as well as I could when I was out in public. *This is what will get me liked,* I told myself. *This is how I will belong.*

The problem with all that pretending is that when you do it for the majority of the time, it doesn't count as "pretend" anymore. I noticed that the loud, funny girls in my elementary school class started to "tone down" their personalities in front of the boys around fourth or fifth grade—and if they didn't, they'd often get into fights with them, so I started to view their silence and spark-less-ness as a protection mechanism. I noticed the adults in my life would talk about how "bad" they'd been that weekend regarding what they ate, even though I was a part of so many of their social gatherings (where we'd all join together as families, eat the best food, and laugh so hard we'd cry)—so I started to view food as something with either "good" or "bad" repercussions. I noticed in almost every TV show or movie I watched with my older cousins—who were way cooler than I was and therefore so were their *TV Guide* selections—that the confident female characters were often villainized when they walked into a party or down a school hallway with self-assuredness. The quiet ones usually ended up being the heroes, but only once they did something (or someone) to elevate their social status. I remember watching *Grease* for the first time and thinking it was so cool of Sandy to throw away the poodle skirts and bow ties and instead tease her hair and slip into spandex. I watch it now and cringe, and sometimes my heart breaks a little for the sweet blonde Olivia Newton-John, who was made to believe she needed to leave herself behind in order to be accepted. Because I'd started to believe it too.

As our collective game of pretend plays out, the lines get blurred between where the make-believe begins and ends. We immerse ourselves in our fabricated shame and guilt—the exact shame and guilt our culture benefits from.

And as we immerse ourselves, our talk follows suit.

Casual Negativity

Casual Negativity is what I call the automatic negative talk (self-talk and otherwise) that we use over and over again without thinking and without emotion attached—the kind we use so much so that it becomes a part of who we are.

When people talk about negative self-talk and shifting it, they'll usually say things like "Don't be so mean to yourself." As if we insult ourselves on purpose. But negative self-talk is a lens we interpret our Self through and a language we learn to speak unintentionally. We learn this just like we learn any other language: by internalization and immersion. And what better way to learn a language than by practicing the phrases we use most often?

If you're learning Spanish, for example, it's pointless to only practice in your head. You've got to get interactive. You practice by talking to people in simple, easy-to-understand ways.

Hello. Goodbye. I'm sorry. I'm well, thank you. And you?

becomes:

"Hola." "Adios." "Lo siento." "Muy bien, gracias. ¿Y tú?"

When you're learning self-talk, it's a different story. The words you say out loud must match the feelings in your heart.

And that's where things get lost in translation.

I want to fit in. I want you to like me. I'm hurt. Can we connect?

Morphs and masquerades as:

"I'm so weird." "I was so bad." "I don't care." "Why can't I get it together?"

Those self-disparaging phrases of comparison and censorship I'd heard all my life weren't confined to my own family and friends. This kind of talk is a *colloquial cultural epidemic*. And it's been passed down to us, from both those who came before us and those who are all around us now. Casual Negativity isn't a coincidence. It's a natural result of a bonding mechanism that we've used for decades, one where we take that self-deprecating, self-effacing, self-loathing self-talk and beam it back outward, reinforcing our own and others' self-judgment by vocalizing the Casual Negativity we've absorbed.

How many times have you joined in when your friends or family start criticizing themselves, "empathizing" by sharing what dissatisfies you about *yourself*? We use Casual Negativity—and hear it being used—all the time. What we don't realize is that the way we talk rubs off on others, making it seem commonplace and even *acceptable* to speak this way. Even when we don't realize we're speaking it. (Not that you needed studies to prove it, but studies have found that revealing shared negative sentiments can create a deeper feeling of closeness between people than revealing positive sentiments can.)[2]

Let's stick with the Spanish example. If you decided to go live abroad in a country where the vast majority of the population speaks Spanish as its primary language, you'd not only try your best to string together the phrases you know, but you'd probably also study during your stay, so that next time you were with a group of people, you could have a conversation. Language, after all, is such a large part of how we connect.

Is it any surprise, then, that Casual Negativity is so common? We immerse ourselves in it not because we want to be mean to ourselves, but because we want to speak the language others are speaking. It's a bonding tactic above all: we self-deprecate to relate.

But Casual Negativity isn't just how you bond with others—it's how you develop an unhealthy relationship with your Self. What might seem like a few negative comments here and there start to work their way into your verbiage and morph into a daily diatribe that's on loop both out in the open and under the surface. And most of the time, you probably don't even realize you're doing it. Sure, the internal negative self-talk that's on loop within us most of the time isn't great, but Casual Negativity is *especially* harmful. If this is what our *emotionless* self-talk sounds like, how can we ever expect to conquer the negative self-talk that's *filled* with emotion?

We rarely realize how often we use Casual Negativity. It happens so much that we don't know how to get out of the pattern.

And so we don't.

Sculpting Your Self

We are each clay—the remnants of those who came before us, both sharp and soft, made up of not only the DNA strands of our ancestors but the belief systems and values and fluent languages of everyone who's ever stood before or beside us. What will we be shaped into over time? To be determined. But the only way to truly become who we know we're meant to be is by embracing those jagged edges and deep crevices of profound feeling and unique perspective. They're not weaknesses or flaws—they're the scoring necessary to fuse together all the various unique forces that make you You, and create your Self.

Our culture looks down on emotional scoring. We're not supposed to have jagged edges, peaks, and valleys. We need to be perfect to fit in with the rest of the world, and if we're not perfect, we at least need to be the most curated, socially acceptable form of un-perfect possible, which is its own form of perfection itself. Unemotional, agreeable, soft, sweet, flat, pristine, and perfectly smooth—or a little rip here, an aesthetic tear there, no more, no less. And so we soften our edges and fill up our valleys so that all we're left with is a neutral plane.

But what people might not realize about clay pottery is that underneath the crescent handles and delicate detailing, there's a labyrinth of jagged edges fusing it all together. It's not beautiful because it's been smoothed out—**it's beautiful because it's embraced its edges.**

Yes, my grandmother was fluent in Casual Negativity, but I highly doubt she sought out to learn it. And while I don't intend to tell a story that's not mine, there are clues scattered along the way that might suggest how her story took shape. She was the product of a time when women couldn't get their own credit cards (until 1974), could be fired for being pregnant (1978), and weren't protected by any sort of sexual harassment laws (a term that wasn't even officially defined by the Equal Employment Opportunity Commission until 1980)—and that was just in the United States. This was a time when, legally, women could be refused service in English pubs for spending their own money (until 1982 in the UK), couldn't own their own homes in Ireland (1976), and could be exchanged for dowry in India (1961—even though it continued well after the Dowry Prohibition Act was passed).[3] These are just a few examples of the kind of world my grandmother lived in. My grandmother, and probably yours too, and your great-grandmother, and her mother before that, lived in a time when the world at large was violent toward women at worst, invalidating at best.

I wonder if somewhere along the way, women learned that if they were cruel to themselves first, then maybe, just maybe, the world's cruelty wouldn't hurt so much. Just The Way Things Are. No use questioning it.

~

You might not be able to remold your biological DNA—at least not just yet—but the language you use to tell your story is something you're able to reshape and retrain second by second. It's not just words or emotions: it's the fabric of your Self.

And unlike the physical stuff, the shifts you make when it comes to your emotional center are shifts that won't just affect the generations after you who will be looking to you for how to live their lives, but all the others around you who are taking cues from you as to what it truly means to *belong*. Because who we are isn't only shaped by DNA strands and ancestry factoids; it's shaped by the people around us. We have way more influence on each other than we even realize.

In a way, I think my life's quest to shift our self-talk as a society has been fueled by my belief that Dione deserved better from her generation. She deserved to have these kinds of self-aware and self-empowered conversations in *her* communities, starting when she was young. She deserved to sweep herself off her *own* feet before anyone else could.

She deserved to believe the words she painted on her lips with Chanel before she even opened her vanity drawer—colors with names like *Tempting Tangerine*, *Provocative*, *Rebelle*—instead of waiting for those words to work their magic via a red-rouge affirmation. She, at the very least, deserved her own credit card sooner than age forty-five.

But it wasn't her time. It wasn't her era. And from what I knew of her, it wasn't in her nature to make the choices to challenge her society.

As I share all this with you, I'm balancing the reality of multiple truths. Dione lived a life filled with travel, love, togetherness. She soaked up life like a sponge in warm water, like I soak up your emotions before you've said a word. And yet. If I'd asked her at the end if she would have done anything differently, I honestly don't know what she would have said. Whether that's because she wouldn't know what to say, or because she wouldn't have known anything different, will remain my own unsolvable mystery. She created her own world and was also a product of the world around her. Both can be true at the same time.

Before she died, she gifted my mother and me her old journals and photo albums. I was not prepared for what I found in them. No, not shocking family secrets (sorry, didn't mean to lead you on there). But intricate details describing the micro-moments in her life, combined with the photographic evidence. The thoroughness of this *life-log,* if you will, helped me see her in a way I never could have otherwise: as unmolded clay, a mish-mosh of minerals and particles of those who came before her and were all around her. As I read and looked and noticed each micro-moment, I saw her evolve from childhood into teendom into her early twenties. And what I noticed was a woman who was just the same at nineteen—the year she met my grandfather and was swept off her feet—as she was at ninety. A new wife and a new mother and newly-inducted adult-life-liver while her girlhood was still vying for her attention. Frozen in time like clay not yet finished.

I think about her death, and I start to get angry. Angry that she won't be here anymore. Angry that I get to live on and succeed and fail and laugh and cry and experience so much I can't tell her about, stuff that she no longer has the chance to experience. And then I feel silly, as I remember all the people I've loved and lost at ages and stages way too soon. *How foolish of me*, I think, *to be angry that a ninety-year-old doesn't get to experience this world anymore.*

But it's not because of her age that I think this way; it's because of all the healing and liberation I hoped she'd live to see. In my conviction to shift the self-talk paradigm of our society, I thought that maybe I could help shift something in *her* as well. Or even if not shift *her*, I could help heal her lineage, and that would be quite something; a quite-something she'd be around to see. I know, I know—proverbial old dog, proverbial new tricks. Once all the negative self-talk you've learned is in your system, it's a struggle to shift it. That's why most people don't. And most people aren't ninety years old, with ninety years of self-talk steeped into their system.

As strong as she was, Dione was still human. Her strength didn't show up like my strengths, or my mother's strengths, or my aunts' strengths, or my cousins' strengths. They were all her own. She was a collection of high-highs, low-lows, and everything in between, shaped by every micro-moment that had been pulverized into fine particles and sculpted her into who the world told her she needed to be.

I know and always knew my grandmother loved me fiercely. More than just how a grandparent is supposed to love their grandchild, or at least that's what it felt like. I used to think it was because of a special collection of reasons and similarities. A shared love of beauty. Art. Culture. Family. Conversation. Giggles.

But once I began digging into her old journals, I started to realize that her love for me might have also been a sort of longing. I was maybe the kind of person she would have been in her alternate life, if she'd been born in a different time, with a different world molding her, with a culture embracing her edges instead of flattening them out to be Just So. As beautiful and rich of a life as she lived, I have to wonder what kinds of pages she might have turned if her world had told her other stories.

In her book *Tiny Beautiful Things,* one of my favorite writers, Cheryl Strayed wrote to a reader of her "Dear Sugar" advice column who had asked her to help him make a big life decision. She said,

> I'll never know, and neither will you, of the life you don't choose. We'll only know that whatever that sister life was, it was important and beautiful and not ours. It was the ghost ship that didn't carry us. There's nothing to do but salute it from the shore.[4]

I often wonder if I am the "ghost ship" carrying the life my grandmother did not choose to lead or would have chosen in another universe.

Side-Stepping the Freeze

We all have the ability to become frozen in time—so stuck in our ways that further molding ceases to happen. Whether it's because of a choice we make that leads us down a very specific path or a loss we experience later in life that makes us want to stay exactly as we are, there's always something tempting us to put down the water dish, stop morphing, and dry up before realizing who we're meant to be.

My heartbreak sometimes makes me want to freeze. And my heart breaks constantly. I wonder sometimes if I was born with a more fragile heart than others, and then I remind myself: my heart is no more fragile than any of the other billions of beating, breaking hearts out there. Some of them have just been pretending for so long that the cracks remain hidden on the inside. I might not know what splinters each slit into so many pieces that the cracks become chasms, but I know each of us is walking around with our own inner rifts. To pretend is to freeze for the sake of fitting in.

I know I could remain the same person I am today—a version of Me my grandmother would recognize and relate to if she were to meet me again decades from now. But I can't. I know I can't because freezing myself in time won't just *not* bring her back, but it also won't fulfill the dreams she had when she started our family. It won't magnify the joy she experienced, or heal the wounds she carried, or add any more paint to the canvas of her life. It won't serve my friends, my family, my cousins, my coworkers, my colleagues, even the strangers I meet at the store or on social media who I don't even realize I'm impacting and are impacting me too.

Freezing myself in time would be the easy choice, but the easy choice isn't always the right one.

The tougher choice, the one to keep going and growing and evolving, is the one the world needs me to make—and the one the world needs you to make too.

~

I've had so many versions of strong women in my life and so many conflicting forces coming at me all at once. We all have our strengths and our weak spots, our helpful and our hurtful forces, and what's so cool is that each of us has a completely different configuration and combination of them all. The thing that makes it cool isn't just the fact that we're all "unique"; the thing that makes it cool is that we quite literally have a *world* of choices around us to help us make the change we wish to see and be the change we hope to be. One person can't be your everything—no one can—but you can take a little lesson from here and a touch of inspiration from there, and write and rewrite your own story. Not just for you and not just for the future, but for all the other people around you right now who are taking cues as to what it means to walk through this world.

We can't do anything about our past, but we sure as hell can do something about our present and future. For they too, one day, will be lost and in the past for us—but will be a very real part of someone else's story and inner workings. Learning how to move through shame, change, loss, growth, guilt, grief, and all the tough truths of life in a way that's right for you, in line with your own ethics and values, is a story you can always rewrite—for you, for those who came before you, for those who come after you, and for all of those who are next to you right now.

Maybe I hoped I could unfreeze that nineteen-year-old inside of my grandmother before she died and help her find, be, stay, and *want* her Self, on her own terms. But just because her breath has stopped doesn't mean her story has. Her leaving the room is my tipping point—this time in a different direction. If I cannot do it for her, I will do it for me, and I will do it for all the women who are around me, and all the women who will come after me. We will side-step the freeze and sculpt a Self together—shaping it and molding it and scoring it like clay, keeping it malleable and warm under our fingers until we fuse together to become who we know we're meant to be.

Chapter Three

LONELY IS LOVE WITH NOWHERE TO GO

I don't know who decided that college is supposed to be the so-called best four years of your life. I'll believe in Santa Claus before I'll believe in that.

I'm eighteen years old. I'm sitting on my twin bed in my freshman year dorm room, in the first year of my drama major, in a building filled with at least a hundred other Theatre Kids like me. I've filled my side of the 150 square feet allotted to me and my roommate with floor-to-ceiling photos of me with friends doing fun things. Most of it is all show. As a freshman in college dorms, it seems to be an unspoken rule that you plaster any and every corner of your allotted wall space with evidence of how loved you are by everyone in your life outside of college—all the people you knew "before you got here." And so I find photos to fill the empty spaces—photos of me with boys I barely knew, at parties I attended for an hour, in group hugs I only really joined because hugging is one of my Love Languages, and I will hug almost everyone and anyone (with consent!) no matter whether they're my bestie or not.

My emerging anxious and depressive spells have been kicking my ass for months, and the more time I spend around the other kids, the more alone I feel. But this is the nature of college. You're around others 24/7—no space and place to just *be.*

I'll get used to it and learn to love it. Best four years of my life, right?

And this is when my lifelong high proprioception starts to eat me alive, which is a darkly humorous turn of phrase for what happens because eating isn't really happening, and I rarely feel "alive." I feel myself in space, my body and energy stuffed into a life that doesn't feel like my own. I have long since internalized that I'm here to be an example for others. To be mature, talented, beautiful, smart. To follow systems, set expectations, stay in line. These are the habits I've honed. I feel myself pretending to be Good College Girl so that I can fit in. It doesn't feel right. And the quest to fit in, of course, is the demise of us all.

My demise comes in the form of an eating disorder. Counting, restricting, under-eating, and over-exercising all become a numbers game and motivation. These are things I'm good at. These are things I can manipulate and control.

On this particular evening, I'm lying on my bed, staring blankly out my window. I watch as a group of fellow freshmen friends from my dorm bounce-walk down the paved path to their cars, where they'll drive off to the gym, then see a movie, then head to a party. I feel relief mixed with an unignorably deep pang of longing. I know my habits haven't been normal, but I can't seem to break them. To fit in with my peers, it feels as if I'll have to "let myself go," as I've heard it referred to by nearly all the grown-ups in my life. I will have to forego the advice of every magazine article I've read and ignore the butt of every joke I've heard made about our campus's fully stocked food commissary. I will have to do the thing that makes me weak and a non-example: I will have to not diet and not exercise.

But to belong to myself, I will also have to be okay with it. Which I am not.

I look out the window and grab a pear from my mini fridge at 7:15 pm. Eating it feels like rebellion, and then it feels like wrongness. My high sensitivity starts to kick in, but this time it's different. The mix of relief and longing and rebellion and wrongness is signaling to me: *Something is wrong. You can't keep this up.*

I look to the pictures on my wall, but they provide no comfort. They never did. A fake life I was posturing to lead.

And so I log my pear in my food journal.

Loneliness

Lonely hits at the most unexpected times—in line at the grocery store, walking out your door into the sunshine of a Sunday morning, propped up on your elbow on a half-made bed, listening to new music at 2:00 am. It comes when the world is quiet but your insides are screaming. When everything around you is vibrant and thriving, and you tiptoe in gingerly. When you open the refrigerator and realize you need to buy something other than condiments and wine.

Lonely hits you when you look in the mirror and don't recognize yourself like you used to. There's something different in your eyes. *What is it? Oh, that's it. Time.* It's the strain from holding them so wide open all the freaking time because a broken gaze is a missed opportunity. Lonely is the realization that even your own personhood is not a constant.

Lonely is the brutally self-aware, the uncharacteristically quiet, the plant that's suddenly stopped blossoming. Lonely is the song you *try* to sing. It's wishing to sing and not getting the chance. It's all of the trying and wishing, really. Lonely is the necklace you wore so well that's now neglected because you can't get the tangles out. It's the change that comes with the time and the transience of life in general.

Lonely is a contradiction: vague yet clear. Lonely is living in footnotes and swift asides and question marks lined up like window decorations.

Lonely is what happens when you question the way you give.

Lonely is what happens when you question the way you *are*.

Lonely is love with nowhere to go.

Losing My Voice

I sometimes get asked about how I "got over" my eating disorder. How I "recovered." And I always answer . . .

. . . well, before I answer, I clarify that recovery isn't linear. It's a two-steps-forward-one-step-back process that looks different for everyone and runs on its own timeline. Especially when your eating or body-related disorder is vague and lives in hazy parentheticals. I ate (but only specific amounts and specific things). I rested (but only when I "deserved" it). My life was about getting good grades, being cast in as many student-directed plays and musicals as possible, micro-managing my schedule of food and fitness, and having something to show for these socially lauded successes (because if no one could see them, were they really successes at all?). I was so very high-functioning to the world around me—but on the inside, it was a different story. I had pretended for so long that I didn't have any cracks on my surface, when in reality, I'd flattened my surfaces so finely that there was nothing inside to hold me together. We all shatter when we pretend.

And after I clarify *that*, I tell them my recovery wasn't about "fixing" a "moment"; it was about finally taking a good look at what I'd been burying and battling my entire life: a whole host of unattainable dichotomies. A desire to fit in *and* stand out at the same time. To shrink myself down *and* share my gifts in a big way. To be perfect enough to be aspirational *and* flawed enough to be relatable. My body wasn't the problem; it was just the easiest thing to manipulate in a world that felt so far out of my control.

My desire to fit in and be accepted had become the most important thing to me. But I knew deep down my values weren't worth sacrificing. I walked around with a constant, dull pressure to abandon myself in order to be loved—to dive head-first into being the most extraordinarily talented human being on earth *and* the most social, most college-y college girl there ever was—and then felt shame that I couldn't bring myself to do it.

So I did the things that would help me check out and dissociate without having to do anything I didn't want to. I auditioned for every show and got into many. Rehearsals, though, only made me feel more lonely when I got home. The only place I felt like I could let go and be my whole self was on a stage, honing my craft and playing characters completely different from my age or life stage. Ironically, my pretending usually peaked offstage, not on.

I needed another strategy to check out—one that ideally made me feel like an adult and was culturally celebrated. Controlling my body seemed like a grown-up, socially acceptable way to dissociate. It wasn't about my body. It never was. I had become so lonely in the skin I was in that it was making me disappear.

And so when I heard that voice—*something is wrong*—I was forced to address where that debilitating loneliness had entered in the first place.

Disconnected

I was born in the '80s, which means I'm a child of the '90s, which means I'm part of the last generation that can simultaneously be tethered to technology and vividly remember a time without it. I entered college in 2004—the year Facebook, then *The* Facebook, was slowly rolled out across university campuses. The only picture you could add was a profile photo, there was no wall of comments or updates, and one of the main purposes was to link up with potential friends who shared similar interests (and classes) at your school. When I received my very first college class schedule, I typed each course into the dull grey boxes provided to me, then eagerly clicked on each class to find out who else I could expect to see on my first day. The new friend possibilities were both exciting and nerve-racking. I wondered if I seemed cool-but-accessible enough for College Friends.

Think-pieces on millennials, Gen Z, and technology like to blame our culture and younger generations' "loneliness epidemic" on social media, but I don't think that's it. On social media, the periphery fades away—all that deep context that comes from standing in the 3D presence of another person—and we're left with strings of words, two-dimensional photos, and videos that play on loop. Social media is like a magnifying mirror for all our preexisting social habits. We're more connected than ever but feeling more disconnected at the same time.

I once read an essay in *The New Yorker* by journalist Nausicaa Renner about how social media was making it harder for us to evolve beyond our past selves due to the constant connection to ex-lovers, former friends, past coworkers, and people who entered our lives at a time when we weren't who we are now.[1] It talked about how conversations and moments are immortalized on the internet—how it's like we're juggling the task of driving forward while constantly looking in the rear-view mirror. And when we feel like we can't be who we are? Enter: loneliness.

And yet, aren't we doing this anyway, *off*line? Holding each other—and ourselves—to outdated expectations, and feeling like we've lost a little bit of who we are when we falter or fall short? The stifled sense of Self, the blocked energy exchange, and the questions that arise from all that's unsaid—they suffocate, and they hurt. Loneliness is asking questions that aren't heard, or holding back answers we long to give.

Lonely isn't a relationship status. Lonely isn't crowded or alone. Lonely is the aching for wide-open exchange. And no matter how many friends you have, how great your love life is or how perfect your job seems, lonely is the confusion that sets in when you wonder, when you hold back, or when the external facets of your life become a guise or overcompensation.

And the tricky part is that lonely cannot be solved by being social, going out, or striking up a conversation. Our bonds over anger and fear are real and run deep and way too often hijack our conversations. Fear, anger, and negativity are *emotionally heavy*—they evoke something strong and primal when spoken out loud. And when we feel lonely, awkward, uncomfortable, they can become our default bonding strategies.

So no, I don't blame social media. Our loneliness would exist with or without it because social media is just our way of communicating boiled down to its common denominators. If we're complaining out in the world, our complaining is highlighted on social media. If we're faking it IRL, we're probably faking it on social media too. If we default to self-deprecation in life, then there's a good chance we're using social media to offload that buildup of self-loathing onto others. Our loneliness isn't fully *caused* by social media, social media is just a place our loneliness gets amplified. We're being limited versions of ourselves—both online *and* in real life.

People get used to the version of You that you present to them. If you're constantly surrounded by people who have a limited view of who you are . . . then living your full spectrum of Self out loud is risky business.

Choosing My Self

My wake-up call doesn't come from my concerned boyfriend, or my exasperated younger brother, or my patient parents, or my tear-stained best friend. It comes from my voice teacher.

Myrona is like a second mom to me in college—my professor during school hours, my voice teacher and mentor in between classes. I admire how to-the-point she is: pragmatic and direct, and at the same time managing to hold space for me to feel my feelings as they bubble up. I don't feel coddled by her, which I love, and she praises me when I succeed, which I also love (I'm still very much a people-pleaser).

And so when she speaks, I listen.

My weekly voice lesson, on one particular week, is what does it.

I'm standing by her piano, as I always do, and holding on to its lid for balance, as I've begun to do recently. Our exercises have been exhausting me more than usual, and the vocal trills she's leading me through are taking all the air out of my system.

We wrap up. She pauses. And she speaks with a tone I've only heard her reserve for the most tender moments in class—the moments when she's preparing to hold space. The ones when someone is either on the verge of an artistic breakthrough, or on the verge of giving up entirely.

"I don't know what you're doing, Katie . . . but you've got to get it under control. Your other professors and I notice. We're worried about you—and it's starting to affect your voice."

I lose my breath, and not because of the trills.

She's completely right.

My most prized possession—my voice—it's fading away.

Trying so hard to be the most likable, most beautiful, most disciplined, and most mature has slowly been robbing me of something that's made me the most *me.*

My voice is an extension of my Self. It makes me whole.

But if I keep living this status quo, my voice will be lost.

And what rattles me the most is that I haven't even realized I've been doing it to myself.

Caging my Self has made me so very lonely. I've been locking my Self away around others and only letting her live on a stage, where the accountability is off because I can blame any quirks or imperfections "on the character" (a scapegoat for my own Self-ness, whom I continue to be at odds with once I step offstage). I've been giving my Self less and less room to exist out loud, and now here I am, beginning to lose the only part of her that I've allowed to run wild and free.

In this moment, I need to decide what's more important to me: my status or my Self.

I choose the latter.

Somewhere to Go

If lonely is love with nowhere to go, then the antidote must be to give it somewhere to go.

Okay, sure. But what does that *mean,* and how do you logistically do that? If someone had told me that if/then "solution" in the midst of my darkest moments, I would have nodded politely while telling them in my mind to go kindly fuck off.

How is it possible to give your love somewhere to go, when you feel disconnected from the whole world around you? Where do you even begin?

You begin, I've found, by focusing not on where you'll give your love a place to go, but on when you feel your love naturally *come alive*.

The trick is to not only notice the micro-moments, but do something about them. To be a Professional Noticer is to pay attention to when the richness and depth of your inner life asks you to bring it out into the light of the outside world. The difference between bridging that gap and deepening its chasm is the attention you pay to the sweetness in the longing. Because longing can feel callous and it can feel cruel, and those feelings can distract you from the sparks hidden underneath. Longing, after all, is bittersweet: it's bitter *and* sweet. The former does not, and cannot, negate the latter.

~

I find group fitness while on the journey of creating my new normal. (Recovering from an eating disorder, I've noticed, isn't so much about *getting back* to normal as it is about the process of *creating* a new normal as you navigate the baby steps of your own nonlinear recovery path. In this new normal, the disorder or addiction is still a part of your story—it's just not the defining chapter.) While I struggle with exercise bulimia when I'm alone at the gym—working out pathologically and often compulsively to control not only my body but my emotions—the urge to purge and punish disappears completely when I'm in a class. Whether it's a yoga class or indoor cycling class, I adore the sense of personal accountability that exists when I'm around others. A sense of community while still being in charge of my own personal experience. I love that I can feel fulfilled and embodied instead of desperate and dissociated, and that there's a clear start and stop time that prevents me from dragging my sweat session on and on. I love moving to the music on the beat, and actually being able to keep the beat to begin with (something that happens so rarely in the dance classes required by my drama major that I almost don't graduate after a notably horrendous semester in Tap 101 where only my right leg can master a kick-ball-change). Fitness, it seems, allows me to move in a way that feels free and expansive. In a way, it feels like the way my body was *designed* to move. Combine that with the community atmosphere and the life lessons expertly woven into the instructor's coaching, and I'm hooked. This feels like ME. This is a feeling worth following.

But at the same time, my disordered years have made me acutely aware of the fitness industry's failings. The fitness and wellness narrative glorifies thinness, smallness, and purity of lifestyle choices like food and exercise—the exact same "purity" that has, in the past, insinuated maybe my eating disorder *isn't all that bad.* Maybe even worth celebrating. Ever heard the phrase, "You can't unsee it?" You can't unsee your experiences with an eating disorder or addiction. And like a relationship that ends sour, you can either let that relationship dictate your narrative moving forward, or you can view it as something that led you to become the person you are today.

So while I can't unsee what I've seen in the years I've been sick, and can't un-feel the feelings of loneliness and loathing I've become accustomed to for so long, after a few years of taking classes that make me feel appreciative of myself instead of ashamed, I also can't un-know that there's another way to not just move, but live. The fitness and wellness industry can do so much better—and maybe, just maybe, I can help it do better. For all the deeper reasons as well as total control of playlist curation (as I once went to a class where the instructor played dance remixes of musical theatre songs that should never be made into dance remixes, and I couldn't un-hear those cringey beats), I decide to become certified to teach indoor cycling classes myself. To be able to be on a stage, but also be able to be exactly who and how I am—and uplift others at the same time? Hell yeah.

Inadvertently, this decision is what helps me realize how important it is to have a sense of Self *wherever* I go. Once I realize that there are places out there where I *don't* feel the pressure to pretend, I become fascinated by where else that sense of Self can take me.

This is also the early 2000s. Online communities are starting to blossom, and as an introvert, this is both novel and thrilling. I start to seek out places online where I can be a part of the same kinds of communities I'm finding in real life through fitness. When I do, in the form of "healthy living" blogs and direct-to-email newsletters about living mindfully, I love them so much that I start to pitch them my writing services. I have an inkling that I can help be a part of the new, emerging "self-care" conversation—or at least curate a good playlist to listen to while it's happening. Pretty ladyballsy, as I'm a musical theatre major with no writing credits to my name. But I studied creative writing and journalism at my liberal arts university, and have always excelled at putting words to abstract thoughts or connecting disjointed facts. I figure that what I lack in journalistic experience, I can make up for with enthusiasm and assuredness.

I hear a voice inside me say, without emotion or reason: *Do it.* And instead of arguing, I agree. Why not try?

Fortunately, enthusiasm is what they want, along with a willingness to try out something new. I begin freelance writing for email newsletters and blogs as a side hustle, and I eventually start my own. I learn in real time, on the job. I soak it all in. I bathe in the self-knowing I can feel emerging. I begin to realize I feel more at home and like myself when I teach and write than when I'm learning lines and performing a character. Crafting transformative experiences that stick with people way after they leave me, whether on a page or a podium . . . this lights me up in a new way that pretending rarely did.

The proof I gather, and keep gathering, all leads me to the same place. After four years, I begin to realize that I haven't been wrong about wanting to be on stage—I've just misidentified the kind of stage I'm meant to be on. I can no longer unsee what I've seen: a Me that's started to come alive in a way she rarely does anymore while acting, but used to way back when. The same type of aliveness she used to feel while drawing. The same aliveness she felt just before she was told to get back in line. And I know I need to move forward with that feeling and see where it takes me.

I often tell people that getting certified to teach was the best decision I ever made. Finding group fitness exactly when I did—at the peak of my sickness, during the transition from college life into adulthood, in a period of deep questioning and darkness—changed my life. It opened my eyes to what it means to truly live well, made me curious about myself and others, and sent me down a path of trying to figure out what, as my friend Dr. Carrie Kholi-Murchison calls it, *inclusive actualization* truly looks like.[2] How to create a sense of belonging, fulfillment, and meaning for anyone and everyone, no matter who you are or where you've been. It all began by coming together with forty other people, in a sweaty room, on bikes that go nowhere, all moving forward fearlessly through resistance together, turning obstacles into opportunities, and fighting for what we believe in.

Did this choice flip a switch and "heal" me forever and ever? No.

But.

It gave my love somewhere to go.

And that was an important start.

Addendum to Loneliness: Most People

What we do in group fitness is simply practice for what we do in life. In that room, no love is too small, no life is too sparse, and no responsibility is too insignificant. I notice these micro-moments of self-recognition and togetherness in class so I can notice them out in the world. One, I always realize, tends to bleed into the other.

I used to teach at this huge gym right in the middle of Sepulveda Boulevard. One of the biggest gyms on one of LA's most sprawling streets. The parking garage alone filled up the space of an entire block. Driving in, you could feel engulfed by the enormity of it all. But when you walked through the sliding doors and into the group fitness studio, everything changed. The experience became intimate. You were seen. You mattered. You could let your guard down and come alive.

One day after teaching a particularly euphoric indoor cycling class, I teetered with my gym tote to the third floor of the massive parking garage as I always did—except this time, my senses felt on higher alert. I felt more dialed-in than usual. Was it the group that showed up? Was it the playlist I created? I couldn't pinpoint one thing specifically. Maybe it was all of it and none of it at all. Maybe I was just ready to notice what had been there all along.

And then, I saw it: a pigeon no more than three feet away from my little silver car.

I walked closer. It didn't budge.

I thought maybe it had been wounded somehow, even though I couldn't see any visible injuries. Or maybe it had just woken up from an ill-placed nap.

But as I inched closer, it moved centimeters away from me, revealing something unexpected and, in my mind, even worse: a round white egg.

There it was, sitting on the cold concrete saturated in days' worth of car exhaust and caked sweat, propped up and surrounded by no more than 10 to 15 twigs. A last attempt at some sort of shelter, some sort of home, some sort of safe-haven-meets-throne. I watched the mother bird, this little creature that was probably both bravely on guard and intensely terrified. Slowly, literally millimeters at a time, she eased back on top of the egg. She fluffed her feathers, just like in a Pixar movie, and slowly, so slowly, settled back down on her baby.

I broke down.

My first thought was to call the local wildlife rehab center. Visions of my first-grade class field trip to an animal sanctuary and the baby bunny fiasco of 1995 (a story for another time) came flooding back to me as I reassured myself: *It'll be okay. It's their job to be empathetic. It's their* job *to know.*

They were open—yay!—and a call center receptionist answered with no clue what was about to be spewed down the line. I frantically explained my scenario—*parking lot, pigeon, nest, gym, indoor cycling*—and, judging by their silence, I realized they might think I was some twentysomething who got a little too high on something other than life and a little too invested in something perfectly mundane. Los Angeles, after all, was filled with pigeons. Why, the call-center-answerer-person might think, would *this* person care about *this* creature? I steadied my voice to signal that I was totally serious and asked them: "What do I do now?"

They slowly explained: there weren't really protocols for animals that weren't wounded or endangering others, and pigeons weren't really that high up on the protocol list to begin with.

They directed me to animal care services. The animal care services voicemail directed me to their emergency hospital. The emergency hospital voicemail directed me to a recording about birds, which mentioned absolutely nothing about nests, eggs, or parking lots in the middle of Sepulveda Boulevard on the third floor of a gym. I called again and pressed all the numbers just to be sure I wasn't missing something. Press one for a wounded bird, two for volunteer opportunities, and so on and so forth. I pressed zero for the main office.

Voicemail. No one answered. There was nothing I could do.

My mind couldn't grasp it. *Why did this pigeon choose* this *place to build her nest? Why did she choose* this *corner to lay her egg? Why didn't she hide in a hidden corner of the rafters among the electrical wires and dust mites and dark abysses where she'd never, ever be seen? Why did she have to choose this place, out in the open, instead of settling for the man-made darkness where her chirps would echo, and passers-by would mistake her song for a faulty smoke alarm?*

I sat there in a panic, thinking about how nobody would even notice until it was too late. That the crew hired to clean the garage overnight would hose away the nest, egg, and bird, that a car would run it over early the next morning, or that someone who didn't know any better would try to Do The Right Thing and move the egg, and maybe the mother would never find it. I texted my friend, who had the brilliant idea to get cones and create a little barricade for the mama bird and her eggling. I sprinted down to the first level of the garage by the maintenance closet and found three cones, then another one upstairs by a pile of broken plastic bins. I walked up to the security guard, tear-stained and tired, and prefaced my story with "I'm not high, just empathetic." He helped me build a sign, marking where the bird was, and assured me he'd tell the maintenance crew not to mess with it. I built my pigeon barricade. An hour and many deep breaths later, I drove away.

~

My intense emotional reaction confused me at the time. My tears, my determination, it all seemed to pop up out of nowhere.

I know myself better now. It wasn't about "saving the day" or even Doing The Right Thing (which many times is only the right thing for *us* and not for *them*). In that little bird, I saw the whole world. I saw each one of us collectively and separately, all trying to live fully and grow wholly and build our legacy while at the same time living and growing and building it all on cold cement under jarring fluorescent lights in the only structure we can find for ourselves when we'd so much rather fly free.

We're made to believe that the only space available for us is on the cold cement floor and that the deadly hoses and crushing cars and other people acting with their ego instead of their empathy and calling it the "right thing for everyone" are just occupational hazards of being human. That there's nothing we can do. It's Just The Way Things Are.

In that moment when I hovered close to the haphazard twigs, I feared the mom would be scared off for good. In that little eternity when I unrolled a strip of tape long enough to wrap around the metal-wire fence, the security guard, Ray, watched me and commented: "Most people wouldn't even notice."

Lonely is love with nowhere to go.

We run things over and call it roadkill. We say it's just how life is, how this world is. It's just what happens. But it's not. It is, but it's *so* not.

Things get run over, and we keep going, and we force ourselves to forget because we say that if we can't understand, we can't do a thing.

A twisted game of Survival of the Fittest. We've evolved in ways that allow us to build highways, commission strip malls, and lop off whole chunks of a mountain to develop a community of condominiums, but somehow haven't evolved in ways that force us to sit with ourselves and our decisions before we make them. If we think too much, we're told, we miss the opportunity. If we think too much, we're warned, we might not ever get where we want to go. And if we think too much, we're cautioned, we run the risk of feeling too much, and making choices that challenge the status quo of Just The Way Things Are.

Most of these tiny creatures are born into the lie we've told ourselves about Just The Way Things Are. They didn't know the trees, the acorns, the Disney-esque thickets. They only know the concrete jungles and fake fluorescent sunlight. The power lines are their trees. The moldy sandwich scraps on the sidewalk, their acorns. The sprawling avenues and boulevards, their thickets. Our asphalt world is not where they're supposed to be, and yet, we just expect them to be there.

And they don't know how to adapt. They don't know that an airplane is not a bird, and a car won't just leap over them like a rabbit. It breaks my heart when I see a squirrel running up a lamppost, or a chipmunk flattened on the road, or a rat trap in an alleyway, or a nest perched on a concrete floor of a parking garage. They don't know that this isn't how life should be.

I saw the way this sweet little bird hovered close by even when she got scared. She would not fly. She did not dart. She took careful steps from side to side, keeping one eye on her egg and one eye on me. I saw how she fluffed and pillowed her feathers and how, as she sat ever-so-carefully in her makeshift nest, she cocked her head down to the side to make sure that everything was exactly as it should be and that she was exactly as she should be.

She was brave not *because* she was nervous, or *in spite of* being nervous. She was brave because she knew she had more important things to focus on than her fears.

Lonely is love with nowhere to go.

We all have something to love. Something we nurture, something so beautiful it's worth the risk of the careless drivers and the leaf blowers and the hoses that water everything down so that what's left is an impeccable void.

What is your beautiful *something*?

A partner? A child? A friend? A pet?

How about your Self?

What if you nurtured that?

What if you loved *that*?

Isn't it worth it to face the careless drivers and leaf blowers and hoses if you're able to live, grow, and build your Self on your own terms? Isn't it worth it to fluff your feathers out in broad daylight, use what you've got, and side-step the most fatal risk of all: the risk of living a life that's immaculately innocuous?

You only have twigs?

Use them to build your throne instead of holding your legacy inside.

You only have a concrete floor?

Let the world see you in broad daylight rather than push yourself into its dark corners.

You're told this is Just The Way The World Is? Just The Way Things Are?

Open your mouth and tell the world you refuse to budge, because you know that for every parking garage there once was a plot of land that held fertile soil, and you'll be damned if those trees can't and won't someday grow again.

Lonely is love with nowhere to go, so give your love somewhere to go.

No love is too small. No nest is too sparse. No responsibility is too insignificant.

We are not what life makes of us. Life is what we make of it.

Most people wouldn't even notice.

But then again, you're not most people.

Chapter Four

THE REIMAGINATION

Somewhere inside you is a Self that was meant to live out loud. Because of that, you'd think it should be simple to be You.

But your Self is not the obvious choice.

If finding your Self isn't a quick thing, being your Self doesn't just come naturally either. And staying your Self isn't even remotely easy. Actually *wanting* the Self that shows up for you on top of it all . . . well, that feels like the hardest task of all.

The greatest opportunities don't come without obstacles, and the most worthwhile things are rarely simple. But we often don't realize that a "normal" life is usually full of obstacles; that anything worth doing is usually complicated as hell. *There must be something wrong with me,* we think. *I feel so stuck, so alone.*

And so we *self-help* ourselves. We dive into books and websites doling out prescriptive advice on who we are and aren't. We fall for the clickbait that promises happiness rather than the clickbait that promises paparazzi photos and celebrity gossip, and we applaud ourselves for our restraint. We watch movies about women who begin their journey lost and alone but feel empowered by the time the credits roll. If we're lucky, we even get a super-short, super-cute scene tacked on after the final credits slide off the screen, making sure everything ends on the lightest of light notes.

Don't think I'm putting myself on a pedestal here. I'm not above immersing myself in the vortex of self-help—or *self-improvement*, as it's called more often now. My life was changed forever when I was gifted my first self-help book on my thirteenth birthday: a cleverly, *wink-wink* titled collection of self-awareness prompts and affirmations by Iyanla Vanzant called *Don't Give It Away!* I learned it was possible to be fully self-expressed by reading the works of mentors-from-afar like Oprah Winfrey and Anna Quindlen. I've never really been able to watch most mainstream movies (because, Highly Sensitive Person—hello loud noises and jumpy surprises), but I make a point to watch anything about a woman rising. I love a strong female lead and a well-told story. And c'mon—who doesn't love a post-credits scene? More movie!

But I also know exactly what I'm being sold, and I know to take it with a grain of salt: the idea of Living Your Best Life.

The myth that those self-help books and girl-powered movies are selling is that to choose and *want* your Self is a before-and-after kind of thing. You feel lost, and then you feel found. You're living the worst, and then you're living the best. Living Your Best Life is like the after shot in a "before and after" diet campaign that tells you to *just do this* to *look like that.*

But diets don't work. And photos don't tell an entire story.

Lost In Translation

That voice in your head is shit.
Don't let your thoughts bully you around.
Inner monologue? More like inner bitch. Don't give her the power.

"Empowerment" has been trending for at least a decade now, but somehow, we're still here telling our negative self-talk it can go screw itself.

Most of us are programmed to interpret the world in very black-and-white terms. There can be no middle ground when it comes to right and wrong, and when we disagree with something, we typically villainize it rather than try to understand where it comes from (or what the real solution should be). Good versus evil. Us against them.

A formula that's easy to understand and easy to master. It's primal. Or at least, it feels that way. It's only natural, then, that we'd choose sides as we listen to our self-talk and let one extreme bully the other into submission.

Some people like to give their internal, critical voice a name. And for some people, providing that separation is useful. It allows them to distance themselves from the harsh, usually untrue things their inner voice likes to say. For some people, it works, or at least works well enough.

I, however, have never been able to separate my inner voice from myself. Because the thing is, it's all a part of who I am. Maybe my brain is playing tricks on my heart, maybe my inner voice is misguided at times, but at the end of the day, it's all just me, telling myself what to believe.

If this sounds like you, welcome to the club. Some days are hard for no specific reason at all. And some days are hard for all the reasons in the world. People might suggest that you need to tell yourself to *snap out of it*—to tell your inner critic to shut the hell up. And that might work for some people. But it's *never* worked for me. Identifying my negative self-talk as someone other than myself, someone who's a villain—a bully—only puts me on the defensive and gives me yet another thing about myself to dislike (on top of whatever it is I'm negative self-talking about).

Turning your negative self-talk into an internal villain is a catchy empowerment technique. Empowerment, for the record, is defined as "the process of becoming stronger and more confident, especially in controlling one's life and claiming one's rights." Yet I find it hard to see how throwing insults at insults can make you feel anything but more aggressive and afraid. Even if on the surface it seems like telling your negative self-talk to eff off brings a sense of power, what kind of habit is that helping you build? They're just harsh words to combat harsh thoughts. Abuse masked as empowerment. Which, to me, is anything but empowering.

Instead of fighting against what is, why not try fighting for what could be?

Instead of taking sides, why not confront the perceived enemy?

Instead of viewing your inner monologue as separate from your "true" self, why not aim to understand what it's really trying to tell you?

Mental Mean Girls

I'm the founder of a platform called WANT: Women Against Negative Talk. WANT gives people tips, tools, motivation, and inspiration to shift their self-talk patterns. Through multimedia content, events, partnerships, and more, the point of WANT isn't to give you all the answers to your macro-issues, but to help you ask better questions in the micro-moments. We live in an increasingly complex world, and the goal of WANT is to help you redefine positivity in a way that's not only realistic, but sustainable.

When I first started WANT back in 2007, I loved the acronym of W-A-N-T and the way it helped people understand our, and my, mission in a quick way. As it evolved, though, I wondered if the name no longer served the platform. *Instead of fighting against what is, how about fighting for what could be*—was the "against" part no longer aligned with WANT's mission? If words are so important, did these words still work?

And then I realized that the meaning went way deeper than that.

So much of our day-to-day energy is spent navigating the things, systems, and feelings we feel like we've got to fight against. Not wrong. Not bad. But it's only half the equation if the goal is real, lasting change. WANT is about looking at your first-impulse desire to fight against what feels like no longer serves you and *morphing it.* Not ignoring your impulse altogether, but getting curious as to what it means. Because behind every person fighting against their Self is really a person who yearns to *want* their Self. And that is a journey worth going on.

WANT isn't just an acronym—it's a metamorphosis. From finding to being to staying and beyond. A journey toward *wanting your Self,* unfolding.

This isn't about telling "your mental mean girls to shut up" or "banishing your inner bad guy." I can understand how some people need a metaphorical smack upside the head to catapult change into motion. But I don't think that's what builds kinder habits, in the long run, and I don't think that's what makes the changes we're going for *last*.

Because here's the clincher: the quicker we are to find fault inside ourselves, the quicker we are to find fault outside ourselves. The quicker we are to tell ourselves to "get over it" or "snap out of it" when we're feeling down, the quicker we are to do the same to our friends who crave our compassion. What happens on the inside gets reflected on the outside. We can't speak one language internally and genuinely speak another externally. It's a negativity loop that goes on and on and on—all in the name of self-love.

Teaching yourself a new language, whether it's Spanish or self-respect, is a process. Sometimes it's as simple as going word by word, phrase by phrase.

Your mind and heart are smart. They're not giving you information unless they think you need it. They're most likely just trying to protect you from disappointment, shield you from loneliness, or numb the pain that's predicting what other people might "find out" about you so that it won't hurt as bad if/when they do.

Your inner voice is just accustomed to using negative self-talk as a warped defense mechanism—a defense mechanism you don't need.

Calling a very real part of who you are a mean name reinforces and strengthens those negative-talk muscles that have been trained over the years. And it focuses on the problem, not the solution.

Berating a part of who you are is not the answer. Tapping into a new reserve of power to retrain the voice that so longs to be helpful *is*.

Next time you're tempted to call your inner voice a harsh name, sideline the smack-talk and reframe it as something *more*. Self-talk isn't good or bad. It's simply information. And if you and your mind and your heart are all on the same side, there's a very real possibility that the information your self-talk has to serve you is more valuable than it seems.

For example: could it be that your negative self-talk is . . .

. . . an invitation to explore?

. . . an opportunity to rise?

. . . a clue to an imbalance?

. . . a way to practice moving forward through fear?

. . . a wound to be nurtured?

. . . a signal for help?

. . . a cautionary tale of what it looks like to not be self-actualized?

. . . a sign of neglect?

. . . a cry for attention?

. . . a distraction from the truth?

. . . an inkling of what you cherish or value most?

. . . a language that's been inherited from someone else and internalized as your own?

. . . a sign of burnout?

. . . a call to action?

. . . an empathetic pathway?

. . . a clue as to what needs some extra love?

Remind yourself that it's not you versus your mind. Not good versus evil. They're all on the same side, fighting for the same life.

Living Your Best Life

We are who we believe ourselves to be. Our story is shaped by the words we use to tell it. So I've got to wonder if we're really doing ourselves justice by reaching for a life that's The Best.

Where did our cultural obsession with Living Your Best Life even come from? The commercials, probably. Those damn before-and-afters.

My earliest micro-moments helped me conclude very early on that my Best Life was one where I was *good.* Being a Good Girl = Living My Best Life. Being smart, nice, pretty, talented—but for everyone else, not for myself. Being loud when you want me to be. Being soft when you need me to be. Never speaking out of turn. Never making jokes. (Sidenote: I was convinced for *years* I was the unfunniest person I knew. I later realized I wasn't *not* funny, I just couldn't bear the humiliation when I got a side-eye or people didn't laugh at my jokes. There is nothing Best or Good about humiliation.)

But "best" is numbing. In reality, my Best Life isn't being a Good Girl, or Bad Girl, or any one type of human at all. I don't know how to Live My Best Life, or at least in the way people say. It's not that I don't know how because I haven't tried. I don't know how because I don't *want* to know how—how to be The Best on all days in all ways. You need the balance and the spectrum—the highs, lows, and everything in between—to actually create a life. If you only strive for The Best, and then everything is The Best, then is *anything* really The Best?

And moreover, if you don't hit that "Best" marker, is everything else a failure?

My real-deal Best Life isn't one that *feels* like I'm at my best all the time. It's the one where I feel the *full spectrum* of my experience—the heartbreak and the heart-opening all at once. We need contrast. One isn't better than the other, and one isn't worse.

I often wonder if our cultural obsession with rightness, perfection, specialness, and success would be different if we stopped making Living Your *Best* Life the goal and instead aimed for Living *Your* Life. Bests rendered irrelevant.

Who would we discover?
What would we find?
Would we be our *whole* selves?
Would we learn what it truly means to live?

Self-Concept

Psychologist Carl Rogers defines self-concept as the organized, consistent set of perceptions and beliefs about oneself. It's fluid and in-process, but specific and identifiable in any given moment.[1] Your self-concept is an idea-based definition of your You-ness, one that you've created from all the beliefs you have about yourself and the way you perceive people responding to you. Self-concept is the broadest answer you have to the question "Who am I?"

According to Rogers, your self-concept has three components: your *self-image*, *self-esteem*, and *ideal self*. These can change over time, just like your self-concept can, based on the story you tell about the life you live.

Each one gets a little more specific:

- **Self-image** is the answer to the question "How do I see Me?" It includes physical features, social roles, and personality traits. Your self-image is how you feel about that definition of your You-ness. It's the lens you look through to view your self-concept.

- **Self-esteem** is the answer to the question "How valuable am I?" It's usually comparative and fluctuates based on the way we evaluate ourselves.

- **Ideal self** is the answer to the question "Who would I like to be?"

If this is all true, then the answer to summarize my self-concept for the first two and a half decades of my life was: *I am here to be special.*

And when I land on that, it's easy to see how that one theme wove its way through all the sub-components of my self-concept for the first two and a half decades of my life:

- My self-image was: *I am not special enough.*
- My self-esteem was: *Other people are more special than me.*
- My ideal self was: *I must be the most special.*

What *is* special, even? In the mind of a Theatre Kid, it's role-snagging, award-winning, accolade-receiving, and applause-getting. My therapist likes to remind me that anyone who ever once "did theatre" rarely ever just did theatre. They were *obsessive.* If you were a bona fide Theatre Kid, you usually started performing at a pretty young age. While other kids are listening to Top 40 hits and debating which boy bands are better, you're analyzing bootlegged Broadway videos and getting into debates about which cast albums are the best. You're in lust with everything about the theatre, and lust feels like love when it's extreme enough. Success is defined early for Theatre Kids, and "special" is defined very specifically. Roles. Gigs. Award shows. Applause.

And so you develop an idea about success that is less about what you do than about how others *respond* to you—but you're young and in love, so you think it's the other way around. If you're already a high achiever, your high achievement goes into overdrive. You are defined by how extraordinary you are and how often you're rewarded for it.

This isn't unique to theatre. No matter what sphere you're in, if you identify with a specific idea of success for long enough, it starts to shape your self-told story. And if that idea of success (and what's more, the pursuit of it) is something you've married your identity to since childhood, it's very likely that over time, the story you shape becomes less and less malleable.

Eventually what happens, or at least what happened to me, is you start to realize that those narrow expectations don't meet the vast reality in front of you. You notice that all you ARE is very different from all you've been made to believe you SHOULD be, and you assume the disconnect is your fault. You think life isn't supposed to be as complicated as it is, because if that were the case, you would've learned that somewhere along the way. And if it isn't supposed to be this complicated, then it's probably complicated because you're doing something wrong. You cling to the highs because it seems there are so many lows, and you cling to the parts of you that are easily understood and agreed upon by the world because everything else seems too contradictory and confusing. It feels like there's only so much room in the world, and if you dare to cross any kind of boundary, you'll be thrown out forever.

I thought that living out my dream of being an actor would be *it*. It would be the thing that made me feel whole and alive. Which it was, until it wasn't. The reality of who I was inside rarely matched the reality of the roles I was cast in or auditioned for, and that feeling of being my whole self on a stage started to fade away. Pretending through the thing that used to light me up was not a game I wanted to play. I started to feel that "this isn't it" feeling, but was so scared to stray from the path I'd carved out for myself that was familiar to those around me—the people from whom I craved validation, took my cues, and who I wanted to please. I worried that I'd created a mess. I worried I no longer had the capability to be special or extraordinary because the talents that I thought existed for everyone else to enjoy weren't being used like they had before. I realized I had opinions worth holding, and values worth sharing, and goals that weren't motivated by anyone else but myself. And what scared me was that I had spent an entire lifetime pretending to be a Me on the outside that I was just now realizing didn't match the Me I *knew* I was.

Sometimes it's not the big discrepancies that get under our skin. It's the small, seemingly dull details that only we notice exist. And as a lifelong Professional Noticer, I knew they existed. The differences between the Me I pretended to be and the Me I knew I was meant to be were small—but all those small choices and changes piled up like bricks in my mind, and became too challenging to carry and impossible to ignore. I had been living out my life based on a former version of my Self—one who existed differently on the inside than she did on the outside.

The Rebirth

Moving past the visions and dreams of your past can feel like losing a lover. The first time I thought that acting might not be the sole vessel through which I wanted to give myself to the world, my eyes stayed red for days from crying. The first time I realized I was unclear as to whether or not I wanted children, I had a meltdown. The first time I found a soulmate-friend outside my comfort zone of shared upbringing, I felt like I was cheating on my entire past. At the time, it felt like a breakup. At the time, it felt like a loss.

How strange, as each experience or epiphany that triggered a sense of loss or wrongdoing was actually opening a door and showing me to my true Self. Although, come to think of it, sometimes people confuse self-actualization for something worthy of an accusation . . . so maybe the fact that it felt so wrong wasn't as abnormal as I thought.

Your visions and goals are always in flux. Some are not better or worse than others. They're just different. Hanging on to past ideas of what you "should" do can put self-actualization on standby and screw you over in the long run. Who you are during one season in your life is neither the end-all-be-all nor invalid. It's a fragment of you. Information. A small yet important page in the story of the You *you* know you're meant to be.

It can feel scary to move forward beyond a past version of your Self, but there's no reason to mourn.

Moving forward is not a death of who you were—it's a rebirth of who you are.

You are more than your past aspirations. You are more than the ideas your ten-year plan expressed. You are more than the connections you made long ago. You are more than what's been passed down by everyone who came before you and what's been molded by everyone who's now around you.

And yet these are a part of you. Who are we to say we know what our journey will look like in a decade, or if we'll feel the same way then as we do now? We're always in flux. The important thing is to feel deeply and express yourself authentically every step of the way.

Had I never wanted to act, I would have never learned to perceive the world around me in such great detail with such empathy. Had I never felt so much passion for something that was so different from the things my peers felt passionately about, I would have never known what it is to pour my soul onto a page. Had I never envisioned my life the way I thought it would look by now, I would have never met some of the most influential players in my life's journey. I am still that same girl who thought success lived solely on Broadway, who expected her kindergarten buddies would be her friends forever and that her life should unfold looking almost identical to her mother's and her mother's before that.

And yet here I am, no Tony Award in sight. I'm surrounded by friends from all stages of life, connected to my past but fully invested in my present. I look toward the future, not with a predictive eye but an openness to the expansion I know I will experience. I cannot possibly know what my story will look like in ten years—or even two. I have not broken up with my past visions; I have let them morph and blossom. I have not buried my Self; I have let her come alive into the now.

Your Self, Out Loud

Somewhere inside you is a Self that was meant to live out loud. You'll so rarely get permission from others to be your Self. That kind of go-ahead isn't really *permission* anyway. It's validation. It's someone else saying, "I bless you to do this or be that because it's what I deem acceptable and how I can guarantee my support."

And so, you must reimagine the parameters of who you know your Self to be. You must courageously move into your own greatness, despite others' thoughts, and grant yourself permission without someone else raising their hand and declaring, "I second that decision." You must feel the fear of judgment, disconnection, loneliness, and sit with it, examine it, and move forward through it. Finding yourself isn't about abiding by a past vision of how you once were, and finding yourself isn't about searching for a new you. Finding yourself is about coming home to the You that was always there, about living intentionally and focusing on your own unique bottom line. There is information everywhere—even in the darkness.

When I was seventeen, I ripped the following Wendell Berry poem out of one of my mom's copies of *O, The Oprah Magazine* and taped it to the wall in my childhood bedroom, where it's lived ever since. I've cleaned out my room and my parents have redecorated, but the poem remains on the wall as an ode to my past, a reminder of my present, and a call to action for my future Self. It's called "Do Not Be Ashamed." I reread it often.

It begins:

> You will be walking some night
> in the comfortable dark of your yard
> and suddenly a great light will shine
> round about you, and behind you
> will be a wall you never saw before.
> It will be clear to you suddenly
> that you were about to escape,
> and that you are guilty: you misread
> the complex instructions, you are not
> a member, you lost your card
> or never had one. And you will know
> that they have been there all along,
> their eyes on your letters and books,
> their hands in your pockets,

their ears wired to your bed.
Though you have done nothing shameful,
they will want you to be ashamed.
They will want you to kneel and weep
and say you should have been like them.
And once you say you are ashamed,
reading the page they hold out to you,
then such light as you have made
in your history will leave you.
They will no longer need to pursue you.
You will pursue them, begging forgiveness.
They will not forgive you.
There is no power against them.
It is only candor that is aloof from them,
only an inward clarity, unashamed,
that they cannot reach.

Moving forward on the journey of reimagining your Self will force you to face shame.

Keep going.

You might feel uncomfortable, awkward, wanting to crawl out of your skin as more of You gets unearthed and unleashed.

Keep going.

Your greatness might scare you or knock you off your feet.

Keep going.

Place your kindness at the helm, your courage at the mast, and your heart at the forefront. When you come from a place of radical empathy and self-love, others can't help but follow suit.

We all have a Self inside us that is aching to live out loud. When that ache is stifled, it comes out in ways that hurt us all—in anger, prejudice, violence, war. It's up to us to give ourselves proof of all we can be, and as we do, we set the example for others, and provide proof for them too.

Wendell Berry's poem goes on:

> Be ready.
> When their light has picked you out
> and their questions are asked, say to them:
> "I am not ashamed." A sure horizon
> will come around you. The heron will begin
> his evening flight from the hilltop.[2]

Your dawn is on the precipice of its break. Your Self is not the obvious choice. But I promise you—it *is* the right one.

Part Two

YOU NEED A SELF

FIND YOUR SELF

BE YOUR SELF

STAY YOUR SELF

WANT YOUR SELF

Chapter Five

THE REDEFINITION

Shifting your self-talk is a two-part equation. There's the *self* part, and there's the *talk* part.

Most people jump straight to the latter and focus on the *talk* first. But we talked about this in earlier chapters: you're not most people.

Starting your shift by focusing on the *talk* part of the *self-talk* equation is like sucking on a cough lozenge to cure your chronic colds. Maybe it'll get you to stop hacking in the moment, but if you're getting sick all the time, there's probably something more going on than a seasonal sniffle.

Self-talk is so ingrained in us that it's chronic. The *talk* part is symptomatic. It's the *self* part that's at the core of the shift and is key to learning the positive, self-loving language you long to live out loud.

The real, lasting work of shifting your self-talk doesn't start by finding nicer words. It starts by sifting through the years of shame, blame, and pretending, and finding your Self underneath it all.

It starts by rewriting the story you've been telling—and redefining the words you use to not only tell this version of it but describe what you're after. Beginning with the redefinition of what *positivity* and *self-love* really mean in the first place.

Carousels

My amusement park ride of choice as a highly sensitive kid was the carousel. No big drops. No unexpected moves. No aggressive sounds or strobe light effects. Just an expected gallop in the round. For three whole minutes, I could get on my favorite horse and escape from everyone and everything around me.

I'm a Libra, and true to my astrological nature, I appreciate aesthetics. So of course, part of the appeal of carousels was their prettiness. Anyone who has ever visited an amusement park or fairground knows carousels are very pretty. Porcelain hollow horses and spherical molding on loop. And most carousels cost cents to ride, so it's easy to just stay on the gorgeous ponies and go around in circles ad nauseam. A tactic I employed in 1995 on my first trip to the Santa Monica Pier, when the roller coasters and target-shooting games felt too overwhelming to even walk around. Those were scary. The carousel, though, made me smile. If I just stayed on long enough, I could avoid all the other stuff and ride the pretty ponies until it was time to go home. So I did.

And then . . . it happened.

The song on the loudspeaker changed.

Bryan Adams's "Have You Ever Really Loved a Woman?" started to croon in my eight-year-old ears.

Have you ever heard that song? Because if so, you already know this song is *not* meant for eight-year-old ears. Mind you, eight-year-old me had just recently learned about sex and, to her horror, just recently realized how practically every song on the radio is about it. This was the '90s, and "sex positivity" wasn't mainstream yet, even though my elementary school taught us all we needed to know in an age-appropriate way that was exactly that. No shame. No stigma. All honesty and information. We learned the facts, maybe with a lighthearted emotional anecdote here or there to make sure we weren't too scared or scarred. I was neither. I was just . . . eight. And very much not on board with this whole sweaty-seeming thing.

So I was at the age where sex seemed like a very gross thing adults enjoyed doing for who-knows-what-reason. I didn't want to know. I *certainly* didn't want to be sung to about it. Being stuck on a carousel going around in circles while having Bryan Adams's advice about what to do when you really love a woman echoing through the chamber felt like a very specific kind of hell.

My horse rounded the bend and the song continued.

Some lyrics about holding and touching a woman.

I saw a couple making out on the bench by the door.

I circled again.

The verbs in this musical instruction manual were escalating now. Breathing. Tasting. Feeling.

Quick check—yep, still there. They were really going at it.

I focused intently on the walls, trying my best to tune out this very all-around PG-13 moment.

I almost succeeded.

Until I heard Bryan Adams clearly and passionately croon the line about seeing his unborn children in this woman's eyes.

NOPE. THAT'S IT. I'M DONE. I WANT OUT.

Let me tell you something.

That was the longest carousel ride of my life.

And let me tell you something else: never again did I make the mistake of thinking I could avoid feeling uncomfortable by staying put on a pretty ride that goes nowhere.

Dead-End Optimism

So much has been said about how our culture has a negativity problem. Which it does . . .

. . . but it also has an Optimism problem.

To be clear, living with an optimist*ic* outlook on life is a strength. No doubts there. Living optimistically usually means you're forward-thinking. You naturally see what *could be.* You find the beauty in the seemingly possible instead of the darkness in the seemingly inevitable.

Please don't get me wrong—optimism (lower-case O, neutral tone) by itself isn't bad at all.

However.

Just like anything, we've got to be mindful if we want to make optimism work the way we intend it to.

If you pay very close attention, you can feel the disconnect when optimism starts to go downhill. Maybe you'll hear someone mention "good vibes only." Maybe you'll be told to "look on the bright side." When it happens, that well-intentioned optimism shuts out reality as a means of avoidance—a form of toxic positivity—and chalks it up to a glass-half-full mentality.

How does this happen, though? How can something so inherently good betray us?

I call it Dead-End Optimism.

Dead-End Optimism is when you rely on a positive outlook to ignore, shut out, fabricate, or gloss over the important and valid realities of life. It can gnaw away at your spirit and your relationships, minimize your experiences, and roll a haze of oblivion over your existence. And it can lead you into a cul-de-sac of toxic positivity with no way out.

Dead-End Optimism makes me dizzy—just like carousels. It turns me away from reality in favor of the shiny, pretty thing around the corner. I get on board and go in circles over and over until I lose my bearings.

The thing about carousel rides is that they need to end at some point. At *some* point, the machine slows down, and the music fades. You get off your literal high horse, and you're faced with the world beyond the beautiful lights and porcelain creatures. Stay on too long, and there's a good chance you'll stumble off a bit more than wobbly.

When you find yourself caught in the nonstop carousel ride of Dead-End Optimism, one of two things usually starts to happen:

1. **Eventually, it breaks down after going around and around for so long, and so do you.** There's only so much you can give, and only so long you can force a smile or look for the silver lining in pain.

Extremes lead to breaking points. Nothing can sustain the highest highs or longest rides forever.

2. **It becomes nauseating and obnoxious—something other people don't want to go near.** It's cheesy and trite at best, ignorant and entitled at worst. Ignoring the realities of the world around you, dismissing the "bad" feelings of others, and attempting to write over any sort of uncomfortable or unpleasant experience alienates you from not just your community, but from your Self. You lose track of real life and become a part of a fairy-tale world playing on loop. And then there you are, alone on a ride going nowhere, clinging to a fantasy you know deep down isn't real. (And sometimes, if you're particularly unlucky, a song will start playing, and you'll wonder why you ever got on in the first place.)

Pragmatic, Proactive Positivity

I'm able to see the good in most things. One of my friends even calls me "aggressively optimistic." And when we're all stuck in the collective doldrums together, I'm often asked how I stay so hopeful. "Give me your secret," they ask. "You've got it all figured out."

I don't have a secret. I don't view myself as a glass-half-full kind of person, and certainly don't feel like I've *got it all figured out*. The title character in *Pollyanna* was admirable but always bugged me a bit (which made me feel guilty, of course—sorry, Hayley Mills). I loved the dance sequences and cartoon penguins in *Mary Poppins*, but the Practically Perfect parts of the famous nanny never resonated with me. Come to think of it, I much preferred her subtle snark over her organization skills.

When asked for my "secret," I reveal that I'm not really an Optimist (capital O, chipper voice). Or at least how others expect me to be.

I'm Pragmatically, Proactively Positive.

To me, positivity is about looking at what's in front of you and being proactive, not reactive. My brand of positivity isn't about what's happy instead of sad; it's about what's pragmatic instead of unrealistic. With this definition, "happiness" or "good vibes" are rendered irrelevant—which I guess is my secret of sorts, because it's what allows me to *sustain* my positivity. It allows positivity to permeate ANY kind of moment, without breaking me down, cutting me off from reality, or pressing the fast-forward button. Presence and positivity work hand in hand.

The myth we're told when it comes to "being positive" is that positivity is goodness, and goodness equals happiness. I have never, ever experienced that to be true on a lasting basis. Happiness is fleeting, and goodness is a one-trick pony. Real positivity—the kind that *lasts*—is pragmatic, *proactive* positivity. It happens when our love of life, love of others, and love of Self not only transcends the pitfalls and darkness that come our way but transcends the peaks and lightness as well. Real positivity doesn't make happiness the goal—it makes You-ness the goal. All of you. No matter the circumstance or emotion.

Life's ups and downs are inevitable, and some moments will seem more hope-filled than others. So what can you do about those moments that feel like there's no hope to be found? You can see the facts in front of you and the projected outcomes ahead, and you can root for what you hope will happen while also recognizing the various realities of what *could* happen. It's not about ignoring that things aren't perfectly in place or might go awry (or maybe they already have). It's about taking in the world as is, seeing the full spectrum of its experience and existence, and choosing to proactively fight for an outcome that uplifts us collectively.

To shift away from Dead-End Optimism and into Pragmatic, Proactive Positivity, we must let go of rushing into the search for how good things can be in the future (or not), and instead, sit with how good things are right now (or not). We must begin to look at the glass not as half empty or half full, but as a glass that's being sipped from every moment. You have a glass, and you have water. That's a start.

Shifting from one to the other begins by moving forward through rough obstacles and uncomfortable feelings instead of around them and granting ourselves permission to let our *self-like* ebb and flow.

You read that right. Self-*like.*

Self-Like vs. Self-Love

Think about your most lasting, enduring relationships. Friends. Family members. Significant others. There are definitely times you don't like what they have to say or what they're doing, right? Obviously. With vulnerability and intimacy comes the fact that you don't always like what you see or hear. Healthy relationships create a safe space to explore what you like and don't like as you learn more about who you are and move forward on your own journey.

So why should it be any different with the relationship you have with your Self?

Disliking a part of your Self sometimes doesn't mean that you can't love your Self at the same time, at all times. You don't love your Self—your body, your brain, your heart, your spirit—because you're waiting for payback or payout. You love your Self because you love your Self. Period. It's *unconditional love.* And if there's anything I know about unconditional love, it's that it does *not* equal unconditional *like.*

What holds us back from true self-love is the idea that we're supposed to like our Self 100 percent of the time. Because chances are, if you're a living, breathing human being, that's just not going to be the case.

Like, *ever.*

When we mistake *self-like* for *self-love,* we send a message to ourselves that not *liking* how we show up in that exact moment must be an indication that we don't *love* who we are fully and completely.

"Love" is the goal self-help culture sets for us. That's a good goal in theory. But rarely do we hear about the nuances of self-love. And *words matter.* When chosen over and over again, this super simple yet highly limiting word choice makes us believe we can only love or loathe ourselves. No in-between liking or disliking allowed.

Practicing this *self-like vs. self-love* distinction is work. It's unlearning years of verbal cueing and retraining yourself to see more than two options—love and loathing—when it comes to how you feel about your Self.

My Self speaks to me daily, and I don't always like what I hear:

- When my physical Self feels uncomfortable or doesn't look the way I think it "should" look, even though I know I think that way because of decades' worth of internalizing diet culture and toxic beauty standards—in this moment, I do not like the way my body *is*.
- When my mental Self jumps to conclusions or becomes defensive, even though I *know* that conclusions are risky to jump to and a hyper-protective defense rarely produces a truly proactive offense—in this moment, I do not like the way my mind *works*.
- When my emotional Self whines for validation and permission, even though I *know* neither will take away my pain or shame—in this moment, I do not like the way my emotions *respond*.

But none of these dislike-able moments define how I *really* feel about my Self. In reality, I love my Self despite those things, and I love my Self for those things. I love my Self for telling me what's up, for waking me up to parts of Me that need some TLC. Sure, we fight sometimes, but my Self and I know how to fight fair. We know how to keep respect at the core of our conversations and use explanatory "I feel" statements instead of accusatory "you are" ones (my therapist would be so proud)—and we're always solution-oriented. The more I remind myself that I'm in a long-term relationship with my Self, the easier it is to keep recommitting to our common values and goals.

Positivity Proof Points

Pragmatic, Proactive Positivity relies on the kind of self-love that's unconditional, that's unbreakable, and that no high-high or low-low can affect. And it's important to remember that neither positivity (the real kind) or self-love (the unconditional kind) asks you to be any other way than who and how you are.

Let's try this out together real quick:

> I know that, even on my worst days, *I am kind.*
>
> I know that, even in my toughest times, *I have tenacity.*
>
> *I know that, even when things feel hard, there's got to be a way forward.*

When I say these things, I'm not being impulsive or grandiose. I'm not employing "wishful thinking." I'm simply stating what I know to be true.

These are your positivity proof points. They're objective reminders of the things that make you YOU. They're a part of who you are, whether you think them daily or not, no matter where you go or how you feel. The trick here is that positivity doesn't need to be mysterious or magical. The sturdiest, most grounded positivity is based in the truth that's already there. Especially when it comes to your Self. If, like me, you always tear up at that one scene in *Hook*—you know the one, where the Lost Boys see Peter Banning for who he is after he's forgotten for so long—you'll understand the simple yet profound power of self-recognition. *Oh*, there *you are.* Your magic was always there.

Think about these for a minute to gather your proof:

- I am___________ (a characteristic you're proud of, like: kind, hilarious, generous, a good friend, loving, true to my word, compassionate, analytical, perceptive, a great listener, driven, etc.)

- I have__________ (a quality that helps you through tough times, like: resilience, perspective, humor, stellar gut instincts, non-attachment, etc.)
- I know__________ (a belief *you already hold* that makes you feel expansive, like: I am doing the best I can, I can find community anywhere, I'm not alone, I can face any challenge, my life will be an adventure, etc.)

Your positivity proof points don't need to be polished or poetic. All they need to be is true-to-you. They're evidence you can begin to draw on to build unwavering self-love. You've got this because you already *are* this.

Sorry to break it to you, but there is no grand expedition when it comes to "finding" your Self.

Because finding your Self is not a search. It's a dig.

It's an adventure, sure, but it's not about finding what could be, *out there.* It's about uncovering what already is, *in here*. It's okay to not like all parts of your Self all the time, or not prefer the way those parts are in any given moment. I'd even go so far as to say it's *healthy* to not like all parts of your Self all the time. Isn't that what the strongest relationships are like? There's always tension that inevitably pops up. Always dissonance that arises when you least expect it. The key is to remember what's underneath.

When it comes to your relationship with your Self, it's always on your side.

Things might get rough. You won't always agree.

But your Self is always there for you—even underneath the rubble of resistance.

It always wants you to listen.

Please don't shut it out.

Chapter Six

LOOSENING THE GRIP

Growing up in Southern California meant access to a slew of quintessential summertime experiences. Beach days were most days. Board shorts and flip-flops, the unofficial uniform whether you were a surfer or not. And as soon as the cold-for-Los-Angeles weather would subside (which is the unofficial start of summer in LA, which is usually sometime around April), my parents would corral my younger brother Alex and I into my mom's green station wagon, and we'd take the hour-long journey from the 101 to the 405 to the 5 freeway to my own personal promised land: Disneyland.

At Disneyland, I was acutely aware of who the *real* stars of the show were. The rides were exciting, but to me, they were far from the main attraction. As soon as I entered the park gates, I kept my eyes peeled.

At any moment, I could see *them.*

The characters.

Whether it was Pluto the dog or Donald Duck or the ultimate of ultimate celebrity sightings—Mickey and Minnie Mouse—getting to share a moment with my animated role models was my top priority when I was at The Happiest Place On Earth. I loved the human "princesses" too (I was still very much obsessed with all things Ariel), but something about the fully-costumed animal characters, ironically, seemed more . . . believable? *You can't fool me, random lady in a princess dress.* But giant Mickey Mouse—you're obviously the real deal.

Some kids carry souvenir autograph books with them from character to character when they go to Disneyland, collecting signatures like sports fans collect baseball cards. Not me. I didn't care about signatures. So impersonal. All I wanted was a meaningful moment—and a photo to remember it by.

When I finally saw a Disney character walking along Main Street, my heart fluttered a little. I waited patiently in line for a photo, and then when it was my turn, they welcomed me in with a wave hello and open arms. They gave me a hug and I wrapped my arms around them as tight as I could in return. I buried my head in their synthetic fur and for a second, time would stop. I was loved, I was seen, I mattered, and I belonged.

Touching moment, right? Yeah, that's what my parents thought too. Until the photo opportunity was done, my turn was over, and to their embarrassment, I wouldn't leave the character's side. I wouldn't cry or scream; I just wouldn't *go.* Alex got his hug and hurried back to my parents, ready for the next adventure, but I stayed put by the giant mouse or the chipmunk or whoever. Other children and their families would proceed to walk up to take their pictures, which then became group photos since I was still there standing slightly to the side like an awkward extra wheel. But I didn't care. I was there for love.

When my parents would finally coax me away (probably by the promise of another character to meet down the lane, or the sideways look of another parent trying to get a picture without me in it), I'd keep turning back to look behind my shoulder until I couldn't anymore.

God forbid I became just another kid they met that day.

God forbid I was forgettable.

~

I am a recovering Stage-Four Clinger. And it's not just the characters at Disneyland that I'm talking about here. I cling to people. I cling to places. And most of all, I cling to ideas—none more than the ideas I have about my Self.

Becoming attached to something or someone is almost always at least *in part* about becoming attached to the story you've written about it or them in your head. Attachments are usually less about the actual things and more about your relationships with them.

My clinging isn't physical, and it's probably not the kind of clinging anyone else would notice but me. My mind goes into overdrive, like a frantic puppy who senses its human is about to leave for the day. I both dissociate and grip harder.

I feel myself clinging when the story I've told myself starts to develop holes in it. "You are *this*" and "you can *do that*" get challenged by real life, and I take a microscope to myself, dissecting every little decision and every possible perception.

WHAT'RE YOU DOING? WHO ARE YOU WITH? WHAT ARE YOU SAYING AND THEN WHAT DID YOU SAY ABOUT IT AFTER? YOUR VOICE—MAKE IT SOFTER—YOU MIGHT COME OFF AS STUCK-UP IF YOU'RE LOUD—BUT NOT TOO SOFT—THIS IS YOUR MOMENT!

I look for all the ways my self-woven tale has started to unravel, or could possibly unravel, and I swoop in with the SuperCling. I'm basically my own biggest helicopter parent.

I've softened my voice and dulled my presence in a room because there was that one time I was spoken over and shamed, so it's probably just safer for me and better for everyone if I nod my responses and silently smile my sentences. From staying in line to "Living My Best Life," I know what a Good Girl looks like, sounds like, acts like, and *re*acts like. Good Girls do not raise their voices. Good Girls do not get the luxury of healthy discourse. Good Girls are agreeable and easily agreed upon, or they're not Good Girls at all. I've known the value of being a Good Girl—love and acceptance by a world that prefers you to stay small—and sacrificed my Self by clinging to the story of my goodness.

I've chased after goals long after I've wanted them, because I've invested so much time, money, and energy in them for so long. And even more than that, I've gotten other people to believe in me and invest their energy too, so it's probably just better for everyone if I remain who they know me to be. I started to realize that I didn't love being in the world of acting way before I made the eventual pivot, clinging to the goal of being a Tony Award–winning actress for way longer than I related to it. The signs were there, of course: auditions I skipped if they didn't feel "just right," bitingly bitter feelings about the way the industry treated young women, journal entries I wrote admitting that acting was not the center of my life like it seemed to be for my peers, confessional notes I posted on social media acknowledging that I didn't love escaping into a character and way preferred to be Me. There were clues; there always are—we sometimes just choose to ignore what they tell us.

But I'd made it a goal to be a Tony Award–winning actress when I was thirteen years old. And went to college to study to be a Tony Award–winning actress. And spent lots of time and money on voice lessons and acting classes and headshots and audition outfits. And invested so much energy on Tony Award–winning actress-ing. And got everyone I cared about in my life to believe in me. Even when I felt myself clearly not lit up by my work, I stuck with it. Not out of tenacity, but out of loyalty to others, and out of loyalty to that thirteen-year-old's dream. Maybe one day I could live up to her idea of success. Only then would I be free to create a new one. *Look what we did!* I'd tell her. *Now you can pivot. Now you've crossed it off.*

Clinging is a survival strategy, albeit misguided. Any time I cling, I submit to a feeling of scarcity—there's not enough, I'm not enough, I better not make any sudden moves, it could all go away tomorrow—and set a robust stage for my Fraudy Feelings to waltz in and snag the spotlight.

And so I cling tighter.

All the Fraudy Feelings

Harvard Business Review says that Imposter Syndrome is "a collection of feelings of inadequacy that persist despite evident success. 'Imposters' suffer from chronic self-doubt and a sense of intellectual fraudulence that overrides any feelings of success or external proof of their competence."[1]

But Imposter Syndrome isn't just about intellect. It shows up *everywhere.*

I call these Fraudy Feelings: the emotions that arise when you question your sense of belonging or rightness.

Here's a collection of Fraudy Feelings I've heard over the years from friends, coworkers, family members, clients, mentors, mentees, and myself. Note if any resonate with you:

Am I too selfish?

A pushover?

Am I too strong?

Am I too loud?

Too quiet?

Did I come off wrong?

Will they take me seriously?

Am I really good enough . . .

Wise enough . . .

Strong enough to weather this life I've constructed . . .

. . . or have I just made everyone believe I am?

Will they find me out?

When my Fraudy Feelings fire up, I worry that I've created a mess. That I'll never be able to live up to the expectations I've built for myself. I'll never forget when a coworker once called me *enigmatic.* A mystery. "Who *are* you even, Katie Horwitch?" he teased. It was the first time I realized I might not be the person I'd always told myself I was in my internally self-narrated tale.

I'm too introverted and too solitary to be the kind of companion I feel I should be and have always told myself I am.

I'm too much of a team player to be the kind of leader I know I can be and have always told myself I am.

I'm too interested in day-to-day micro-moments to seek out the big adventures I know are there and have always told myself I should go after.

I'm too private to be public.

Too soft to be tough.

They'll find me out. I'm sure of it.

I used to believe that when you became more self-assured and successful, your Fraudy Feelings just melted away. Or at least melted away quicker than they would if you weren't so self-assured and successful. *Nuh-uh.* The irony is that as you become more and more You, you open up way more doors and windows for Fraudy Feelings to enter through. Your Fraudy Feelings don't melt away—they amplify and attack.

The good thing is, you've now got *way* more introspective ammo to battle them than you ever did before. You know to take a closer look at what your self-talk might be trying to tell you. You know the difference between real positivity and Dead-End Optimism. You know that temporary self-like and unconditional self-love aren't the same thing. And you know, most of all, that the small moments aren't really so small at all.

But even so, it might start to seem like you're in a constant battle with your Fraudy Feelings instead of a sometimes-tiff. That doesn't mean you're doing things wrong. It means you're doing things *anew*. You've got new strategies, which means of course you've got new struggles. The difference is that you're paying attention and moving *through* them instead of ignoring what's tough and moving *around* them. This is the opposite of wrongness. This is what it means to grow.

Moving through your Fraudy Feelings is empowering, scary, and 100 percent worth it. And sometimes, all it means is taking a second look at what's already there.

To Me, I Belong

If you're even peripherally aware of the world of self-improvement, you've probably heard the phrase "belong to yourself" before. Belong to yourself before you belong to anybody else. You belong to You. It's a pretty phrase and a cute quotable.

But when you jumble the words around a bit, you'll notice something way more interesting underneath . . .

I belong to me.

Make the last two words the first two. Add a comma.

***To me,** I belong.*

Say the same thing in a different way.

***In my opinion,** I belong.*

True belonging is about full possession of yourself, sure.

But it's also about *believing* in your capacity to belong wherever you go.

That belief is *deeply* rooted in a sense of purpose and passion.

Fraudy Feelings, then, surface when your sense of purpose and passion don't have solid ground to grab onto and healthy soil to feed them.

Negative self-talk might sometimes seem like it pops up out of nowhere, but when you boil it down, many times it's *filler* for uncertainty: lack of clarity around who you are, no plan on how to be that person, and an absence of ownership of what makes you YOU. I'm not saying "finding your purpose" is going to solve all your problems and transform you into a positivity unicorn. And I'm not going to tell you that planning out every step of your journey, Excel-spreadsheet-style, is a fool-proof plan. What happens when you inevitably change and grow, as human beings do?

But I *will* say this: with confidence in what I call your *Through Line,* you might start to notice less of the negative self-talk you use to sabotage yourself when things start to feel like they're on shaky ground, or when they're maybe going—cue horror movie narrator voice—a little *too well.*

What Is a Through Line?

What is the common theme in everything you love?

What is the common goal in everything you do?

Those are the building blocks of your Through Line.

We're all equipped with a Through Line; something we're wonderful at and are meant to give to the world. And while some people might suggest mantras or affirmations to help you "be nicer" to yourself, it's my firm belief that you can't shift your self-talk in a real, lasting way without finding your Through Line first.

Why? Because embracing your Through Line goes deeper than what others can see. It's about having a sense that everything fits into a larger, bigger-picture version of who you are. That alignment can lead to not only a feeling of purpose, but a feeling of fullness. Like you're using everything you've got. Your Through Line adds a sense of cohesion to choices that might seem unrelated, and encourages you to explore as many interests or paths as you please. From the outside, it might look like you're pivoting—but on the inside, you know you're just fulfilling more and more of your purpose. Once you find your Through Line and shift your actions to *deliver* it, a long-term sense of Self is exponentially more likely.

If negative self-talk is (at least partially, at most totally) about a lack of clarity in purpose or meaning, then let's get clear. You might have one Through Line or a couple. Here are three steps to find yours:

Step 1: **Make a list of everything you love to do or experience.**

And I mean *everything.* Notice the little things that fulfill you. The tasks themselves, but also the meaning behind those tasks. Not so much the superficial Whats, but the hidden *Whys.* The things you seem to get absorbed by that fill you up from the inside out.

Don't worry about cohesiveness. List as many actions, experiences, and instances as you can. Cooking dinner, one-on-one time with friends, business strategy, binging on horror movies—it's all fair game.

Step 2: **Find a common theme and goal within your answers.**

Try to find a mode, a feeling, or an output. Maybe not *all* the things you listed out fit together, but I'll bet *a lot* of them do.

Look beyond the obvious—the fact that you love to bake and you love to have spontaneous dance parties around the house might seem unrelated, but when you look deeper, you might realize what you actually love is the act of creating something that brightens up *someone else's* day. You love to bake, but you love it most when you're sharing your treats with friends. You love to have spontaneous dance parties, but you *really* love them when they're shared, because they make your roommate/partner/family member/cat/dog fill up with joy and laughter. *There's where your magic lives. That's your Through Line.*

Step 3: **Formalize your Through Line Statement.**

Once you've got the pieces of your Through Line, it's time to put the puzzle together. Take your answers from Step 2, and use this formula to create your Through Line Statement: **I [common theme in everything you love] to [common goal in everything you do].**

Need an example? Here's what my exercise, and my Through Line, looks like:

Step 1: **Make a list of everything you love to do or experience.**

I love writing, singing, people-watching, having unfiltered and authentic conversations, listening to podcast interviews, discovering new music, running outside, teaching fitness classes, taking fitness classes, performing, photography, singing and dancing at concerts, laughing out loud at movies, spending time with my family and soul-friends, reading nonfiction books or books written in the first person, public speaking, taking small chances, painting, drawing, playing board games that may or may not bring out my inner competitive Monica Gellar (I'm usually more of a Phoebe type, but whenever Monica's competitive side comes out on a *Friends* rerun, I relate on deep levels).

Step 2: **Find a common theme and goal within your answers.**
The common thing I love in the majority of my answers is being able to use my voice in some way. Whether it's literally using my voice through conversation or song, or figuratively using my voice through my style of drawing or the way I move my body, I can see that when I love something, it's usually because I'm showing up as myself not only fully, but out loud.

But I can also see that when it comes to most all of the things I love, they don't exist in a vacuum. There's usually someone else involved, and I love when I can help them feel a sense of self-expression. The times I feel like I love those full-voiced things the *most?* When what I do can set off a chain reaction in someone else and help them use their own voice, literal or metaphorical, too.

Step 3: **Formalize Your Through Line Statement.**
What happens when I put the pieces together? I get my Through Line: **I use my unique voice to its fullest to help others find, use, and *own* theirs to its fullest.**

But wait . . . *how does this connect to playing board games or singing and dancing at a concert?*

We learn best not from textbooks or bullet-pointed protocols, but from each other. (Ironic, I know, as this is a book, and it has a few bullet-pointed protocols sprinkled into it.) "Picking up on everything the adults do" doesn't end in childhood. It's the way we learn to coexist in the world. At least, how we learn to survive. At most, how we learn to thrive.

I see my "voice" show up not only when I hold a mic and stand on a stage, but also when I write or draw on a page. My "voice" even shows up in the way I move—not graceful per se, but a style that's all my own.

I love listening to podcast conversations and reading books written in the first person because they spark a discussion inside my head—I can almost hear my voice chiming in with the author or speaker—and I love taking those discussions out into the real world and turning my community into my very own unofficial book club or listening group. If I look closely, everything I love has my Through Line of "using my unique voice to its fullest to help others find, use, and own theirs" running through it.

When I think of my Through Line, I'm reminded that there's no time to shy away from my Self. The way I think, feel, move, and interact with the world could become a part of someone else's Emotional DNA without me knowing it. So I better be intentional about using my voice to its fullest, making sure I am more of myself each day, not less. If honoring exactly who I am helps someone give themselves permission to do the same, I'm on track. I stand for love—of others, of my Self, and of your Self too.

Loosening the Grip

It's easy to talk negatively about yourself when you feel out of control, or like the least "expert" in the room, or wonder if there's something else you should've done (or not done). We all face tense, anxious, awkward, or bang-your-head-against-the-wall scenarios throughout our lives. Sometimes, things just don't go the way we prefer they would.

But now that you know your Through Line, you can choose to invest your time and energy a bit more mindfully, and make more decisions that are proactive, not reactive. Whenever I feel stuck or useless or squashed down and dull, I ask myself: *Are you using your unique voice right now, and is it resonating with the best parts of others?* If the answer is no, even if I can't fully escape the scenario, I divert my attention and try to place myself in a position where I *can* use my Through Line to its fullest potential, however big or small that might look from the outside. I don't need to shift everything, and even if I wanted to, most of the time I can't. But I can shift *something*. And that something matters.

Keep your Through Line Statement handy by writing it on a sticky note and placing it somewhere visible. When your Fraudy Feelings bubble up, go back and look at it. See if you can identify a nuance of your Through Line that exists in your current situation. And try again. Maybe it's even time for you to revisit the exercise altogether to make sure your current Through Line is still resonant. Trial and error isn't about racking up your failures; it's about changing up your approach so you can find the most successful successes that work for *you*.

I'm not saying that once you figure out how or where you shine the brightest, you'll always be shiny and sparkly. Life wouldn't be life without mistakes, missteps, and those moments when we feel our lows the deepest. But if you're intentionally placing yourself in scenarios where you can use your Through Line—whether it be with a group of friends, a relationship, a job, a hobby, or even a random conversation you're having—you'll start to feel those highs a whole lot higher, and your life will start to feel a whole lot more cohesive. And most importantly, you'll feel like exactly who and how you are in the moment, instead of thinking you must abide by a set of rules and descriptions that no longer serve you.

~

Loosening your grip on an idea you've built up about a person or a place is tough. Loosening your grip on an idea you've built up about *yourself*, though—well, that's next-level. You're You, after all. You can't escape You.

But why keep clinging when there's so much adventure ahead? Clinging isn't an act of love. It's an escape. When we cling, we bring in the ships and shut down the lighthouses. We call off the search party and refocus our energy on keeping ourselves captive. The more you cling to how your story is "supposed" to unfold, the less chance you have at delight and awe and all those other emotions in between.

When new, exciting opportunities come my way—an invitation to something special, a friendly friendship gains soul-status, a YES to that

YES I've been pursuing for months or even years—I feel my Stage-Four Clinger walking into the room with a megaphone ready to yell at me and a cane ready to pull me off the stage.

And when that happens, I have to tell her no. I have to tell her that as much as she has tried to take good care of me, she has not always been right. She has *rarely* been right, actually. She has the best of intentions, but comes from the wrong place. My inner Stage-Four Clinger wants so desperately for me to find my Self—but she wants me to do it by sticking to a set of outdated ideas I've had about myself that I made before I even started to live. Like that kid hugging Mickey Mouse and not letting go out of fear that she's forgettable if she doesn't work hard to give someone else reason to remember her by. Like that kid who wants to let her Self shine but is afraid of what might happen if she doesn't stay in line.

My inner Stage-Four Clinger is so afraid I'll fade away if I don't make a lasting impression, and simultaneously afraid I'll be in the wrong if I try.

I tell her I appreciate her concern. And then I keep living.

I still make choices that feel more in service of an imaginary version of Me—one that's led by her Fraudy Feelings—than the Me I am right now.

But I'm learning to loosen my grip. I'm learning that a true embrace will linger way after I let go, and that I don't need to cling tight to be deeply felt.

Clinging to a vision of who you should be or could be will never reap the kinds of rewards you'll get when you honor who you are right now and live on purpose, with purpose.

You belong to yourself.

To yourself, you belong.

In your opinion, you belong.

And go from there.

Chapter Seven

INTERNAL GPS

At twenty-four, I was convinced I had the worst luck ever. In no way was this more exemplified than when it came to me and my shitty-ass car.

The summer between my freshman and sophomore years of college, I'd gotten into the worst car accident of my life. And not like a *jarring-but-mostly-annoying* fender bender. The kind you have nightmares about and wake up from upon impact. (It should be noted right now that I've had vivid nightmares my entire life. I'm a chronic nightmare-r. And while I rarely remember my good dreams, I remember my nightmares forever.)

I was driving north on the freeway, heading back home after a gig for a new surfer-girl-adjacent clothing line. The kinds of clothes that twentysomething girls wore in the early 2000s to look like they hung out at the beach all weekend, when in reality they were probably sitting in their cars in traffic for hours upon end just like the rest of the city (maybe clothes made for twentysomethings are designed so you can emulate the life you want to live instead of actually living it. Maybe that's one of the reasons so many of us feel so behind in our twenties).

The gig was a modeling gig. Modeling was something I'd been secretly interested in since I was a kid, even though I felt like I wasn't "supposed" to be interested in it at all. *Don't get full of yourself,* I thought. *You're vain and conceited for wanting this, so you better pretend like you don't. Get over yourself, Katie.* As someone who spent her time striving to be seen while at the same time apologizing for it, this all tracks.

When I dove into my acting career, I was excited to learn how many times actors were sent into auditions for modeling jobs in addition to film and TV jobs. It felt like a good way to excuse my interest in it. Modeling, it turns out, is really just acting frozen in time.

In hindsight, photo shoots were a charged space for me as someone who struggled with body and Self issues. If they went well, I felt amazing. If they were anything less, I'd spiral. But I didn't realize that pattern, or if I did, I didn't care enough to change it. I kept saying yes when the opportunities came up—not only did I need the money and the work, but I also craved the validation. I loved knowing that someone else saw me in a way worthy of being captured and frozen, extending a fleeting moment into eternity (or at least however long that image would last).

But saying yes because you want someone else to say yes to you is a risky move, and leaning your permanence on someone else's lens is dangerous territory.

I drove home that afternoon and reflected on the day I'd just had. As a woman on a set, I can't tell you what a difference it makes to have other women not only on set with you but in leadership positions calling the shots. This was not one of those cases. While the (female) designer was present and as encouraging as could be, the (male) director was another story. On the cusp of nineteen, and not in very good mental health, I felt great about myself and my body . . . until I was standing in front of the camera next to someone else. I fought not to compare myself to the other lanky models: my mind told me my legs were too short, my skin was too oily, my arms were too hairy, my face was too round, and my body took up way more space than all the other girls despite being a good four inches shorter than them all. My heart was persistent in its attempt to remind me that I'd felt great just minutes before, and that the narrative of Skinny Is Better and Sexy Is Specific was bullshit.

No size is better than another. Sexy is subjective. You're just fine, Katie. You're just fine . . .

As I posed leaning causally-but-actually-very-strategically against a prop linoleum patio table, I heard the director call out to the stylist to adjust me.

"She doesn't have one—[glances to me] you don't have one!—but it looks like she's got a tummy pooch. Just tilt her hips and raise her shorts like this. Katie, stay right there, don't move. We'll adjust you."

I'd go on to replay that comment in my head for years when anyone pointed a camera at me.

Tummy pooch.

Don't move.

We'll adjust you.

More than the words themselves, I'd replay his tone—one that made it clear he saw something wrong with me. Of course my abdomen had curve and softness to it—that's how my body was built (and how many women's bodies are built, by the way). But apparently, that needed to be our little secret. His comment made the flame of my body dysmorphia flare into a wildfire. Even now, almost two decades later, I can't stand the words *tummy* and *pooch* like some people can't stand the word *moist.*[1]

Driving home that evening, though, it was all I could hear. *Tummy pooch. Tummy pooch.* Until it wasn't. I heard a *screeeeeeeech!* coming from somewhere behind me. My eyes darted to my rearview mirror, and I saw, two cars back, a small grey four-door sedan zigzagging its way through every single lane.

I could barely attempt to get out of dodge before he *whacked* into the side of my car and I went spinning. I tried to gain control, but in a matter of milliseconds, I slammed face-first into my airbag as my car crashed into the center divider.

There was silence.

And then I started screaming.

My tummy pooch didn't matter anymore. My life did.

It took months for me to sit comfortably in a car again, let alone drive. And when I did, in a new car specifically splurged on for its safety features, I struggled to trust myself on the road.

~

And thus began my string of self-proclaimed "bad luck." My safe not-as-new-anymore car broke down three times in the span of two weeks, the third time in the middle of a downpour where I was stranded in a 7-Eleven parking lot for two hours until roadside assistance arrived and the mechanic casually told me the transmission had blown out. Turns out, the "brand-new" car I'd been driving was a lemon (a cute term to describe a very not-cute defective vehicle). We waited another forty-five minutes for a tow truck to come and take my untrustworthy vehicle away for good. I got a new car but the same bad luck. Its hubcaps were stolen repeatedly for a good five months in a row. First, the fronts, then the backs, then the hubcap thieves decided to get fancy and take a random one, one at a time. It got broken into in my own parking garage, and all my belongings were stolen from the trunk. The rental car I used while my car was in the shop got rear-ended at a stoplight. I got a new rental. I got clipped on the freeway. I got my actual car back. It got broken into again. My debt was racking up right along with my shame. At this point, it was almost comical—but I was in no mood for comedy (I wasn't even in the mood to contemplate the concept of *coincidence*), so all I saw was my dirty rotten bad luck everywhere.

My anxiety began to spike each time I got in the car to go somewhere. I triple-checked every light, every switch, and every mirror. I got honked at for going too slow and yelled at for pausing too long at stop signs. But I kept triple-checking and going slow and pausing for three counts of Mississippi—*one Mississippi, two Mississippi, three Mississippi*—because who knew what could be lurking right around the corner that I somehow managed to miss?

The story started to be written over the next handful of years. Even though the words didn't match the reality:

Katie must be a really bad driver.

It must, somehow, be my fault.

Lessons on the Road

In life, we're often presented with the same lessons over and over again until we *finally* learn them. Not every single shitty occurrence is a "lesson," of course (sometimes, things are just awful with no reasonable explanation—"everything happens for a reason" is a phrase I wouldn't miss if I never heard it again). But the ones that *are*? If we resist the lessons, life will *push-freaking-back* with more situations and more complications, which—surprise!—are more chances to learn. Because life (or the universe, or Source, or God, or whatever it is you want to call that thing that's bigger than you are) will rarely flat-out give you answers, it'll give you *opportunities* to answer your own questions. It's a principle that's withstood the widsom of centuries, from passages in religious texts to advice given by executive coaches. Ask for strength, get opportunities to be strong. Ask for bravery, get opportunities to be brave. Ask for self-confidence, get opportunities to stop letting yourself down.

My mistake at twenty-four as a "really bad driver" was that I was asking for confidence, bravery, and strength—but was showing up with doubt, panic, and excuses. My luck wasn't running out. I wasn't irresponsible, clumsy, or doing things wrong. I was just coming to the realization that everything I thought I wanted out of my life wasn't actually what I wanted, and I was resisting that change *hard*. I was beginning to transition away from a career in the entertainment industry—but still going out of my way to attend auditions because I felt like I "should" keep auditioning since I'd committed to it for so long. I was posturing like I'd "fully recovered" from eating disorders and body dysmorphia by eating and exercising "normally" in public—but in private, I'd begun binging on anything I could find in my fridge, abusing over-the-counter laxatives, and sweating through rounds of sit-ups (like I said before, recovery is rarely linear—even when you've seen the change that's possible on the other side). I was telling lies while convincing myself I wasn't lying at all; *I was just omitting truths*. I was spending frivolously to make myself happy and distract myself from my lonely uncertainty.

I was transitioning out of a whole stage of my life I wasn't yet sure I wanted to leave behind.

It was like I was being told to get in my car, leave my gloomy but pleasant-enough town—a place I knew well and was comfortable with—and start driving because there was a warm and sunny destination in my future. But also not being told where that destination was or what I should expect once I got there. All I had to go off were *feelings* about what could be, but at this stage of the game, *feelings* weren't enough to convince me that the challenge would be worth it.

And so of course, my main mode of transportation was breaking down on me time and again.

I had to figure out where to go next with my own internal GPS.

The Confidence Myth

I get asked all the time about how to build self-confidence. "I want to feel good about myself," the person usually tells me.

And I tell them that if feeling good is what they're after, then confidence is the wrong thing to be focusing on.

But if they truly want confidence, that's another story.

If you look up "confidence" in the dictionary, it's got a few standout definitions: "a feeling of self-assurance arising from one's appreciation of one's own abilities or qualities" and "the state of feeling certain about the truth of something" are two of them.

And then there's my favorite: "the feeling or belief that one can rely on someone or something; firm trust."

Confidence, then, isn't about feeling good about yourself. "Feeling good" is irrelevant. Even the dictionary says so. Equating "feeling good" to "being confident" is a myth.

Confidence doesn't always feel good, but it always feels *right*.

Confidence is trust. Period.

Confidence is about recognizing, appreciating, and *trusting* the *truth* of who you are in any given moment.

My multi-year car metaphor—my major distrust of the road ahead and the vehicle driving me forward—began in that moment when my car flew across the freeway lanes. I don't find it coincidental at all that as I drove home, I was focused on what I believed to be the truth of how I looked to others, which really was one man's subjective opinion while manufacturing a 2D image of me for a specific catalog spread. No, I don't find it a coincidence that as the car behind me zigzagged from lane to lane and knocked me off course, I was in the middle of questioning my own truths. Yes, those questionable truths were about my body—my *vehicle*—but at that time, I was unable to separate my Self from my vehicle. I was my body. My body was me. My truth was not that I had a body; it was that I *was* my body. I'd felt great that day on the inside, until I walked on set and gathered evidence to support the story that I wasn't great enough on the outside. I didn't know what was true. And when one wheel falls off your truth wagon, trust becomes a road you can only hope to drive on.

Adding Back the Truths

We all have an internal GPS—one that already knows where we're meant to go. And that GPS is fueled by truth and self-trust. And because truth is essential for trust to exist, we'll tackle it first.

It's way easier to tell myself I'm "omitting truths" when what I'm really doing is dancing around so many unsaid lies that my mind could be mistaken for my Bat Mitzvah party. The phrase alone should be a red flag—*omitting truths*; you're actively removing pieces of reality from the equation. What happens when you've taken the truth out of the room? You dance with the lies and call it life.

Truth omission is a way we feign trustworthiness, but it rarely works as planned. That's because truth is *exactly what's needed* for trust to exist. With others and your Self. If you've lost touch with your trust, you've most certainly lost track of your truth. The former cannot exist without the latter. That internal GPS will break down, and your transmission will explode. Believe me—I've seen it happen in real time. And as nice as they are, roadside assistance won't be able to save you and put it all back together again.

Getting back in touch with truth begins by taking a look at where you're getting stuck, preferably *before* the breakdown happens. It requires you to take a tough but necessary look underneath the hood of your human vehicle and address what's gotten out of alignment, whether you believe it's "bad enough" to fix or not. Think about it: if your car has a screw loose or an oil leak, and you say it's not "bad enough" to repair and go about your day, you're playing with fire. You don't ignore it as long as you can (even though a lot of drivers do), and you certainly don't go and buy a whole new car just because you don't want to deal with it. You get that sucker fixed before it ends up crushed like a soda can on the side of the freeway. You take care of the problems you have now, because those problems will probably show up no matter what car you get, and that makes for a pretty expensive lifestyle of avoidance.

~

It wasn't that I only had bad luck with my car. My internal GPS was so out of whack that I was being sent messages, loud and clear, to get a trust-and-truth tune-up. I was just too focused on the way I thought things "should" be, and the stories I'd told about how it all "should" unfold.

Instead of ignoring signs of un-alignment like I did—persistent frustration, bitterness, anger—or reactively buying a brand-new soul-car by putting a Dead-End Optimism spin on things, do some proactive Truth Maintenance *now*. Maybe before you even realize you need it.

When I feel myself getting stuck and losing touch with my truth—and therefore, my Self—I ask myself these four questions to keep me aware, honest, and proactive:

1. **Is my self-talk really about what I say it is?**
   Before anything, I get clarity on what it is I'm actually talking about. If I'm complaining about something, or getting down

on myself for speaking/acting/being a certain way, I ask myself if there's anything underneath. Am I using the subject of my negative self-talk as a scapegoat for something deeper? What am I self-talking about—*really?*

2. **Do I really want the reality (and result) of making a change, or do I want whatever the process of trying to figure it out gets me?** Just because you're saying negative words or thinking negative thoughts doesn't mean there's not a positive intention behind them. Our own individual histories of using negativity as a bonding tactic can run deep into the roots of our first, most primal childhood needs. Sometimes we insulted ourselves out loud to get someone to negate them and say loving things to us. Sometimes we wanted attention or sympathy. And sometimes, we'd self-deprecate to relate.

 Psychologists Mary Ainsworth and John Bowlby wrote about something called "attachment theory" extensively.[2] Attachment theory is about the patterns we developed in childhood to adapt and feel secure in our environment. And relying on tumultuous tactics to create a sense of security and ease is a sign of anxious attachment.

 Maybe you're using those same tactics now to get the validation, love, attention, care, or connection you want. And let's be clear: these things aren't bad things to want! They're human desires that follow us through all stages of our lives. It's just important to identify those things if they're what you're *really* after. Not just so you can shift your negative self-talk, but so you can get what you want in a way that's healthy for everyone involved.

 Take an honest look at what the reality of your resolved situation would look like, and work backward. If you're truly interested in making a shift, your words can be a way for you to figure things out and eventually reach that conclusion. (More often than not, I just need to "talk it out.") But if you're not interested in shifting something, your words can be a way for you to stay stuck in the same refrains. Only *you* know what you're truly interested in, and whether you actually want to put the work in to make shift happen.

3. **Am I using negative talk to distract or *convince* myself that I'm doing something to activate change in my life?**
   Negative talk, specifically complaints and grievances about yourself or others, is incredibly distracting, yet *convincing.* It's a form of procrastination, really—like creating a never-ending to-do list, or staring at a computer screen for an entire day with your inbox or spreadsheets or whatever-it-is in one window and all the social media channels you follow in another, then telling yourself at the end of the day you were "trying to work." Sure, you checked your email a few times or wrote a few sentences for your latest project, but if you were to *really* look at your day, you spent more time distracted and stalling than getting down to business and working.

   At twenty-four, in the midst of what will now forever be known (to myself, and now you) as the Era of Car Woes, I distracted myself a LOT. I vented to friends about how vapid I felt Hollywood was, when in fact, I was trying so very hard to fit in and figure out who casting directors might want me to be instead of honoring who I knew in my gut I was meant to be (I didn't want to not book jobs). I was living in an apartment with roommates who watched loud, violent movies outside my door until 2:00 am—and instead of having a conversation about how the noise affected my sleep, I complained and cried to friends about how tired and anxious I felt (I didn't want to seem uptight). I started hooking up with someone I was enamored with—but I was never honest and up-front with him about how I felt (I didn't want to seem needy), so of course he started dating someone else, and of course I felt betrayed. And it was all happening at once.

I vented about it all in my journal as tears plopped onto the pages, the splattered ink mirroring my murky mood. I felt sad and taken advantage of . . . but at the same time, I felt like the feelings I was having were enough to signal I was on the right track. I'd think to myself: *Admitting there's a problem is the first step to healing the problem, right?* It was just that it wasn't my first step, it was my *only* step. On the inside, I was throwing a raging pity party, which made me feel like I was paying attention to the problems enough that maybe, *just maybe,* they would go away on their own. On the outside, I was doing close to nothing . . . other than venting and lamenting about the way I wished things would be.

Acknowledgment is an important step in doing the work, yes, but it's not the entirety of the work itself. Don't let the way you speak about your life get in the way of you living it.

4. **What's my priority? Is this one of them?**
So you've identified and acknowledged what you don't want. If you're truly interested in change, it's time to figure out what you *do* want—and moreover, whether you're making it a priority. Sometimes we don't realize what our true priorities are until we're asked to name them. But it goes beyond that: a priority, to me, means there's something important to you that you're not only able to name, but willing to address. There's a difference between being capable of doing something, and being willing to do something. The former is an ability. The latter is a choice.

If you're interested in making a change and it aligns with your priorities, congrats on the clarity! You know what matters to you and you're focused on it for a reason. If you're not truly interested in making a change, though, it's time to go back and investigate what information *could* be hidden in your negative talk. Is it a cry for help? A clue to an imbalance? A sign of burnout? (If you need some help figuring it out, flip back to the list of things your negative self-talk could be telling you under the "Mental Mean Girls" section of chapter four for support.) Let go of what you think should matter to you, and start to lean into what actually *does.*

Open Road

Twenty-six hit. I'd racked up a total of almost seven years behind me of car troubles and complaints and not trusting myself on the road ahead. I woke up one day, literally sick of my own bullshit defense mechanisms (I say *literally* because I'd binged the night before, maybe for one of the last times). There was a world waiting for me outside my door, and that vague feeling of rightness—the one that had whispered *You Are Ready* for so long—it had grown into a roar.

I have no explanation for you other than the fact that inner voice was telling me, with certainty: *You know.*

You know what you know, and you know what you don't know.

And most importantly, I was both okay with it all and ready to do something about it.

Knowing you're ready for "something more" is half the battle. Taking steps toward the idea of "something more," even if you don't know exactly what that looks like, is a whole other thing entirely. And being okay with those steps you're taking is the difference that makes the difference—if the reality of "something more" is what you're truly after.

After focusing on the negatives for so long, I wondered if it was less important that I focused my energy on *not doing* anything that dimmed my own light, and more important that I made a concerted effort to *start doing* all the things that lit me up from the inside out. I got clear on my complaints, and realized that at the core of it all, I was distracting myself from *being* my Self out loud. I decided I was sick of complaining, sick of sidelining myself, and sick of feeling uncomfortable inside and out. So I did my best to distance myself from situations that made me feel weak or less-than and instead spent more time in places I felt like myself—like that person who could feel the way she wanted to feel at the end of the day when she got home and looked in the mirror and asked herself if she'd been true to her word and followed up with her actions. I got honest with myself about my priorities and realized they were not what I once thought they were—but instead of trying to cling to scraps and salvage them like I'd been doing, I started to put the things I felt strongly about on my plate first instead of the things I realized I was only prioritizing out of habit. I committed to using my unique voice to help others find, use, and own theirs—because I realized that when one voice speaks truthfully, it gives others permission to do the same, and I was no longer interested in a world without an internal GPS. I spoke up for others. I spoke up for myself. I also moved out and found new roommates.

Did this fix everything? No. But. It helped set the next chapter of my life into motion.

And my car issues disappeared.

Whether they weren't actually there anymore or I was just too busy paying attention to other things, does it really matter?

Part Three

YOU NEED A SELF

FIND YOUR SELF

BE YOUR SELF

STAY YOUR SELF

WANT YOUR SELF

Chapter Eight

BUILDING YOUR TRUST FUND

I was once asked what would happen if I didn't put together a list of every second of every day.

No exaggeration. I used to do this:

"7:12–7:14 am – brush teeth.

7:15–7:17 am – wash face.

7:18–7:20 am – walk to closet and pick out clothes."

(And so on and so forth.)

I don't remember what my response was exactly, or if I even *gave* a response other than "I just couldn't." Living list-less would *never* happen.

I think back on that time in my life and sometimes wonder what my deal was. Did I feel my world would crumble? Did I think I would forget to brush my teeth? Tie my shoes? Walk out the door?

But in hindsight, I know why I let these lists dictate my every move so strictly:

I didn't trust anything. Or *anyone.*

Least of all myself.

Self-Doubt

Self-doubt is what happens when you know who you are, but don't *trust* who you are. To be your Self, you must *live* your truth. It's not enough to just find your Self, you've got to *be* that person out loud.

The knowledge of who you are doesn't create trust—the *implementation* does. The less often you're actively the You you know you're meant to be, the more you'll doubt if that person is even worthwhile in the first place.

I often use self-doubt to protect myself from hurt or disappointment. When I start to doubt myself—my capabilities, my relationships, my character—I formulate questions or negative statements in my mind as a sort of shield. Because if I've thought of it first, I tell myself, I'm prepared. Disappointment won't come as a surprise, I convince myself, because I've made doubt a part of my truth.

My list-making, twentysomething self was young and on her own. And while she told everyone she loved flying solo—preferred living without roommates, enjoyed days on end by herself—in reality, she was flailing. She was trying to find structure in a world that had always provided structure *for* her, and it wasn't working. *Adjust me, please.*

Her life was a list; her growth was a chance; her world was full of deceit. It was lonely. She didn't know where she could give her love a place to go. But hey, she crossed off everything on her agenda, *so that's success, no?*

(No, it's not.)

Self-doubt makes us believe our successes depend on a very specific set of factors and bullet points lining up just like so, but success is not a list to be crossed off. Seeing your impact can be a metric or byproduct of success. But when you're truly successful, there's a whole boatload of impact you might never see. Lives you might never know you touch. Exciting roads you might not know you're venturing down until way after the fact when you look back and realize that everything good you ever experienced started with one tiny choice, one small step, and one ripple that created a wave. Because success isn't about accomplishments, it's about finding your Self, then being that Self out loud.

Self-doubt is a sign we're losing our footing in who we are. We begin to believe we don't have any power, when in fact, we have *all the power*. We've just forgotten it.

To feel self-doubt is to be human. Self-doubt isn't meant to be stuffed down and felt *around*. Self-doubt is change and growth knocking at your door, a feeling that's meant to be acknowledged and felt *through*.

However, self-doubt without boundaries can reshape the core of who you are. Yes, you *do* need to acknowledge the full spectrum of your emotions—but if you allow doubt to fill your mind with every possible outcome (even if it's a means of protection), you risk completely missing out on growth and experience. You'll be shielded from hurt, yes . . . but then what? The would-be thrill of joyful success is replaced by mere relief of a changeless plan. The story you tell yourself, about your Self, begins to include more and more defining phrases like, "I can't . . ." and "I'm not . . ."

~

Knowing why you need a Self is important.

Committing to finding your Self is vital.

But *knowing* and *finding* only make a difference when you start to put them into practice—and start to BE your Self out there in the reality of your own life.

To be your Self, you must live your truth. And to live your truth means trusting it.

You can't control who knocks on your door—but you *can* decide when to open it and who to open it for.

You've got your truth.

What does it take to *trust it?*

Integrity

When you think of the word "integrity," what comes to mind?

Is it a person? An action?

Does it bring up an intense response? An apathetic one? Somewhere in between?

For a long time, integrity was one of those words that I didn't have a clear definition for but knew I should care about. I don't remember when I first heard the word uttered or the context in which it was said, but I *do* remember the feeling I felt when I heard it. This was something that mattered. A LOT.

Integrity, according to the Merriam-Webster Dictionary, is "firm adherence to a code of especially moral or artistic values."[1] My dad would use the word a lot as my brother Alex and I entered into teendom and young adulthood. Hoping to provide a moral compass to his kids, he'd always tell us that if you could look in the mirror at the end of the day and say you'd been true to yourself, that was what mattered most in life. That, to him, was integrity.

I always took his words to heart . . . but also felt like there were missing pieces. I struggled to identify what *true to myself* really meant. Did it mean that I tried my hardest or best? Did it mean I stuck to my word? Did it mean I fit into the parameters of goodness and rightness and socially applaudable-ness? As a Highly Sensitive Person, I both felt that this concept of integrity was super important and struggled when I noticed there were days I tried my best, and did what I said I'd do, and hit all the Goodness marks, but felt disconnected from what I assumed that living this term out loud was supposed to make me feel.

As I've gotten older, gained more life experience, and worked with both fitness and mindset coaching clients who struggle with the same ideas around integrity, I've begun to realize that integrity isn't just about truth—it's a *cornerstone* of self-trust.

Integrity is when your intentions and your impact are in alignment. When what you think, what you say, and what you do match up.

How does self-trust fit into this mix? It goes back to what my dad said about staying true to you. Kind of. In order for you to trust your Self, you need to give yourself a *reason* to do so beyond mere belief. It's a two-part equation: who you believe your Self to be on the inside, and how your Self is *actually* being on the outside. When you show your Self you're committed to what you say you're committed to, even and especially in the hard moments, that trust begins to follow suit.

Intent is not much if the impact doesn't align. And "But I meant this to be . . ." isn't a valid argument here: if you want something to have a certain effect and it doesn't, and you're not willing to change the action to get the intended impact, then you've got to ask yourself how committed you were to that intention in the first place. Maybe it was never really about the intention you thought it was—and it was really about posturing to be someone you wish you were, or about being liked by others. Or maybe pivoting to get the intended impact feels too vulnerable, so you don't: in a society that doesn't make it easy to make mistakes and then course correct, being left to do it on your own can feel daunting. No matter what the reality of the situation is, intent without impact *doth not* integrity make.

That self-trust that's so vital to your journey of finding, being, staying, and wanting your Self relies on your integration of the word "integrity" into your life. Matching the outsides with the insides as much as you can, and working to bridge that intent-impact gap as *well* as you can, over and over again.

Some of us, though (myself included!), don't always know the ins and outs of our intentions. And without clarity and specificity about our intentions, we're more likely to fall back on whatever's habitual or expected. Not because we want to do it, but because we're used to doing it.

In order to trust your Self, you've got show your Self you're worth trusting.

What better way to do so than get crystal clear on what there is about your Self to trust?

Pre-Paving

I first learned about the concept of pre-paving from life coach Jay Pryor. I had them on my podcast, *The WANTcast*, years ago, and in our conversation they introduced me to this exercise originally devised by Abraham Hicks.[2] Pre-paving, as Jay described it to me, was basically a way to envision the outcome of an event before it takes place. Pre-paving is more than visualization—it's mentally planning and preparing for the outcome you want before it occurs.

As I began digging deeper into the work of shifting your self-talk—not just the *concept* of shifting it, but real, lasting ways to help as many people successfully shift it as possible—I wondered: *If we can pre-pave a specific outcome of an event, why can't we pre-pave a specific outcome of who we are?*

Trust and truth are the sturdy foundation for building up (or breaking down) anything Self-related: self-talk, self-confidence, self-love. They're the pavement on the road to being the You you know you're meant to be. If telling the truth to yourself is like clearing the path, learning to trust yourself is taking those first few, strong steps.

If you don't pre-pave your Self, the world will happily do it for you. This is where the trust and self-doubt issues come in. When we leave our self-definition up to others, we're essentially saying, *Tell me who I am and what I do, because I don't trust myself with Me.* Submitting to society can feel like a relief in the moment—ah, fitting in—but perpetuates the idea that we cannot and should not be trusted to craft our own lives.

In my acting classes and rehearsals, we'd work on the "character development" of our roles—the process of fleshing out a complex, nuanced, and true-to-life person that gets your audience believing in who they are. Character development tells the story of who the character is beyond the words on the page.

If the most important story you tell is the one you tell to yourself, about yourself, then think of pre-paving as "character development" where you're the character in the story. You're fleshing out the complex, nuanced, true-to-life story behind what makes you You.

Trust in any relationship—including the one you have with yourself—is the result of being true to your word by following up with actions.

Pre-paving, then, is the word you can be true to as you walk through life, the way to Be your Self even and especially when self-doubt sneaks up on you.

Pre-Paving Your Self

Pre-paving your Self looks at who you are and helps you get clear on how you want to *be.* You can pre-pave your Self for one-off micro scenarios—a tough conversation, a big ask, a tense moment, a first date—or you can pre-pave your Self in a more general sense, looking at your life as the macro scenario. You can pre-pave your Self during easy times, hard times, or in-between neutral times. The most important thing is that you do it enough times, and in enough instances, that you get into a habit of specificity and intentionality.

Ask yourself these seven questions, in order:

1. How do I want to look?
2. How do I want to act?
3. How do I want to sound?
4. What are the one to three points I want people to hear?
5. How do I want people to feel after they've left me?
6. How do I want to feel after leaving a situation, completing a task, or finishing a day of life?
7. What three Anchor Words (that I will remember no matter what or where) can I use to ground me and remind me of the Me I'm meant to be?

A note about the difference between Anchor Words and positive affirmations: positive affirmations are usually referred to as positive words or statements that help you build a positive mindset and counter negative thoughts. Positive affirmations aren't necessarily true in the moment, or at the very least don't feel true—they're words or phrases the person saying the affirmation *wants* to believe are true but doesn't in the moment. But non-believable affirmations can be tricky. If you don't believe what you're saying, it can do more harm than good (remember that University of Waterloo study from the prologue?). I know this. I tried this. Even with this book, I was told I should write "I am a Published Author!" on my whiteboard and in my journal every day while I was first pitching agents and getting rejection letters (or radio silence). Apparently, it was supposed to help me envision myself as a published author or manifest it into existence or something. It did the opposite. Eventually, I had to stop writing this affirmation over and over. I knew what I was writing wasn't true in the moment. I could feel self-doubt creeping in, and I started to become less driven to make this dream a reality.

I'm not against positive affirmations. Positive affirmations might help some people get out of their own way—and like the University of Waterloo study proved, they're a fantastic tactic to reinforce proactive positivity when you're already there, helping prolong the magic and cement those truths as part of your self-told story. That's important. But like we've already talked about, the talk part of self-talk is symptomatic—and so replacing a negative statement with a positive one might not work long-term in the way you're told it will. Positive affirmations are great, but often not enough to create change on their own. It's not about throwing out that tool entirely; it's about adding more tools to your kit.

Anchor Words aren't created to counter a negative thought or phrase. They're identification of what already exists. Usually, they're nouns or adjectives. Anchor Words exist to remind you of who you are at your core, not train you into becoming *someone* or *something* else. They maximize and spotlight the You that's already there.

Go figure, when I embraced the truth of my situation ("I am not a Published Author *yet*, but I want to be and am committed to making it happen") and reminded myself of my Anchor Words, my self-trust and drive returned.

And that's because the beauty of Anchor Words is they're words that remind you of who you already are. They're already true, and what's more, they're already believable.

My Pre-Paved Self

Pre-paving is what you make of it. It can be a super cerebral manifesto for your way of life, or it can help you navigate the tiny moments in life that aren't really that tiny at all.

Here are examples of both kinds of pre-paving—macro and micro—from my own life.

My overarching, pre-paved Self looks something like this when boiled down to its simplest terms:

1. **How do I want to look?**
   Purposeful.

2. **How do I want to act?**
   Mindfully and empathetically.

3. **How do I want to sound?**
   Grounded.

4. **What are the one to three points I want people to hear?**
   That they're capable of creating change in their own lives and in the wider world, that the process of shifting their self-talk begins with exploring who their Self is in the first place, and that they have the power to rewrite their own story, over and over again.

5. **How do I want people to feel after they've left me?**
   Powerful, energized, seen, and self-assured.

6. **How do I want to feel after leaving a situation, completing a task, or finishing a day of life?**
   Like I used the full spectrum of my Self.

7. **What three Anchor Words (that I will remember no matter what or where) can I use to ground me and remind me of the Me I'm meant to be?**
   Worthwhile. Visionary. Fearless.

If you're reading my Anchor Words and feeling like they're pretty bold statements, you're right. They are. Anchor Words are chosen because they bring up big feelings. They're words that feel like your truest, fullest Self, and resonate with you for specific reasons you can identify. For example, I chose *worthwhile* because it reminds me that my thoughts, ideas, and presence matter. *Worthwhile,* to me, renders winning and losing irrelevant. *Worthwhile* is my Self no matter what or where or when or how or why she shows up. *Visionary* and *fearless*? They remind me that when those worthwhile ideas and dreams are crystal clear, I should lean all the way in. Getting this granular about my word choices helps my Anchor Words not only feel impactful, but easy for me to remember.

I am constantly visiting and revisiting my overarching Pre-Pave, fine-tuning to dial in the exact words and phrases that describe who I am and what I stand for.

Pre-paving might seem like it's only relevant in the big, sometimes daunting moments—like an important decision that needs to be made or a scary obstacle that you find in your way. One of my favorite examples of a pre-paving exercise I did, however, was one of my smaller, more mundane ones. It took place in one of those tiny-but-not-really moments a few years ago.

My husband, Jeremy, and I both worked from home at the time—a feat, considering the size of our studio apartment—and while it was brand new to him, I'd been working from home on and off for years (Side note, this was in the early months of the pandemic, so jetting off to somewhere like a coffee shop or library wasn't an option.)

I'm very used to our entire apartment being my office and (hello to my fellow creative introverts) am most productive in complete silence. However, there's no way in hell you can experience complete silence when you're working with another human in a home that's only one room big. You each have your own working styles, unconscious habits, ideal environments—and ways to process the stressful stuff.

Jeremy, I learned, processes the stressful stuff by blurting out phrases and derivatives of four-letter words. Usually, there's a *fuck* in there somewhere.

Fuck balls!

Fucking piece of shit!

Piece of fucking fuck!

And then, complete silence.

The emotions in his outbursts don't stick with him. I, on the other hand, sponge them up and hold on to them. And headphones don't help because being a Highly Sensitive Person and emotional sponge, I can feel the energy they create whether I can hear him or not—even whether I'm *looking* at him or not.

His colorful exclamations during that coworking-from-home time were like a motorcycle revving up its engine and driving by my window. They shocked and rattled me for minutes after they happened, not only interrupting my workflow but putting my anxiety on high alert to detect the nonexistent danger around the corner.

This, I realized very quickly, was not going to fly.

I have a history of not addressing things that make me feel hurt, feel sad, feel startled, or could possibly be perceived as negative by someone else. From training myself to be grateful for "even just the opportunity" to do unpaid acting or writing work I definitely should have been compensated for, to not raising my voice in middle school when I witnessed brutal bullying on the bus, to being teased for being "too sensitive" and then unable to calmly express why that seemingly harmless phrase hurt me so deeply—I have a history of *not* being my Self and *not* saying what I mean. Especially if I can convince myself they're small moments that "aren't really a big deal."

But in order to have healthy relationships, with others and your Self, you've got to be your Self, and you've got to say what you mean, mindfully. Not just in the big moments. In the small ones too. Small stuff can turn into big stuff when brushed off and ignored.

I knew I needed to address Jeremy's outbursts for my own focus and well-being—but I also knew that sharing a space wasn't about him catering to *my* wishes (or me putting myself on the backburner for his sake). I wanted to approach this tiny-but-not-really conversation honoring his Self . . . and also mine.

And so I pre-paved how I wanted to show up:

1. **How do I want to look?**
   Engaged and curious. All-in with my attention.

2. **How do I want to act?**
   Empathetic and solution-oriented.

3. **How do I want to sound?**
   Calm and eager to find a middle ground.

4. **What are the one to three points I want him to hear?**
   I want him to hear how exactly his outbursts affect me (and why headphones don't help).
   I want him to hear that I understand that this work situation is new for both of us—and I'm eager to learn what he needs to function at his best.
   I want him to hear that I respect this space as *our* space, and he's safe to feel whatever he needs to feel within these walls.

5. **How do I want him to feel after our conversation?**
   Respected and connected. Like a team.

6. **How do I want to feel after our conversation?**
   Respected and connected. Like a team.

7. **What three Anchor Words (that I will remember during this conversation) can I use to ground me and remind me of the Me I'm meant to be?**
   Team, kind, proactive.

When we talked, Jeremy shared that his work-related outbursts weren't usually about any sort of notable anger or frustration; they were a way for him to blow off steam in a moment of irritation and move on. They were mostly habitual at this point, but sometimes, they did help calm him down. We both agreed to do our part: he agreed to try to find alternate ways to process irritating moments so I wasn't rattled by them every five minutes. And I agreed that when he *would* erupt out of nowhere, I'd remind myself that it was a reflex and coping mechanism on his end, not a cause for alarm on mine—a habit he'd developed when he was within his own four walls and had no one else sponging up his *fuck-shits*.

Neither one of us was in the right or in the wrong. It wasn't *about* being right or wrong. It was about me being my Self, and him being his Self, and strategizing instead of stifling. When we stifle our Self, even in what seem like the smallest moments, the ramifications can last a lifetime.

Shedding the Armor

I think back on minute-by-minute-list-making Katie, and I imagine how she would simply stare wide-eyed at the Katie of today. She would probably cower, check her words, move with caution. Which makes me sad. No trust. All doubt.

I'm not that person now. Not today.

I trust my trajectory, and I trust my heart. I trust my brain to put words to feelings, and I trust my soul to speak silently when no words suffice. I am in this life to live my truth, which means to *trust* my truth, which is subjective but glorious and most importantly all mine. I am in it to see the beauty in a puppy sniffing its way down the street as it explores the world on the other end of its leash. The uncontrollable fits of laughter so strong they render us silent in our gasps for air. A small idea turned into a world-rocking epiphany. The creased circles under eyes lacking in sleep but gleaming with excitement for a new hour.

Clinking ceramic mugs in cheer. The sigh of a long day that continues to be long. The way you can hear a smile from miles away. The way the sun ricochets off a blade of grass. The way every once in a while, my heart quite literally skips a beat. Hold up your hand and you can feel it; it really does.

I am slowly learning to let go of my lists and shed my armor by planting my feet in the ground of my Self. I give myself integrity checks on the regular—does my intention align with my impact, and am I giving myself reason to trust not only my commitment to my Self but my follow-through?—and pre-pave the macro- and micro-moments often. The more certain I am about what makes me Me from the inside out, the less I allow self-doubt to deplete my self-worth.

I no longer make lists defining my days by the scheduled-out seconds, because I trust that I've got my own back. Most of my lists now (besides grocery lists and weekly to-dos) are ones filled with future plans and budding ideas. These are not my truths—not yet. These are arbitrary. They're coals for an eventual fire and steam for a to-be-wrinkled cloth. My truths are my Self in the now. That, I can believe.

I trust my Self, and apologize profusely for my apprehension by opening up to her fully, hour after unplanned hour, minute by unplanned minute.

Chapter Nine

EMOTIONALLY HEAVY WORDS

I got a lot of wonderful qualities from my mom, Amy: her leadership skills, her laugh-till-you-cry laughter, her zest for life and all its little adventures.

I also got her really colorful language.

Okay, so I'm not sailor material per se, but just like my brilliantly brazen mother, I'm not one to censor myself in a real-life conversation. However, there are a few words I always try to catch myself on, no matter how many F-bombs I let fly. Because strangely enough, they're some of the most commonly used, nasty four-ish-letter words—even though no one's ever told me to censor them.

~

One of my favorite childhood authors, L. M. Montgomery, was impeccable with her words. In *Anne of Green Gables*, she even wrote: "I read in a book once that a rose by any other name would smell as sweet, but I've never been able to believe it. I don't believe a rose WOULD be as nice if it was called a thistle or a skunk cabbage."[1] I love how sneakily complex this quote is. Maybe you chuckled when you first read it—skunk cabbage, *hah!*—but when you sit with the quote for a few minutes, it starts to morph into a pretty profound lesson, one I'd like to believe she was trying to teach every bookworm kid like me who peeled through her pages: the names we give things, each other, and ourselves hold great weight.

A name doesn't just tell us what to call something; it tells us *how to feel* about it too. Words evoke emotion; they *reek* of feeling. A name is an identity, a word that paints a picture before you even see the scene. It's why Norma Jeane Mortenson—a woman whose name went through several iterations after it was penned on her birth certificate—eventually disappeared and morphed into Marilyn Monroe. Why it's a big deal for *everyone* to be able to get "married," not just have a "partnership" or "civil union," and why it's vital to refer to others by the pronouns that reflect their own gender identity. It's the difference between a "dwelling" and a "home." It's why I go by Katie, not Kate, not even Katherine (my full first name). Heck, it's why the place where the toilet lives is called the "restroom," not the "pee place." Does a pee place sound like somewhere you want to go take a physical and mental reset? (Says the introvert who hides in the restroom at parties and uses them for mental health breaks.) The words we use to name things *matter.*

It's also why when I went to my local bookstore to research "the market" as I was writing the book proposal for *Want Your Self,* I saw a trend of "personal development" (which is what they call self-help books now, which I think is a bit nicer than assuming we're all crying for help) bestsellers dropping F-bombs and B-words on their covers. "Look at us," they seem to say. "We're different! We shake things up!"

And they're super smart to do so. We *already* associate these words with risk-taking, rebellion, and edginess. It makes perfect sense that these somewhat taboo words would appear so prominently on the books of authors who want their readers to know that they *don't* do things by the book.

I call these words EHWs—*Emotionally Heavy Words.*

An Emotionally Heavy Word is a word we use that's married to a unique and fairly universal feeling, and evokes a specific, intense reaction when we say it. It holds the weight of associations and experiences felt across humanity. An EHW is *strong.* So strong, in fact, that it's hard to use the word and *not* feel the feeling at the same time.

Just like those rebellious authors and Norma-turned-Marilyn, we *must* be careful and conscious of the words we choose to use as we speak about ourselves *to* ourselves. If we're already associating a word with a certain feeling—if it already evokes a specific, intense reaction—we'd be foolish to believe we're exempt from the repercussions just because those words are used internally.

Digging into an Emotionally Heavy Word is like playing in the Word Association X-Games. Extreme *thing*-naming. You know the game. Maybe you've played it as a team-building activity at the top of a work meeting, or on a long road trip with kids who kept asking, "Are we there yet?" (Maybe you once *were* that kid.) You pick a random word, then your partner thinks of a word off the top of their head that's related, then you ping-pong back and forth. It's thought that word association can give you intel on someone's subconscious mind. In Carl Jung's article "The Association Method," he writes that words are "like condensed actions, situations, and things [. . .] the stimulus word will as a rule always conjure up its corresponding situation. It all depends on how [you] react to [the] situation."[2]

Everyone has their own personal set of Emotionally Heavy Words that add weight to their world just by being said. And yet there are a few that are so ingrained in our general vocabulary, *so widely weighty*, that they're dragging us down with them in droves.

As you read through the following words in big, bold typeface, pause for a second before continuing. Notice:

1. How does your body feel when you hear these words read in your mind's voice?
2. How does your breathing change, if at all?
3. How does your heart change its beat, if at all?
4. Where does your mind go?
5. What feelings, vague or pinpointedly specific, rise to the surface?

And then keep reading.

An important note: these words aren't "bad" words. Just like I haven't fully nixed the F-bombs from my life, the goal here isn't to cut them out entirely. The goal is to be alert and catch yourself when these words sneak into your sentences, so you can either use them intentionally or shift them into something more. Know that these are words you're on the lookout for. Whenever you're about to say them, or even right after you say them, pause and take note.

Consider the EHWs in this chapter your new self-talk shifters—a new generation of curse words.

H*te

Hate, by definition, is "intense hostility and aversion usually deriving from fear, anger, or sense of injury."[3] It's violent and should be used sparingly. So why do we use it so much, *especially about ourselves?*

Well, for one, we don't censor it in other areas of our life. Just like when you're learning a new language, the best way to let it set into your brain is to practice out loud with other people (more on that later). We take social cues from each other, especially when it comes to how we speak. So when we hear the word "hate" being thrown around as an everyday verb—*I hate this, I hate that*—it begins to feel like something we all just do.

We just *hate*.

"Hate" is a form of Casual Negativity, a little conversational tic that's become normal for many of us. It's much easier and more comfortable to say we hate something than to make an actual change—it's a way to distract and convince ourselves that we're doing something to move forward, simply by dwelling.

It's also an *extremely* emotionally charged word. It gives us something to care about. Because when you say it, you *do* care. Writer and Holocaust survivor Elie Wiesel famously said, "The opposite of love is not hate, it is indifference."[4] Hatred gives us something intense to feel, distracting us from why we feel it in the first place.

And so hatred permeates our lives, our relationships, and our self-image. If we're unhappy . . . if we're upset . . . if we're uncomfortable or unsure . . . we hate. It stirs up an intense reaction that, when repeated over and over, ultimately becomes familiar.

To transcend the hate becomes too risky.

So we don't.

And when we don't, we hold ourselves back from caring for the parts of our psyche that just need a little love.

Back in my freshman year of college, I got into a nasty habit of unintentionally dropping the F-bomb in many of my conversations. I was unaware. And then I was *horrified.* Not because I wasn't a fan of the word (I am!), but because I was using it so flippantly. In hindsight, I'm pretty sure it wedged itself so tightly into my talk because it seemed like something Cool College Kids would do. I wasn't rebellious but might have thought that some part of me needed to be in order to convincingly play the role of Cool College Girl. Now that I look back on it, being a linguistic rebel feels very on-brand.

When someone finally pointed it out to me, I knew I wanted to break this habit before it got out of hand, and I let it slip in an inappropriate situation. I took a cue from an article I read on habit-breaking and snapped a rubber band on my wrist for a month to train myself out of using that R-rated conversational tic. It didn't work. But the embarrassing scolding I got one day from a random stranger (who had a small child, and a *lot* on her mind) did. I finally had a reason that mattered enough to me to shift my language: there were other people listening in and potentially picking up what I was saying.

Out-training your H-bomb habit is something you have to do intentionally (just like nixing the F-bombs I used to drop around toddlers). I don't recommend using the rubber band trick—because (a) it doesn't get to the root of the problem, (b) it doesn't work, and (c) it really hurts.

Instead, here's how I've censored the h*te in my life—strategically placed asterisk and all—and what can maybe work for you too.

Find the Filler: You're saying the word "h*te," but what is that word *really* filling in for? Is it a placeholder for frustration? Is it shorthand for confusion? Maybe it's masking hurt or longing. Whatever it is, it's vital to get clear on *what* exactly stirs up such a violent, visceral reaction. Because while sometimes we know exactly what we're talking about, sometimes it's not even close to what we think it is.

There are so many other more descriptive, accurate, and useful words you can use to express how you feel besides h*te. Pretend like the word h*te no longer exists.

What would you say instead?

How do you really feel?

Do you feel sad? Angry? Jealous? Uncomfortable? Frustrated? Embarrassed? Disappointed? Something else?

Tap into your inner detective and interrogate yourself. Ask yourself what's behind your h*te, and don't stop asking until you have that a-ha moment of *Wow . . .* that's *the thing I've been hiding behind a veil of h*tred.*

No matter how deep we have to dig or how superficial it seems, we never h*te something "just because." Maybe it's because of deep-seated beliefs or temporary sensations. Maybe it's because it triggers something unrelated. Or maybe, it's just because we know we can do better. Whether it's politics, people, or parts of ourselves, we never dislike without good reason—whether we want to admit it or not.

It can be scary to get specific—even confusing at first, since you're so used to using the word h*te. But once you land on the words that feel accurate, you can start infusing those words—and more intentionality—into your life.

Ug*y

I don't remember the first time I heard the U-bomb (should we call it the U-turn?), but I do remember the *way* I heard it used most as I was growing up and learning the language of life: by women—about their specific body parts.

Stomach. Nose. Skin. Hair. A mole here. A scar there. If "hate" was the word used to encompass the whole, "ugly" was used to describe the parts that made it up.

When I looked up the origin story of ugly, I was surprised to see that it was actually formed from a root word meaning *fear* or *dread*. The meaning was "softened to 'very unpleasant to look at'" in the late fourteenth century, my bestie the etymology dictionary told me.[5] End of story.

But *why* was the meaning softened? And if the meaning was softened, does it mean the implication was as well?

The short answer is no. I can only assume that linguists in the fourteenth century began to realize that the word was being used more commonly about stuff and looks than violence and crime (the way people had been using it before). The meaning might have been softened, and the load lightened, but the reaction to it has remained just as hard- and heavy-hitting. Try as we might, we can't just redefine things and call it a day.

Yes, we use the U-word in different ways to describe different things, but when I polled people asking where they used it most in their lives, the answer had to do with physicality *almost unanimously*. While this breaks my heart, it also means that when we find the filler for this particular EHW, it's something that can easily spill over into any other way we'd otherwise use it. Because we make changes when things get personal—and there is *nothing* more personal than the skin we're in.

Speak to the Moment: When you're trying to express how you feel and are tempted to pin the U-label on something, put "like" or "prefer" and "right now" back into your vocabulary. "I don't *like* or *prefer* [fill in the blank] *right now*" instead of "[fill in the blank] is ug*y" separates *what* something (like your body) is from *how* it's responding to a given situation in the moment. The love is there. The love will always be there. But right now, it's a little rough to get on the same page.

Remember, unconditional self-love can coexist with temporarily not liking something about yourself. Instead of using the U-word, confront your Self on what's coming up for you in the moment you're currently experiencing. Go into the conversation committed to playing fair and respectfully. Remind whatever it is you're U-ing about that you love it unconditionally, *but right now, it's a little hard to like it.* Seems like such a small, inconsequential shift, but it really makes a world of difference knowing the uncomfortable feeling isn't a forever thing.

It's okay not to like parts of yourself all the time. I'd even go so far as to say it's *healthy* not to like parts of yourself all the time. That doesn't mean you're broken. It means you're human. Remember the core of self-love: it's unconditional. No matter how rough things get, name-calling is not the answer.

P*rfect

Out of all the words in this chapter, this one might seem the tamest. What's wrong with striving for perfection? Perfection is virtuosity. Perfection is a plus.

But perfection? It's a *scam.*

Forget about Photoshop and social media filters. Perfection, as we typically think of it and talk about it, is a fake ideal. It's less of a specific goal and more of a vague antithesis of everything we find unsatisfactory. It's a trap to fool ourselves into believing that we're failing and need something else to be whole.

In retrospect, the concept of "striving for perfection" has haunted me my entire life (see: most of the stories in this book)—but the first time I can remember the word feeling like a curse word was middle school.

When I was thirteen, I had a group of friends who would call me perfect as a taunt. I didn't have braces. I liked to color-coordinate. I loved school. Remember those multi-colored capris The Gap sold circa 1999? I owned a pair in every color, with shirt, shoes, and butterfly clips to match. My middle part was striking; my bangs cut straight across with no hair out of place. I was easy to be around and nice to everyone. My awkward stage was mostly just awkward in my mind—or so I'm told.

Sounds great, huh? Yeah. Not really. Being teased about being "perfect" made me not only feel constant pressure never to slip up, but also feel detached and alone. When my friends called me "perfect" in that sing-song way that kids do, I felt like they were saying I didn't belong.

At the same time, I felt like my ability to check off all those "perfection" boxes was part of my middle-school identity. I'd just changed schools after sixth grade and was finally feeling accepted in this new place. Any misstep or deviation from whatever I'd been doing felt risky. I felt I couldn't be my full Self at school; God forbid I spoke out of turn or mismatched a sock.

And if I *did* flub up my perfection? I sunk deep into a shame spiral, *fast*. You know those "One Time in Eighth Grade" stories you're haunted by for the rest of your life? I'm still haunted by that one time in eighth grade when I went to an Oscars-themed birthday party hosted by two of the coolest girls in school, complete with awards, a podium, and a loud booming mic—and when I was called "onstage" to "accept" my "award," I was so nervous I mispronounced the birthday girl's name. With so many proverbial marbles in my mouth, I barely said any semblance of a name at all. The whole party giggled callously, as only eighth-grade girls can do—dagger-like giggles.

And then, high school came. The perfection taunts turned into praise, and I just didn't know what to do with it. Instead of being teased for my traits, I was celebrated. My color-coordinated outfits, my love of school, my unbridled enthusiasm, they all became quirks that my high-school friends celebrated. I chose classes where there would be other people who loved reading and analyzing as much as I did and found companionship and belonging among the Theatre Kids who seemed to accept everyone just as they were.

But old habits die hard. Some would have reveled in or rebelled against this sudden energy shift. But I didn't want to rebel. I just wanted to relate. (The closest I got to rebelling was growing out my bangs before sophomore year—and even then, I was worried who I'd be without the "Winnie Cooper" nickname the juniors and seniors had lovingly bestowed upon me.) I'd seen what could be on the other side of this fragile acceptance—taunts, gossip, meanness, other-ness—if I got too comfortable being my full Self. So I downplayed my assets and would self-deprecate to relate. I would go after big things and sometimes achieve them, but if something started to feel too great or too praise-worthy, I would shut off emotionally from it so no one would think I was "too big for my britches." I would obsessively listen to musical theatre cast albums and emulate them in my voice lessons; but if I sang a song and it sounded anything other than how it sounded in the mixed-and-mastered version on the recording, not only would I put it in the vault and never sing it again, I would hold myself back from auditioning for any solos in the choir or roles in the shows that I thought I could be turned down for (or eventually mess up).

Some would call it self-sabotage—but at the root of it, I feared loss. I wanted to guarantee love, and to me, that meant instilling a strict balance of being impressive enough to be likable and normal enough to be loveable. *Please let me be loved,* I'd silently beg with my self-inflicted code of conduct. *Do not love me for my light, because it sometimes gets dark in here, and I can't bear the loss when you realize that.*

If we are who we believe we are, and we are what we tell ourselves we should be, then I guess the silent begging worked. I became a shell of myself by the time I got to college, and in a small way, I think I liked it for a second there. *I am flawed,* I seemed to say. *Now you can see it on the outside too.*

But it didn't feel good after that hot second—and the reversal of my efforts proved to be even more trying for the next decade. Striving to be the perfect student, the perfect friend, and the perfect professional. The most physically fit. The most "balanced" eater. My attempts to feel comfortable in my skin were laughable at their best, alarming at their worst. I needed to feel comfortable in my *Self* first. I needed to stop equating imperfection with submission and perfection with isolation. **I needed to just *Be*.**

If you want to break up with perfection, you might be told to work on "loving your flaws." I don't like calling parts of myself flaws, though. For me, it reinforces a this-versus-that, right-versus-wrong mentality. Sure, I'm flaw*ed*. We all are! Beautifully flawed by our life experiences and the ways we choose to deal with certain circumstances. But there's a difference between parts of me being *flawed* and parts of me being *flaws*. One's an adjective; one's a noun. One's descriptive; one's definitive.

And even more than that: what's considered a flaw now might not be considered a flaw later. Perfection, in the way we use the term, isn't only subjective; it's constantly in flux. Perfection is largely determined by what we're *told* is perfect. It's the other side of validation. When we use perfection as something to strive toward, it creates an assumption that we're not already complete. That we either need to fill a void or change something that's only worthy if it's defined by the P-word.

But when it comes to perfection, there *is* no one definitive definition. Which is what makes this one such a powerful EHW to shift.

Mingle with the M-Word: Next time you're tempted to strive for p*rfection, try shifting your goal to *maximization*. Instead of focusing on your perceived flaws and asking if they're good enough, look at what's right in front of you and ask if you're maximizing, enhancing, and capitalizing on what you've already got. Stuck wanting something you don't have? Start working with the stuff you *do*.

This can work in a slew of scenarios, since the idea of p*rfection can be so all-encompassing. Maximization makes p*rfection irrelevant—which it probably will be not too far from now. No, not the word itself. But the ideal. Trends and *#goals* change by the decade, year, and season, if not the day and week. From body size and eyebrow shape to lifestyle goals and beyond, the scam of p*rfection is that it'll be imp*rfection before you know it.

When you feel caught up in the p*rfection trap, ask how you can maximize and lean into *this* specific chapter in your journey. Shining a light on what's already there, then asking how you can do something proactive with what you've got, helps build a sense of Self that's unshakeable. Not by middle school girls, not by Gap capris, not by age or life stage or anything else. The ideal will always change. The one thing that won't is your commitment to who you are.

I got a lot of wonderful qualities from my mom, her colorful language being one of them. Not just her extensive vocabulary of four-letter-plus words, both commonly bleeped out and made-up alike (ever heard of "shit-ton" as a measuring unit? If not, you're welcome), but also the way she uses words to describe the way she lives and experiences her—as Mary Oliver would say—"one wild and precious life." Those leadership skills, that laugh-till-you-cry laughter, that zest for life and all its little adventures, they're all beautifully expressed through the language she calls her own. And because of that, I've been able to develop my own language to tell my own story.

Just like other choice words and phrases, I sometimes unconsciously slip on these Emotionally Heavy Words. But those instances are now the exceptions, not the norm. And in the last few years, a strange thing has happened: a casual use of these three words has felt uncomfortable and even a little vulgar rolling off my lips. I've noticed that there are very few things I actually do h*te, think are ug*y, or want to be p*rfect in my life—none of which have to do with the way I look, act, or feel on a day-to-day basis. And when I *do* consciously choose to use these words, they're highly intentional.

We all have our conversational tics and our characteristic norms. We all laugh differently; we all lead differently; we all find the kinds of adventures that work for us. The language we use, then, should be a reflection of that—of the nuanced, brilliant individuals we are.

So let *that* language live. Not the easy, violent, unattainable vocabulary that makes us more likely to fight against what we've got instead of fight *for* who we're meant to be.

Take those Emotionally Heavy Words of yours, and turn them upside down. See what's underneath them. And then let whatever *that* is have space at the table and be seen.

Try it.

It's fucking beautiful.

Chapter Ten

TAKE IT OUTSIDE

What's the story you tell people about your life?

Is it filled with detailed truths?

Or generalized reactions?

I'm so stressed.

I'm so busy.

I'm so tired.

I'm fine. Just fine.

I'm sorry.

So many times, so much of what we tell people about our life isn't what's currently happening or how we feel about it: it's a summary of a reaction. Life is complicated—and when we don't want to deal with dissecting its complicated nature, it can feel easier to boil it down to a key phrase we're pretty sure most people won't ask follow-up questions about. Period, end-of-story, shortcut-type phrases. Think about it: when was the last time someone told you, "I'm so busy," and you said, "Tell me more about that . . ."?

The way we narrate our lives to others, though, becomes a part of the story we internalize as our truth.

Which is why we cannot just be our Self on the inside—we've got to live that Self on the outside too.

The Interview

"Tell me more about that."

No, I wasn't in my therapist's office. I was interviewing to be a group fitness instructor at a new gym in town, and I'd just told my potential new boss that while I totally understood its benefits, I didn't feel like the latest, hottest group fitness class craze (that was being added to the gym's schedule all over the place) was really up my alley. It was the equivalent of interviewing to work at a bakery and telling the pastry chef that you "understood the appeal but didn't really do the whole *cupcake* thing."

She leaned in close and rested her chin on her palm—the universal sign for *I'm invested and all ears.*

The fitness world is full of movement devotees—and many strong opinions. Fitness professionals, or *fitpros,* as they're often called on the internet, are notorious for being outspoken about why their way is the best way and quick to tear down anyone who chooses to challenge that. You don't need to look any further than a quick #fitpro search on social media to see a laundry list of conflicting do-this-not-thats. Very rarely do you hear anyone both praise the benefits of an exercise *and* in the same breath say it's not really for them. What follows instead is usually a "my way or the highway" argument that just makes everyone defensive.

My potential boss gave me the gift of curiosity that day, a gift she modeled and helped me practice for years after that once I got the job (spoiler alert!). Instead of jumping to a conclusion about me or defending the industry-deemed amazingness of the craze or trying to pressure me into doing something I didn't want to, she asked me to tell her more about why I felt the way I did. She softened me and made me feel safe enough to dive into the real reasons I became interested in fitness in the first place—which had less to do with athletics or applause from others, and more to do with the mental and emotional gateways it could open *for* others. I told her that I knew my strengths as an instructor, and others' strengths as instructors, and that I would be much more excited to go to those classes rather than teach them, watching the people who were truly excited about this class format as they shined. I didn't want to do something I wasn't skilled at—and wasn't interested in becoming skilled at—just for another chance to be front and center with a microphone.

"I completely get it." She shrugged as she leaned back in her chair. "And I'm so glad you said all that. Not everyone knows themselves well enough to know when something isn't right for them—even when it's the 'cool new thing.' I kind of love that you know what you love and what you're great at, and at the same time are happy to let other people shine where *they* excel."

"Better to be great at one thing than try to be good at everything," she added. "Especially if that one thing is where your heart's at."

A feeling of ease in your Self isn't built in the big, dramatic gestures—it's developed within the tiny micro-moments, like that one gym interview that helped me build confidence to be Me out loud. Over and over, they shape the way you walk through the world.

Practicing Your New Language

What do you do when you're learning a new language? You can't just practice in your head to get really good at it. To become proficient, maybe even fluent, you've got to incorporate it into your everyday life and practice with other people out in the world.

Self-talk isn't inherently good or bad—it's information. It's a language we teach ourselves, and each other, to speak. Negative self-talk, then, becomes about way more than just who we are—it becomes about who all of us are. Every time we put ourselves down, we reinforce that *this* is the language of the land. Every time we show defensiveness or distrust, we subconsciously teach the people around us that maybe they should have their defenses up too. With every action and interaction, we are literally *spreading the word.* And many times, that word isn't all that good.

You can do all the internal work necessary to shift your negative self-talk, but what good is it if you're only using your new language skills on an as-needed basis? How proficient are you actually becoming at your newer, more positive, and more proactive language if you're only speaking it when absolutely necessary—and only within the parameters of your own mind?

Just like you can't learn another language solely by thinking about it, you can only become fluent in more positive, proactive self-talk by also using it in conversation. And when you make that shift happen for yourself, you create a domino effect and help someone else become fluent in it too.

In that interview, my future boss complimented my self-awareness, celebrated the strengths that made me Me, and got curious about my motivations—three Cs essential to practicing your new language out loud.

Compliment Others

Ever heard the advice, "If you wouldn't say it to a friend, don't say it to yourself?" Turns out, this advice works in the positive direction as well.

When you compliment others, whether on a new dress or on their killer smile, you're training your brain to speak kindly. And as with anything else, practice makes permanence. Because we all want to be *seen*, right? Because when we feel seen, we feel that sense of true belonging. So to be seen, really *see* someone else. Start complimenting people in a real, meaningful way that tells people that you see them.

A note on real meaningfulness: waxing poetic doesn't equal real or meaningful. You don't need to have the most words—or the fanciest words—in order to give a great compliment. All you need to do is open your eyes and report back on what you see. Specificity allows us to feel seen. Sometimes the most meaningful thing we can do is notice the details. The things most people might not notice.

Point out the small stuff—the *whys* behind your compliments. Instead of telling someone you like their outfit, for example, can you pair that compliment with something more specific? Maybe you like how comfortable it looks, or the style, or the color. Maybe it's just about choosing a more specific *word* to describe how you feel about it (can you add an adjective before the word "outfit" when you say "I like your outfit," for example?). The goal isn't to win the Compliment Olympics—it's to make your compliments feel intentional instead of on autopilot.

It might seem superfluous or cheesy at first. It might even feel awkward. Do it anyway. When your mind practices the art of reassurance and positive reinforcement, its wires get untangled, and positivity starts to become your vernacular. When you're nicer to others, you're nicer to yourself—and you slowly start making decisions from a place of self-love instead of self-loathing. There's no way we can build those positive-talk muscles in our brain when it comes to *ourselves* if we don't work on building them up when it comes to *others*. They are not and cannot be mutually exclusive.

Celebrate Communally

Remember the study that showed that people create bonds easily over "shared" negativity? While there's no way to totally wipe the world of that instinct, you *can* take steps to counteract it.

Each day, bond with a friend or family member over at least one thing that's positive. Maybe it's a win you had at work. Maybe it's something interesting you learned or a revelation you had during the day. Maybe it's the way you felt or a funny thing you saw. It can be anything. But make sure that neither one of you lets your criticism or cynicism come into the conversation while you're in celebration mode.

If you're in a habit of bonding over negativity or downplaying the good stuff in your life, this might be tough. Give yourself time and patience as you adjust to this new positive and proactive habit of giving the good stuff space to shine.

The hardest part of this exercise for some people is that their friends are . . . *not always on board.* A lot of us are starved for authentically positive connection, which could mean either that people will enthusiastically join in or instinctively repel what's different. It's not their true colors per se—but it might be their true *patterns.* Maybe they also need some time to build this new habit of not raining on the parade!

You can help them out while also helping yourself: if a friend or family member starts to steer the conversation in a negative direction, try saying something like, "I get it, and for right now, I'd really love to keep this conversation positive. Can we talk about all that other stuff at another time?" That other time might come, but it probably won't—and if it does, you can focus on whatever needs to be addressed in a real way. The point here isn't to cast aside a whole set of emotional responses; the point is to let celebration live fully and have its moment.

But sometimes, that doesn't work. And I'd only be speaking to a very privileged, very simplistic situation if I sat here and told you that if those people continue to repel you time and again, "maybe it's time to get some distance." Distance is only possible sometimes. If your attempts at celebration continue to be repelled or criticized by certain people in your life, please know that that doesn't mean you should stop celebrating. Your celebrations are worth having, out loud and in the open, with people who want to celebrate you and you want to celebrate them in return.

Ask yourself: As I continue to practice my new language out loud, who can I count on as my study buddies? Because the other side of this interaction is receiving someone else's celebratory moment and celebrating right along *with* them. Just like the proverbial "putting yourself in someone else's shoes" can help you understand a tough situation, wholeheartedly celebrating someone else's wins can help you understand celebration in general. When we celebrate our steps, whether big or small, we're subconsciously telling ourselves that they're important. And when we acknowledge what's important, change starts to take shape.

Get Curious

Here's what I've learned about curiosity: it's not about being on the same page. It's about leaning in, resting your chin on your palm, and saying, "Tell me more."

Curiosity might be the most important C of all when it comes to practicing your new language out loud, because it's what's necessary for the other two Cs to exist. Compliments can't happen if you're not getting curious about what's worth complimenting. Celebration cannot exist without curiosity around what led you to that particular moment.

An emphatic note: The work of getting curious does not grant a free pass to (or ask you to formulate excuses for) anyone who's doing harm. What it does is amplify the importance of understanding. Which puts the power back in your court if you're interested in making progress, whether that progress is Self-focused or society-focused. We're all a sum of our ingrained experiences and backgrounds—we all bring a different version of the story to the table. If we want to understand our own complex nuances, we've got to try to understand the complex nuances of others too. And not just when it's convenient to do so. Even in the case of the worst problems, it's important to understand the ins and outs of the problem in order to solve it. Otherwise, you're only solving what you see, not what's holding it up underneath (just like repeating an upbeat affirmation won't negate a lifetime's worth of self-loathing; remember, we start with the *self* part of *self-talk* for a reason).

Curiosity means you care. Whether you're getting curious about yourself or others, here are some ways to open up a conversation with the power of curiosity:

- **Share your whys and ask for theirs.**
  In general, people *want* to empathize with each other. Or, at least I'd like to believe they do. However, when all you hear from someone is rage or anger, it becomes really hard not to just shut down and disengage.

It's a lot easier to understand and connect with someone when they explain the *whys* behind their *whats*. Have a "tell me more about that" moment. Dig deeper than what's presented. And when you explain why *you* feel the way you do about something, be sure to back up your feelings with supporting examples. It'll make it a whole lot easier—and feel a lot safer—for the other person to do the same.

- **Ask curious questions.**
  Curiosity isn't just about asking questions. It's about asking the right kinds of questions.

  I ask myself what I call *curious questions* all day. Not only is it a way to face any negative self-talk loops that try to swoop in, it's a way to get clear on what's really in my head and heart. Open-ended questions that encourage specificity—in particular, questions that start with What, Why, or How, but Who, When, or Where work too—can help shed light on decisions that were made, beliefs that are held, and motivations behind even the most auto-piloted actions.

  Asking curious questions is like uncovering a fossil embedded in layers and layers of rock. Each what, why, and how gets more and more specific, chipping away at the surface layers until you're finally face-to-face with the thing you were hoping to find. Or maybe the thing you never in a million years thought you'd uncover. Either way, you've now got a peek into a world you wouldn't have otherwise. (Don't feel like you need to become a question robot, though. Asking curious questions is all about the quality of what you ask, not the quantity.)

  This works for the big things and small things and can turn one into the other or create a mash-up of both. A friend once told me she feared that "everyone" (big thing) would judge her if she made a big life decision—and so I asked: who is this "everyone"? Everyone, turns out, was not *every* single one of the *ones*, but one very specific *one* (small thing) who was very important to her (big thing). What unfolded was a conversation about this relationship, and how it affected her life in ways I'd never realized.

It can feel awkward to ask about someone else in detail if you haven't really done it before—and especially awkward if you're not even in the practice of doing it to yourself. You don't want to come off as condescending, disrespectful, or ignorant. We've all experienced that at some point in our lives. But even (or especially, perhaps) in the face of discomfort, we can't shy away from curiosity. If we do, we're just reinforcing the story that hard things aren't worth our while.

What you *can* do to help those who feel shy or awkward diving deep is encourage them to ask *you* questions and reassure them it's judgment-free to do so. "Why does this scare you?" "What makes you feel strong?" "What is it like to go through [fill in the blank]?" "Why do you feel called to do, or say, or be the way you are?" The more we understand about one another, the more we're able to speak a more proactively positive language with fluency.

- **Talk with, not at.**

It's no wonder "stop feeling this way" self-talk doesn't work the way we intend it to—we're barking orders at our Self instead of leaning in to learn more about what's really going on. It doesn't matter that the orders are "for our own good." They're definitive statements about what you should do and how you should be, without leaving any room for exceptions or nuance.

Just like you wouldn't want to order yourself to simply *stop* feeling a feeling, the same goes for a curiosity practice. Getting curious means resisting the urge to talk *at* someone, and instead learning to talk *with* them. What's the difference? Talking *with* someone is a collaborative conversation, where both people's thoughts weave together, forming a dialogue that couldn't happen with just one person alone. Talking *at* someone, however, is a solo project that happens to be alongside someone else. Instead of a dialogue, it's a monologue with an objective that's not open for discussion. Think of talking with someone as a two-way street that allows turns and U-turns all the way across, and talking at someone as a one-way street with nowhere else to go.

When we talk *at* people instead of *with* people, no matter the subject, they tend to tune out. Instead of focusing on your own response, advice, or expertise, begin your curiosity conversation by standing witness to their emotions, and expressing yours honestly and (this is key) proactively in return. Aim for that conversational braid of words and thoughts and feelings, instead of being two people talking separately who happen to be in the same room with each other.

One last thing: honing a curiosity practice requires commitment. Especially when you're getting curious about the tough stuff. People hold on to their views, their perspectives, and their beliefs in what's possible (or not) for a reason—and that includes you. Whether it was something that happened in childhood or a trigger that lies beneath the surface, no one simply wakes up and decides to live their life, think their thoughts, and feel their feelings out of thin air. Do not be surprised if when you choose to get curious, that curiosity isn't welcomed with open arms.

But just because someone has their wall up doesn't mean there isn't something worthwhile on the other side of the barrier. One conversation might not change anything. But it might change everything. Curiosity is very rarely not worth a shot. And we've got to lean into it with an open mind and full heart if our aim is to see shift happen. On the inside, on the outside. It's all the same language.

Your Self, on Purpose

My earliest memories of being ashamed of my Self all had to do with my relationships with other people. I believed I wasn't good enough, smart enough, or impressive enough to leave a lasting mark. No one told me I wasn't good enough or smart enough or impressive enough. But without words, it was effectively communicated to me by everything from the TV I watched to the women I loved that I needed to be *more* to *matter*. I noticed the kids on the covers of the cassette tape decks and on the stages of *The Mickey Mouse Club* and *Kids Incorporated* with their perfect hair and impeccable style and wished I could be as cool. I listened to my friends' mothers not-so-silently judge one another and wondered who was judging me behind the scenes. I listened to the way women bonded over how much they hated parts of themselves, from their thighs to their thoughts, and I duly noted how it was a quick way to connect and how awful it made me feel for the sake of connection.

I became a master storyteller. Everything was more dramatic in my head. I got even better as I got older. Repetition created fluency.

And then something happened: I started to want to understand and be understood instead of agree and be agreed with. I would look at the reality of the situation and the players in the game of my life, and delicately peel away the cocoon threads protecting the heart of the matter. I started to make decisions honoring who I was instead of who I thought I needed to be and to look toward who I was becoming instead of back at who others had always seen me as.

This *something*—it wasn't one jolt of an a-ha moment that brought me there. It was the tiny micro-moments that built up, one by one. A voice lesson. A car. A bird. A poem. So many small things that were never really small at all. That's the thing about micro-moments. They come in all varieties. And you can't selectively tune out the ones you don't like, because when you tune out one kind, you risk tuning out all kinds. The best thing you can do is notice, lean in, and whisper, *Tell me more.*

I began to realize that my job is not to be special or extraordinary or perfect. I began to realize my job is nothing more than to be

Me, and that I have a voice that's all my own. I began to be truthful with myself during the highs, lows, and full spectrum of my life experiences, and I began to trust myself enough to let that truth live out loud. I dove in and dug deeper when I was tempted to use Emotionally Heavy Words that were reactive, not proactive. I became curious about myself and others.

I sometimes feel like it's only been the last few years, but in reality, I have been on this journey of finding my fullest, truest Self my entire life. And not just finding her, but being her out loud. Over three decades and counting. And just when I think it's over and I've reached Peak Me, something will happen, and I realize there's more. More finding to be done, more being to be had, just . . . more.

The work never ends. The story never closes.

And I don't want it to.

I still tell myself stories that I'm thought ill of, that I'm screwing up, that I'm bound to end up back at square one with nothing. That someone is onto me; that really I don't know shit. That someone is always more qualified, more talented, more beautiful, more special, and more well-liked. Just More. *Who are you, even?*

And when I tell myself this story, I get curious and ask why.

And usually, the story I tell is improbable.

And usually, my story is rooted in a desire to love and be loved, or a fear of being wrong. A premonition that I might have something to be sorry about.

But I know now for certain that my story is not one of a walking apology.

The story I tell is the story of my Self—and she's entirely on purpose.

Part Four

YOU NEED A SELF
FIND YOUR SELF
BE YOUR SELF
STAY YOUR SELF
WANT YOUR SELF

Chapter Eleven

OVERWHELM AND THE ART OF THE PFO

The very first nightmare I remember having was about a stampede. It was so terrifying I fell out of bed, woke up, and burst into tears. In my dream, I was lying in my normal bed, in my normal room, in the normal quiet of the night. There was a faint rumbling—like one of the minor San Andreas Fault earthquakes I'd learned to normalize. It grew. And grew. And as it hit its climax, a whole safari's worth of animals smashed through my bedroom wall. Elephants. Zebras. Giraffes. Drywall crashing and slashing through space, and my framed Disney posters shattered on impact, along with me.

My parents, whose room was next to mine, heard a thud and immediately rushed to my room. They thought I was wailing because I'd fallen out of bed. I was wailing because I'd been trampled. I was five.

My recurring nightmares have now morphed from stampedes to tidal waves. The set is different, but the premise is the same. A clear sky, a quiet street, and I see a wave taller than any skyscraper in New York City towering over my head. As it reaches its peak, it pauses. And then, at rapid-fire speed, it crashes down upon me.

This is Overwhelm. It's a rumbling, a slow and gradual build, one you think nothing of until the rumbling is too loud and the tide is too high, and all you can do is brace yourself for the crash.

What's Overwhelm?

The term "overwhelm" comes from the mid-fourteenth century, early fifteenth century verb used to describe when something is submerged completely. Its origins of "to turn upside down, to overthrow, to knock over" are thought to possibly allude to a ship—which feels right, because, duh, tidal waves.[1]

Now that we're out of the Late Middle Ages, we've turned "overwhelm" into a noun too. It's the *state* of being turned upside-down or knocked over. Overwhelm isn't always about what we're *doing* anymore; it's about how we *identify* in any given moment.

As I lay on the floor in 1992 tangled up in my sheets like a poorly made rubber band ball (I could never master those), I felt the stampede reverberating in my tiny body. When I'm jolted awake in the here and now—*bam!*—by tidal waves so big and ominous they should be in a Christopher Nolan film, my whole body convulses so violently and suddenly that I kick Jeremy awake too.

"What's wrong?" (Poor guy usually thinks something fell on my head.)

"Don't worry, nothing. I just had a dream . . ." (It takes me a moment to get the words out. Things always feel scarier in my mind than they do when I say them out loud.)

I've felt that *reverb* in my life so often that I can now place the meaning of my dreams in an instant. I know when that tidal wave appears, I've got some major Overwhelm (noun) going on, and life is overwhelming (verb) me, and I need to tend to it *stat* before it comes crashing down overwhelmingly (adverb!), shattering me to bits.

Kinds of Overwhelm

Overwhelm *thrives* on extremes. When it rains, it pours. And when it shines, it's scorching. If Overwhelm is about "being overpowered in state or feeling," that means it's not just about the bad times; it's about *any* sustained extreme leading you to feel a lack of control.

When Overwhelm comes knocking, it usually shows up as one—or some combination—of the two types below:

Roughness Overwhelm

The type of Overwhelm we *talk* about the most is the kind when the shit hits the fan, and *keeps* hitting the fan over and over again. Internally, externally, same difference. The objective information of the situation might be totally neutral, but if it makes you feel like you've just been thrown off a cliff, welcome to Roughness Overwhelm.

Maybe you've got a boss who's hounding you for work, and you're feeling the pressure. Maybe you lead a team, and you constantly seem to be picking up the slack for everyone else. Maybe things at home are falling apart or just aren't coming together, and you feel like a failure. (Spoiler alert: You're not. Life is just hard sometimes.)

If Overwhelm has morphed into an identity thing, it's easy to use Roughness Overwhelm to support a negative, self-deprecating narrative. "I am experiencing an overpowering and uncomfortable feeling" becomes "This is a bad feeling" becomes "This is a bad thing" becomes "I am bad at this bad thing" becomes "I *am* bad."

Goodness Overwhelm

It's easy to talk about being overwhelmed when you're overwhelmed by hard things—but it's harder to talk about Overwhelm when things are *good.* Mainly because we think there's nothing to be overwhelmed *about.* Overwhelm, our self-talk says, is about *negativity.* And there's nothing negative happening here. *Snap out of it.*

I'm no stranger to enrolling myself in Camp Overwhelm, usually unknowingly. And many times, it happens when the most *positive* opportunities are at my feet. I end up feeling anxious, self-sabotage, and the cycle repeats. (Or I just have a meltdown. Either/or.)

As a self-proclaimed go-getter, I sometimes back myself into a corner of so much *good* that I don't know what to do with it. My mind instantly starts up with the negative self-talk. The voice gets louder and louder, and I sink into shame from feeling like my Overwhelm means I'm not appreciative:

> *Be grateful, why don't you!*
>
> *How selfish and stuck-up you are right now.*
>
> *You don't deserve good things, because you don't know how to keep them.*

It's easy for negative talk to creep into positive moments—so easy, in fact, that you might not realize you've gotten into the habit of it until the good things come your way and you struggle to embrace them. If you haven't been actively keeping your language in check, internally and externally, the good can feel strange. You're going from one extreme to the other—and are in unfamiliar territory without even knowing it.

We can't expect to truly appreciate the good moments if we haven't been practicing the language to accept them in the first place. Your first response to Goodness Overwhelm might be to complain or downplay the good stuff, or even retreat into self-sabotaging behaviors to subconsciously "balance things out." (Gay Hendricks, psychologist and author of *The Big Leap*, calls this the "Upper Limit Problem"—where we believe we're only deserving of X amount of success, and therefore start to self-sabotage when we reach that level so as not to go higher.)[2] You might even feel selfish or guilty about being overwhelmed in the first place. *If I can't handle the good, am I even* worthy *of it?*

What ends up happening to me in the case of either kind of Overwhelm is that if I leave it unchecked, one small thing inevitably triggers me and sends me spiraling. The whole flood of emotions I've been feeling about how jam-packed life has been or how huge that one transition was or how upsetting so much has been or how I actually don't have it all together like I tell myself I do . . . the force of it all doesn't just *fill* my reservoir; it bursts the dam wide open.

My Overwhelm builds . . . and builds . . . and eventually crashes on top of me.

The work of handling Overwhelm, no matter what kind, is a lifelong practice. There's a reason this chapter isn't called "Beat Overwhelm!" or "Bye Overwhelm!" or "Overwhelm: Get Over It!" You're human, and Overwhelm is another one of those seemingly inconvenient human experiences. Just because you *know* how to navigate the waters doesn't mean it's meant to be a smooth ride.

The solution? Do some preventative care and plan a freak-out. You read that right. . . .

What the Hell Is a Planned Freak-Out?

A Planned Freak-Out, or PFO as it's now lovingly called in our household, is exactly what it sounds like: planning to freak out *before* you freak out. Basically, it's a structured way to lose your shit, then find it again.

Before you start to skip ahead a few pages because this sounds like a *horrendous* idea—intentionally inviting the tidal wave and being like "Hey tidal wave, crash down on me!"—you should probably know I'm married to someone who used to be one of the most emotionally avoidant emotional people ever, and he's the one responsible for the majority of this PFO madness.

The PFO was born out of the minds and hearts of two highly sensitive, highly emotional people who process and express those emotions very differently. There's me, the emotional sponge with all the words who's prone to self-blaming: I'll pick up on your smallest shift in energy and rack my brain for what I did to upset you. I'll accidentally say "love you!" to the barista at the local coffee shop, cower, and then replay the instance in my mind for the next sixty-eight years. I can never visit that coffee shop again. When my emotions feel like all too much, my freak-out moments present as *despair and escape.*

And then there's Jeremy: the grounding earthen shell with the hot liquid magma flowing underneath just waiting to explode. Just like me, Jeremy picks up on everything—but lives in extremes. I often tell him his biggest strength and Achilles heel is his ability to see things from multiple perspectives—hence his grounding force. He takes things in proverbial stride, and while I tend to emotionalize every single instance, he handles one-off moments with a type of composure and levity I can only strive toward. But I've learned not to be fooled when he presents cool-calm-collected under pressure—because when it eventually feels like all too much, his freak-out moments present as a *blazing forest fire of emotion.*

We all handle ourselves differently when things feel like all too much. Some of us shut down completely. Some of us emotionally dump on everyone around us. The common thread? We usually feel out of control and at the mercy of our surroundings.

When we moved to New York City in 2016, I'd lived in Los Angeles my entire life—so naturally, the shift brought up all sorts of emotions, from a sense of freedom and adventure to fear of losing what was familiar. About two weeks before we left, I started to get a little bit anxious. Being the calming force that he is, Jeremy mentioned to me that we should probably plan for at least two to three big freak-out moments in the first few months.

Cool. Okay. Permission. I can do that.

And also, *Sure, right, like I'll even need it.*

Fast forward seven months to December. I'd definitely had my own one-off moments of spontaneously crying or stressing out, but I had yet to sit down and really allow myself to digest what a major life change I'd made earlier in the year. On the first of the month, we sat down together at the end of the day, wordless and frazzled, and realized that neither one of us had truly taken the time to reflect upon and process the enormous change that we'd just made.

I pride myself on being pretty resilient. Sure, if you change the schedule of a day I've meticulously planned out, I'll break out in anxious trembling—but when it comes to big changes, failures, or loss, I take a deep breath and move forward. Is my resilience helpful? For sure. Is it a defense mechanism? Sometimes.

I have a tendency to take my resilience for granted. Because of that, I sometimes downplay huge moments and transitions in my life that are completely worthy of a good old-fashioned freak-out. I don't allow myself to, because my logical brain tells me that I logically know how to handle it. But I'll say it again: just because you know how to navigate the waters doesn't mean it'll be a smooth ride.

So here's what we did: We blocked off a few hours over the weekend just for us. We decided we'd go somewhere, get a nice warm cocktail (because it was cold outside and it felt cozy, but if that's not your thing, you don't have to do it that way), and face it all head-on. At first, I thought we were going to sit and *vent* about whatever we wanted or were worried about and allow ourselves space to stress out, cry, and react however we wanted to in a safe environment. But being the left-brainer he is, Jeremy devised an exercise to provide some structure to the situation (so we didn't, you know, leave even more anxious than before). Our very first PFO.

A PFO isn't about venting or reacting. A PFO is a supercharged journaling exercise that not only helps you outline what gets under your skin the deepest and sends you spiraling into Overwhelm, but also helps you identify tangible action steps forward into a more proactive headspace.

While you can have a successful session on your own, a PFO is best done with a partner, best friend, or someone you trust to keep confidences and (this is important) not judge! Part of the beauty is in the sharing and speaking your words out loud. In speaking them aloud to a trusted PFO partner, you signal to your head and heart that you're in a safe space to acknowledge your feelings. And only when we acknowledge our feelings are we able to move *through* them.

We ended up spending about three hours total on the exercise. And I've got to say it was one of the most cathartic, useful, and impactful exercises I've ever done. Not only did I feel lighter, I felt like I had direction. And maybe even more important than that, I felt like I was taken care of. Like I'd held my Self's hand and said *We got this.*

Since Overwhelm is a human emotion, there's no way you'll ever be able to fully eradicate those times when you start to freak out, or that you'll ever know more or know better than to flip your lid. (A common freak-out, by the way, is something along the lines of: "I'm an adult and should know way more than I do right now." The hallmark of being an adult is knowing you will *never* know it all, so congratulations!) How do you make reactions to freak-outs healthy? You practice freaking out.

Overwhelm at the helm? Going through—or just been through—a major transition? Had a stressful year? Life just feeling like a roller coaster? You might be in need of a Planned Freak-Out too.

Before you begin: something that's important when you're planning your Planned Freak-Out is that you allow yourself the time and space to let anything that bubbles up do so judgment-free. I'm not just talking about if you do this exercise with someone else—you've got to commit to being as judgment-free as you can with yourself. Trust that you're going to get to a positive, proactive place eventually in this exercise. But it might not happen right away. And that is *fine.*

Here's how you plan a Planned Freak-Out. I'll give you the sequence, then share a peek into my first PFO so you have a point of reference:

PFO, Part One:

1. Grab a notebook and open up a spread of two pages. At the top of one side, write THINGS I HATE. On the other side, make the heading THINGS I DISLIKE.

2. Set a timer for twenty minutes and list everything that's on your mind right now that's causing you Overwhelm.

Wait a sec—no asterisk in the word HATE here? Nope—a PFO is one of those times when you actually *want* to lean into that Emotionally Heavy H-word. The point is to face that feeling head-on, so that you can do something about it.

The things you write down in Part One can be general feelings you hate or dislike feeling, or specific things going on in your life right now, or aspects of your life where you're dissatisfied. Nothing is off-limits. The only rule is that this is not a blame game; it's not the time to tell the person you're doing the PFO with what you hate or dislike about them (more on that in a second).

Originally, Jeremy and I set the timer for fifteen minutes but realized that we not only needed extra time at the beginning to sit and mull over what we disliked and hated, but extra time in the middle of it. Once we got into the zone, the words flowed. With a PFO, it's important to recognize and accept that not everything is going to come to you right away. Whether you've been suppressing feelings, there's shame involved, or you've just been accepting vague truths as THE truth, this might take more than a few minutes. Set a timer so you feel a sense of urgency (with unlimited time, you might end up tiptoeing around the big stuff that's hard to say out loud), but feel free to set and reset that timer as many times as you need to in order to get it all on paper before Part Two.

PFO, Part Two:

1. Once you have your two lists, write another heading on a new page: SO WHAT THE FUCK AM I GONNA DO ABOUT IT?

2. Set the timer again, and write down as many specifics as possible, getting as granular as possible.

This is where the power in the PFO starts to take shape. And this is where you get called out if you've slipped and written down a hate/dislike point that places blame on someone else. The *So What the Fuck Am I Gonna Do About It?* section is about taking a stand for yourself by taking ownership of the situation at hand.

(And while no, the cursing is not necessary, I personally find it makes this part a smidge more powerful.)

Giving yourself concrete action steps not only provides you with a roadmap of where to go next, but reinforces a sense of agency around things you might not have been feeling a sense of agency over pre-PFO. The *So What the Fuck Am I Gonna Do About It?* section is when that feeling of being taken care of comes to life. Not only have you acknowledged what's not working for you, you've given your Self tools to move forward instead of staying stuck.

After you're done with Parts One and Two, you might be feeling a mixture of things. Relief. Vulnerability. Excitement. Nervousness. Surprise. This is totally normal. Look at everything you just dove into!

When you hit this midway point, I suggest giving yourself a "brain break"—a few minutes to decompress. Grab a coffee. Sit in the park. Go pet a dog. Enjoy some French fries with your PFO partner. Do something to press your internal "reset" button.

Because you're about to repeat Part One and Part Two—but with love and like.

PFO, Parts Three and Four:

1. When you're ready, open your notebook to a new spread of pages. At the top of one side, write THINGS I LOVE. On the other side, write the heading THINGS I LIKE.

2. Set your timer for twenty minutes and go. Again, write down all the things you love and like. Feelings you love and like. Food. Activities. People. Places. Sensations. It's all fair game.

3. Once you've got your two lists—and you know what I'm going to say next—write in bold letters: SO WHAT THE FUCK AM I GONNA DO ABOUT IT?

When I started writing my lists, I saw some clear themes, which I found interesting. Self-suppression, lack of structure, stagnation, and disconnection were at the root of most all of my hates and dislikes.

To illustrate, here are a few of the things I wrote under the HATE heading in that first PFO:

Feeling ineffective and insufficient.

Feeling like "just another so-and-so"—not feeling unique in any way.

Societal pressures on women and how often I feel trapped by them.

Waiting for validation or permission before I take action.

Feeling like I can't help the people I love when they need help.

Loneliness.

Some of the things I wrote under DISLIKE included:

Low work structure and routine.

When the house is a mess.

Not enough time for long phone calls with my long-distance friends.

Not knowing where my local "spots" in the neighborhood are yet.

Feeling so tired so often.

Waiting for opportunities to show up instead of looking for or making them myself.

On the other hand, self-expression, definition, progress (personal or professional), and connection were at the root of most all my loves and likes. Which all flowed from my pen onto the page.

For example, under LOVE, some of the things I wrote were:

Love and gratitude.

Coffee time in the morning with Jeremy.

Strolling through different neighborhoods.

Helping people feel proud of themselves.

Exercising for my own enjoyment and strength.

Focused, purposeful writing.

Singing loudly.

Great conversations.

Feeling proud of my presence.

Feeling trusted.

And lastly, some things I wrote under LIKE were:

Good sleep.

Good hair days.

Getting paid to write.

Running.

Reading.

Podcasting.

Game nights.

Hosting people at our home.

Daily structure.

Daily flow.

When I started to write my second list of To-Do-About-Its and realized I could just refer to the To-Do-About-Its on the prior page, I saw one more pattern: that stepping up, living *up*, and self-assertion were at the root of most everything I could do to feel the way I wanted to feel.

Note: Planning a Freak-Out is not about expecting the worst. And if your Freak-Out is of the Goodness Overwhelm variety, it's not about waiting for something bad to happen, because "there's always something," and conjuring up that feeling that any happy moment could suddenly become a tragic one.

This is about recognizing your deep and nuanced humanity. You are human. You feel human feelings. And we experience an endless spectrum of emotions throughout our lives. A PFO is like a bowling bumper for your feelings. It makes space for you to feel your feelings and let them roll, then gently bumps them back into a productive direction, so they don't end up in someone else's lane, knocking over someone else's pins.

Jeremy and I now do PFOs together once a quarter and have done so for over seven years. To say I notice a difference in my Overwhelm is an understatement. The most valuable thing about a Planned Freak-Out is that it not only creates order and redirection in the moment, but it also helps you through the real deal when it pops up out of nowhere. Overwhelm can make you freak out gradually, or it can happen in the micro-moments. When stuff inevitably happens, and you have mini-freak-outs, having a PFO practice in place helps you respond as sanely, healthily, and quickly as you can to get back on track, without spending time feeding the negativity (fear, worry, doubt) that inevitably happens in a freak-out moment.

Too Late for A PFO?

I was going to end this chapter with the PFO, but then realized . . . a PFO is Plan A. You can be hyper self-aware, have your PFOs scheduled in advance, and still Overwhelm may catch you off-guard.

Let's say you've missed your window for a PFO.

You're in the thick of a classic FO, no P to be seen.

This is where the real test comes. Are you willing to do the work, but only when it's convenient . . . or are you willing to make shift happen in the middle of the mess?

If you're feeling overwhelmed and start to spiral, I've got you. Here are some ways you can start to proactively persevere through whatever whirlwind you're facing:

1. **Objectively describe what's happening.**

   Overwhelm thrives on feelings to not only rev up its engine but steer the entire ship. Try not to lose sight of where those feelings stemmed from. Otherwise, there's a good chance your negative self-talk will come in and grab the wheel.

   When you're starting to feel overwhelmed—by people, by life, by responsibilities, by the news, by society—take a step back and objectively describe what's happening. For example, instead of "I feel overwhelmed all the time," what if you said "I open social media and look at news headlines and other people's lives for at least thirty minutes at a time, which leads me to feel a sense of dread and comparison" or "I have 400 unread emails that I keep saving for later" or "When people ask me these specific questions, I never know how to answer them" or "I am juggling my work schedule, my life schedule, and my kids' schedules all at once"?

The point isn't to solve; it's to name. Giving yourself an accurate, objective, and specific description of what's going on separates the Overwhelm-inducing thing from how you feel about it, which creates clarity (sometimes, Overwhelm stems from lack of clarity!). Bonus, it can also give you clues as to what you're gonna do about it—that third PFO step—which can give you a much-needed sense of agency.

2. **Focus on getting to Now-Normal instead of Back-To-Normal.** When things suck for me, I want to make them not suck. I try to get "back to normal" or replicate the way things were "back then." *Back then*, of course, being a time when there were limited obstacles and I felt in control. However, normal now isn't the same as normal then. There's a new normal in the Now—one that requires a NOW normal to go along with it.

   Instead of trying to force old habits into a new set of circumstances, why not try focusing on approaching this moment in time for what it is—not trying to make things like they were, but instead trying to work with how they *are*?

   If one thing's not working, try another, knowing that the Now is not the Forever. The name of the game isn't creating a New Normal you'll hold on to for eternity; it's crafting a Now Normal that can serve you for the right-now. If something doesn't feel right, you have full permission to move on. If there's a spark there, try it again. And again.

3. **Perform a simple act of practical self-care.** When the world seems most overwhelming, take life step by step. No choice is too tiny. No change is too small. No decision is insignificant.

   Just start *do*ing. Do one small thing that sets off a chain reaction in your head and heart that tells you you're okay, and that you're capable of moving forward even if you don't feel like you are. There are even studies around habit formation that prove this: when you repeat a chosen behavior in the same context, it starts to become automatic and feel effortless.[3] Why can't that context be Overwhelm, and that chosen behavior be a chosen act of self-care?

Ever caught yourself saying, "Eh, it won't matter anyway," or "It's not enough," or "It's too small to count"? *Welp!* One step is better than no step. And you can't move anywhere if you don't take one step after the other. Send the email. Return the call. Write the thing. Write a *sentence* of the thing. Get your shoes on. Heck, make the bed!

Any time I'm feeling weighed down or overpowered by the sheer force of life, I make sure I practice small acts of self-care at the very beginning (or middle, or end) of the day that make a huge difference. When everything feels tough, nothing feels doable. I tend to procrastinate and tell myself I'll get to things "once I feel better." But once I start doing *a* thing, whether or not it's *the* thing, then I start to feel 2 percent accomplished and 2 percent more likely to do another thing, and another, and another. Eventually, everything feels a little lighter and, at the very least, a tiny bit more manageable.

Need some ideas? Here are some things to do when the Overwhelm is so overwhelming that literally just getting out the door seems like a feat in and of itself:

- Make your bed.
- Brew yourself coffee or tea.
- Send *one* email you've been meaning to send (my own personal go-to).
- Text a friend and tell them how much you love them.

- Trim your nails (the oddly satisfying self-care practice you didn't know you needed right now).
- Read three pages of a book.
- Lace up whatever shoes you exercise in and tell yourself that if you still don't want to move after ten minutes, you can stop.
- Take ten slow, long, loud breaths.
- Do your laundry, then—*plot twist!*—fold your clothes after (instead of leaving them on the ottoman—what do you mean you never do this? Okay, me neither).
- Make or buy yourself a nourishing meal—or pack your lunch for the next day.
- Drink a full glass of water—it's amazing how much simple hydration can do.
- Hug someone you love. (P.S. your dog is definitely *someone*.)

Accomplishing one small thing after another in the midst of an Overwhelm storm helps develop resilience and *proof* that Overwhelm is not your default state. You might not be in control of everything, but there are things you *can* control in this exact moment. Do those things first. And when those things don't seem doable, just do *some*thing.

4. **Schedule white space.**
I am nothing for anyone if I am not *grounding* for myself. And so when shit starts to hit the fan—or when everything, good or not-so-good, feels like it's coming at me all at once—I schedule in *white space.*

In business terms, "white space" usually refers to identifying gaps and areas of opportunity to meet a customer's needs. In design, it's a phrase used to describe the empty space around text and other design elements, usually helping to emphasize them in a way that just wouldn't be able to happen in a cluttered picture. I like to think of the kind of white space used to address Overwhelm as a mash-up of those two: something that allows you to think clearer, see clearer, and declutter your feelings.

White space, when it comes to mindset, is time that's all your own, that you don't plan to fill and don't schedule over. It can be an hour. It can be three minutes. It doesn't need to be formalized as meditation or a "mindfulness practice." It doesn't need to be productive *or* unproductive. The only thing it needs to be is nothing.

I've learned that having time that belongs to me and me alone, time that's like the white space on a canvas—no paint, open to possibility—is a deal-maker or -breaker for me. If I don't take time to reconnect to myself with no external stimuli or things/people to answer to and don't take that time when I need it most, I end up spiraling into the Overwhelm zone. Or if I'm already there, my downward trajectory spins even faster than before.

I practice white space moments for both the moments I'm in, and the moments in the future when I'll need them most. To get into the habit, I try to incorporate them into my day-to-day activities. White space is wearing sunglasses on the subway in order to create a little me-time bubble for myself. It's walking around the block before I go inside and join the party or sitting in the car listening to one last song on the radio to create a moment of transition for myself from one thing to the next. It's hiding in the bathroom before networking or a big family gathering, not because I'm scared or nervous, but because I need a moment to myself. It's what I do when the stakes are low, so I know where to go when the stakes are high. It's both everything and nothingness rolled into one—and often the difference that makes a difference.

5. **Nix the one-sided emotional labor and replace it with a two-sided emotional investment.**
Emotional labor is what it sounds like: doing the emotional work to make something function. It's actually a useful thing but becomes dangerous when it's ridiculously one-sided.

Emotional labor can look like being the one who is constantly dissecting your friend's toxic relationships and convincing them to see the light (then they do it again, and you do it again, and so on and so forth). Emotional labor can look like putting on a happy face for your partner and "being a light" for them as they continuously stew in their own troubles. Emotional labor can mean decoding the unspoken subtext at work so that everyone can get things done. Emotional labor is why it's so exhausting to be a barista or a server or in the hospitality industry in any capacity: You're soaking in the emotions of each and every customer, many of whom are taking their daily aggravations out on you. It's your job to keep the peace and put a smile on their face. (If you're in the hospitality industry, by the way, there are going to be parts of one-sided emotional labor that are unavoidable—and you'll need to figure out your own personal boundaries, makes-and-breaks, and lines in the proverbial sand. But let's talk *outside* of those instances.)

One-sided emotional labor is taxing and gives all your good stuff to others while leaving zilch for yourself. You can't drink from an empty well, so to speak. And it's when we're feeling empty, depleted, and emotionally dehydrated that things turn really dark.

A two-way emotional *investment*, however, is different. By definition, an investment is "an act of devoting time, effort, or energy to a particular undertaking with the expectation of a worthwhile result." Start-ups present investors with data, proof points, and projections for a reason: to let them know their money isn't going to waste, and their investment won't make them go bankrupt. With an emotional investment, if you're devoting your emotional time, effort, and energy to something, you're going to see a return. Emotional investments might not be two-ways in the moment, but you've got proof points that you'll be getting that investment back in your direction when you need it. That's why investors don't just pour money into companies that sound cool, and why it's usually not the best idea to invest in people who aren't going to ever give back to you. *That's not being a friend. That's being a savior, and dehydrating and bankrupting yourself of your most valuable assets.*

There is no "you owe me" or keeping tabs in an emotional investment—there's just trust and mutual respect. Emotional labor doesn't have either. It does, however, keep tabs and tallies so it can pull more from you when it needs to . . . no matter how overwhelmed you might be.

When you feel like the Overwhelm just won't let up, it's super important to protect your well-being and energy so that you have enough resolve and resilience to be proactive, not reactive. Let your loved ones in on how you're feeling so they're up-to-speed on where you're at mentally and emotionally. Then, when and where you can, press pause on one-sided emotional labor. If anything, this is the time your emotional investments should be making a return in the form of love, check-ins, support, or even space while you slowly start to build up your emotional funds again. It's *not* the time for you to spend mindlessly as you continue to overdraw.

6. **Find your personal balance of structure and flow.**
Did you ever watch those educational TV shows as a kid that centered their whole episodes around one thing?

It's BLUE day!

The Letter of the Day is . . . the letter P*!*

Today is all about FARMS! Let's go see how to grow lettuce!

I loved those. How comforting it felt to know that for about twenty to thirty minutes, all I would need to focus on was one thing. Blue. The letter *P*. Farm stuff. That's it. Next time, something different.

When we're feeling overwhelmed, we'll often make decisions based on short-term relief instead of long-term success. As a former chronic list-maker, I know all about this. Remember those lists I used to make by the hour? To say they were failed attempts at getting ahead of Overwhelm is an understatement. If I strayed from even one minute, I felt like the freaking failure of the century. And with 1,440 minutes in a day, that's a lot of opportunity to feel failure-ish.

However, I was right about one thing: structure *works.*

The problem is, most structures that come premade for us weren't really made with us in mind to begin with. From the five-day, forty-hour workweek created in 1926 to multi-month-long workout routines you can download online right now with just one click, the structures that we opt into are often outdated or simply made with one particular audience in mind. Even as this book is being published, the concept of "going to work" is being globally challenged and upended in a way it hasn't been in decades. Whether it's the hours or the conditions, many of us are realizing that the old ways were never working—we just didn't know anything different.

While you might not be able to set your work hours or micro-manage your family's every move, finding a sense of structure in your life can help slow Overwhelm's roll. And it's not just about planning for things to go as planned—it's about planning for the inevitable "life happens" moments too.

When I start to feel Overwhelm getting the best of me, I lean on a strategy reminiscent of those educational kids' shows I used to watch growing up: *themes.*

Whether it's a full day or a few hours, I'll choose a recurring theme to carry with me each time that day or time frame pops up throughout my week. Whether that's something as obtuse as "12–5 pm are my Power Hours" or as specific as "Wednesday is my Community Day" or as quirky as "Friday is Feel-Good Friday,"

I'll give myself a word or phrase to guide my decisions, focus my energy, and wrap my mind around one thing at a time instead of all the things at once. It's a way to both focus in on what matters, and allow myself the wiggle room to adjust based on whatever the day really brings.

Everyone's idea of "structure" looks entirely different, and everyone's idea of "structure" changes. What one week, day, month, or year brings will probably look a lot different from whatever comes next and whatever's come before. It's not about finding what works forever; it's about what works for now. Some questions you can ask yourself when you're figuring out your works-for-now structure:

- What are my non-negotiables throughout the day?
- What time do I like to (or need to) wake up? To go to sleep?
- What would the bare minimum of a "successful" day need to include?
- Are there certain days or times I feel more energized? More drained?
- What do I need to do to end the week feeling the way I want to feel?

After you brainstorm, you'll land on a plan that feels both structured and allows room for the inevitabilities of life. The point isn't to stick to each day's or time-block's theme literally, but to give you a lens through which to view your experience. That sense of inner cohesiveness, even when life feels the exact opposite way, can be a game-changer.

7. **Embrace No, Not Yet, and Come Back to Me Later with This.** When we're overwhelmed, we sometimes forget that we have the ability to choose what we say yes and no to. Not all times, but some times.

   When you're overwhelmed, don't be afraid to say no to additional, non-absolutely-essential asks. This might seem easy when your to-do list is filled with awesome things. But for some reason, we tend to overextend ourselves *out* of that state of happy bliss way too often. If I only had a nickel for every time I've said "Yes!" to social plans, overly anticipating how physically, mentally, and emotionally available I'd be once those plans finally rolled around . . . I mean, I'd have a lot of nickels, for one.

   If you're the kind of person who equates Yes with strength or love, the idea of saying No might make you squirm. But remember that intentionally asserting your Yeses and Nos can be a *sign* of strength and love. Neither depend on how many things you say Yes to, especially if you do so begrudgingly or totally check out afterward. Strength and love aren't a game of *how many,* but *how meaningful.*

   Not feeling the No, or don't want to give such a for-sure answer just yet? Give yourself some space to decide. "Not yet," "I'm not sure right now," and "Can we circle back around on this later?" are all valid answers and alternate options to the Yes you might feel obligated to say. Sometimes, all Overwhelm needs in order to soften is a little space to breathe and think.

8. **Stay present as you step forward.** No matter how much you think about, talk about, or write about the *so-what-the-fuck-you're-gonna-do-about-its* of your Overwhelm, taking action needs to culminate with taking active steps forward. Thinking about and planning for something are both important, but without taking action on those thoughts and plans, you're likely to stay stalled. And not only action, but *aware* action.

Like the Nike ads say, "Just Do It"—but do it with *presence.* Treat the moment you're moving in with the respect it deserves. Instead of treating it like a task you need to check off a list and speed through, approach your action step like a meaningful moment that's one of a kind. Take what I call "mental pictures" as you go by, stopping to notice not only the way things look around you, but also the details of when and where and how you are in this moment. What time is it? Where are you exactly? What's the temperature? How do you feel? Then take another step and another mental picture. Then another, and another. And so on. It's a tricky feat to balance savoring the moment and actually getting things done, but when achieved, it's a surefire way to kick Overwhelm to the curb—because you're experiencing the entirety of the moment you're in without racing forward or looking backward.

This chapter was a big one, I know. Because Overwhelm is a big subject. Not just because it *feels* big, but because it feels a different kind of big for whoever is experiencing it. A bigness that sometimes defies explanation. A rumbling stampede. A tidal wave. Something so big that when you're caught in the middle of it, getting grounded feels all but impossible.

Not all of these strategies might work for you. But maybe some will, at some times. And sometimes, "some times" is enough to see hope on the other side.

When you're overwhelmed, it can feel like the world is pitted against you, preventing you from accomplishing anything or feeling like the person you want to be. But you'll find that once you start to show your Self you've got things handled, once you start *going*, the sunshine is yours for the keeping.

I'm getting better at it. Things that used to overwhelm me no longer do, and the things that overwhelm me now—well, I try to be as proactive as possible. I remind myself I've done this before, I'll do it again, and this is just another instance for the list. And if all else fails, I whisper to myself: *The now is not the forever. This is a moment in time, a chapter of my story. And while it's just one chapter, how I choose to read it will inform how I view the other chapters to come. The storm will pass, the waters will calm, the rumbling will subside. And I'll still be standing.*

Chapter Twelve

TRIGGERED SUSPICIONS

Everyone's got *at least one* zany story when it comes to dating. I never liked to date, so when it comes to zany stories, I have exactly one. Just one. But sometimes, one is all you need to learn what you need to learn. . . .

A few years ago, I was introduced to a man by a friend of mine. We were a perfect match on paper—and apparently, in my friend's mind too. She and I shared a love for moments of kismet, and our breaths were taken away by the prospect of this love story unfolding from afar.

Oh, important note: she introduced us via direct message on social media. He was in Texas. I was in California.

He was a deep thinker and a beautiful writer. He worked in sustainable energy and cared deeply about the planet. His taste in music was impeccable. He was tall, red-headed, handsome. He had a dog!!! Never mind that he and I lived in different time zones entirely. Somehow, this made it more romantic in my mind.

We began a very intimate, very personal relationship remotely, based entirely on the idea that we were a perfect match. We swapped songs, poetry, ideas, dreams. Swept up in the moment and my intuition telling me this is what was supposed to happen, I booked a plane ticket to fly out of state to see him.

This was within thirty minutes of talking to him for the very first time. Ever. Via text message. Not even a voice-to-voice call in the books.

And I was now going to spend a weekend with this guy I'd only "known" for thirty minutes. I'm historically cautious and haven't ever been a fan of the unknown, so from the outside, this was *way* out of character. I had friends telling me it was no big deal, and other friends telling me I was nuts. But since we had a mutual-IRL friend, I felt like I could trust him. I knew in my gut it was the right thing to do.

Two weeks later, I found myself boarding a plane from LAX to Austin. The couple next to me on my flight seemed kind, making cheerful jokes to each other as they sat down. I was drawn to them, and instead of brushing off their conversational advances like I usually would, I leaned in. Turns out, they had a daughter who had gone to my elementary school. We knew at least five of the same people. They were delightful. I never talk to people on flights, but I found myself chatting with these people the entire way.

This is a sign, I thought. *This is meant to be.*

My intuition was already telling me to move forward. Now I was getting even more proof from the outside that this was the romance of a lifetime!

As the plane touched down, the couple smiled and squealed along with me, knowing that I was about to meet my future forever-person. *My guy.* I entered the terminal with my heart beating out of my chest. I walked slowly through the oversized archways that welcomed me into Austin, soaking in the feeling of a life that would never be the same.

I rolled down the escalator.

I saw him.

He was not my guy.

Intuition vs. Triggered Suspicion

Before you start panicking on my past-self's behalf: no, I did not get catfished. He was, literally speaking, *the* guy I'd come to visit. It was just that, in that moment, my intuition told me this person wasn't the person I'd hoped he'd be.

Intuition, by definition, is something that one knows (or considers likely) based on instinctive feeling. It's quick and doesn't register consciously. It's a sense of knowing without even really *knowing* how you know. It's so strong, so powerful, that many of us choose not to listen because it's scary to trust your gut, especially when it senses things you *don't* want to be true or things that don't make sense or have any supporting evidence. Intuition feels so concrete, so objective, that no evidence is even needed for you to know that it's right.

And that can be scary.

There are times, however, when evidence *is* steering the ship. Something reminds you of something else—something else you've already formed opinions about—and you make assumptions based on what that evidence seems to be telling you.

Some call it "jumping to conclusions." I call it a triggered suspicion.

The term "trigger," psychologically speaking, is typically used to describe sensations, images, or experiences that remind you of a specific memory. With triggered suspicions, you form beliefs based on what you're reminded of, instead of what's in front of you.

Important note: a triggered suspicion isn't always a bad thing. It's not always a good thing either. Evidence from the past can be a game-changer, or a deal-breaker. If someone or something has harmed you or someone else in the past, it's not just smart but absolutely essential (sometimes even lifesaving) to keep that in mind as you move forward. I say this before I expand upon anything else here: never just write off a triggered suspicion.

But when we rely too hard on what we're reminded of to tell us what we're experiencing in the moment, our intuition can get drowned out by the evidence we gather. We take evidence from our past to inform our future, and become swayed by what we see. We begin to view the world through the lens of that evidence and those memories, and develop sneaking suspicions we then call "gut feelings." (They punch us in the gut, so this makes sense.) Of course, they feel as natural as intuition does; we've spent so much time living with those memories and festering emotions inside of us that it's hard to distinguish between familiarity and a deeper instinct. We mistake "I suspect" for "I know."

I've got intuition for days. I've learned how to listen to that objective feeling inside, whether I like what it's telling me or not. But this doesn't mean I don't get swayed by my triggered suspicions. When you have a strong sense of intuition, it can be easy to assume it's always running the show. You've spent so much time *just knowing,* you assume that your intuition is always the one calling out to you with a megaphone.

But while it's true that intuition is strong, so are triggered suspicions.

How to Tell the Difference

Both triggered suspicions and intuitive kicks can tell you if something is right or wrong or somewhere in that middle ground. The key isn't to vilify one over the other or separate them entirely. It's to get clear about what's going on, so you can make a confident, self-trusting choice moving forward.

When I slid down that escalator, my intuition told me right away that this was not "my guy"—my so-called forever-person. But it wasn't a feeling of danger or dread; it was just kind of . . . *Meh. Nope.* My gut knew it was over before it began, and it told me so.

But did that stop me? It did not. Triggered suspicions aren't always negative, and the triggers themselves don't always come in negative form. He was clever, attractive, kind, had great energy—there was nothing off-putting whatsoever. We'd already established more emotional intimacy in ten days than some of my previous relationships had established in ten months. We'd talked on the phone for hours, written love letters back and forth—and our friends were more than certain we were the perfect pair. The promising depth we'd established, the on-paper compatibility, and the overwhelming reassurance of our friends reminded me of all the things I'd hoped for in previous relationships but had never gotten (or at least not gotten all at once). I longed for depth—here it was. I wanted someone who wanted the same things I did—here he was. I wanted my friends to be excited about him, his friends to be excited about me, and a melding of friend-families like in the movies—here they were. My triggers were all *positive* things—memories and emotions of what I *hadn't* gotten and longed for in the past, and was getting in the present—and my suspicion was that *this must be it.* So I tried to push away that intuitive knowing that this was not my person. It seemed like I had so much proof to argue otherwise.

I ended up staying with him for two short-but-long months, uncharacteristic of someone who didn't like dating and couldn't stand superficial romance that didn't hit the deeper notes. Or maybe it was totally characteristic: I was trying way harder than my gut wanted me to—forcing happiness and bliss when it was really a romanticized idea I wanted to come to fruition—and told myself that since I was not someone who got involved in flings, this must be the real deal. But if I *knew* this was "it," I couldn't understand why it didn't *feel* like "it."

~

We all experience a mix of both intuition and triggered suspicions daily if not hourly. They help us make sense of the world and inform our choices moving forward. The key is to get clear on which one you're experiencing within your self-talk, so that you can trust yourself to make the right decisions for you.

If you're trying to figure out whether you're hearing your intuition or experiencing a triggered suspicion, here are two questions to ask yourself:

1. **How emotionally charged is this thought/feeling?**

   When you get an intuitive sense about something, it's not because of anything people can see. It feels like a knowing as clear as the sky is blue. It just *comes to you.*

   We all have the ability to tap into our intuition—it's just that sometimes, it doesn't feel logical. Intuition isn't based on evidence that you've gathered from the people and situations of your past.

It doesn't always feel reasonable or rational. And if you're someone who prides yourself on being reasonable and rational, it might feel silly. So you ignore it.

However, if you're being triggered, you've got *all* the emotions and at least some evidence to validate them, so it's really tempting to automatically believe in your suspicion. Whether those emotions and that evidence deal directly with the specifics of the present is inconsequential; in the moment, evidence is evidence, even if it comes from the past.

The thing about intuition is that while emotions might be present, emotions aren't the star of the show. If an idea is bubbling up and it's based on emotion, it's a good idea to double-check where it's coming from. If you're getting that "this is how it is no matter how I feel about it" feeling, it might be your intuition with something it wants to tell you. If it feels like emotions are in the driver's seat, you might be using past evidence to create a current conclusion.

2. **Am I trying to talk myself into or out of this thought or feeling?** Identifying your intuition gets messy when strong emotions aroused by an *action or circumstance* come into play. Strong emotions are evidence that, if used, can always lead you to a conclusion of your choosing.

   When I cannot separate the reality of a situation from the emotions of the situation, I ask myself whether I'm being told something or being convinced of something.

   Intuition always helps me understand whatever situation is at hand, even if I don't exactly know *how* I understand it. It comes to me in the form of statements and instructions sans emotion or opinion.

   Triggered suspicions, on the other hand, feel like there's something trying to *convince* me to buy into whatever's in front

> of me. They come to me in the form of subjective statements and loaded (sometimes judgmental) commentary about what "should" be done.
>
> A good rule of thumb when you're faced with a decision but you're unclear if that decision is being driven by your intuition or a triggered suspicion (or both working together to tell you the same thing!) is to notice whether you're trying to talk yourself into thinking/feeling a certain way or out of thinking/feeling a certain way. If you're trying to talk yourself *into* something, your past might be coloring your present, and it's probably worth a second look. If you're trying to talk yourself *out of* something, you might be working against intuition—and, yes, it's probably worth a second look.

You read that right—both intuition and triggered suspicions might be working together to tell you the same thing. Sometimes they lead you to the same place. Again, it's not about villainizing one or glorifying the other. It's about getting clear on where your self-talk is coming from. But you'll never know if you don't take a second look to deduce what it is that makes you think what you think and feel the way you feel.

There's an old saying that "feelings aren't facts." This is true in some cases. Others, not so much. Feelings and facts can often coexist, overlapping like a Venn diagram. Your feelings can contain facts, or cover up facts, or sit side-by-side with facts. Taking a second look is important, because underneath feelings are always facts about *something*. Maybe they're facts about opportunities that are or aren't right for you. Maybe they're facts about why you feel the way you do. Going with your gut and going with your feelings are two different things. Your body might think you're in a past situation, triggering emotions to try to protect you from whatever that situation ended up bringing forth—protection you do or don't need in the here and now. Or maybe your emotions are telling you to move away or toward something that seems similar to a situation in the past, a situation that's not actually like the one you're experiencing now.

The work of distinguishing intuition from triggered suspicions is nuanced, yes. But it's the work that helps you stay your Self, especially in new situations. And isn't staying your Self worth that work?

Epilogue to Austin

From the moment I descended that escalator, I knew in my gut that the person I'd flown to see was not *my guy*. But I also wasn't getting danger signals to end it and fly home right away. It just came to me as a sort of casual, internal observation. And trust me, I looked for *all* the danger signals and missteps. There were none. I felt extremely safe and cared for, and without any red flags present, my triggered suspicion was *sure* that this was my "perfect match"—and made the whole relationship into a lot more than it ever really was.

I know now my intuition was activated, but not in the way I initially thought. Because alongside the intuitive observation of "this is not my guy," I also felt my intuition telling me: *stay*. At the time, I thought my intuition was telling me this was my person and I just needed to give us time. In reality, it was simply telling me to stay in Austin and spend time with this person, even though he was NOT my person. In hindsight, I believe my intuition wanted me to keep things light and less emotionally invested, to experience what happens when I feel safe enough to embrace the unknown. So rarely had I done that in my life.

I had a blast in Austin. I got on my first stand-up paddleboard. I explored the main street filled with thrift stores and bars and restaurants and buildings that felt like they all had life and music pouring out their windows. I lounged on back porches and laughed with new friends.

Yet I was simultaneously experiencing a triggered suspicion, which got my hopes up way beyond what my intuition *knew* I was there for. Despite the great time I was having in a new place with new friends, I wasn't feeling the connection between me and Austin Man. I convinced myself the romantic bliss would arrive at some point, and so my triggered suspicion kept our relationship going for two more months.

He wanted to fly out to see me the very next month. I knew he wasn't my Meant-To-Be, but I also had this weird, objective feeling—this knowing—that this was the right thing to do. So I didn't stop him. I ran out of triggered suspicions. He flew in for a visit, and we ended it on that trip.

On his flight home, he reconnected with a woman from his hometown, who coincidentally had been in LA at the exact same time. That woman is now his wife.

I couldn't be more grateful that he came to LA—for him, and for me. Him? He found her. Me? I'm a lot braver now. I listen to my intuition a lot closer. I pause before some sort of external expectation takes over my self-talk. If I had never gotten on that plane, I would have never learned how brave and self-trusting I could be. If I hadn't taken that chance, I would have never taken all the chances I've taken since then. For so long, I would say to myself, "If I can do Austin, I can do anything!"

Our relationship didn't work out, but I walked away with more self-confidence—that beautiful cocktail of self-trust and living my truth—than I'd ever had in my life. The big things still feel big, the tough things still feel tough, and the confusing things still feel confusing, but if my intuition is telling me yes, I jump in without hesitation. If it's telling me no, I back away, no questions asked. And if I don't know what it's telling me, I dive deep into whatever my triggered suspicions are bringing up—because there's good information in there.

~

"We're going on an adventure, and you're not going to like it," my friend Jen prefaced as we had dinner together a few months after the breakup. A great way to win me over. I rolled my eyes.

"We're going on eHarmony."

Oh, hell no. I hated everything to do with dating even more than I hated everything to do with cars. Jen was the person who had introduced me to the person who had introduced me to Austin Man, who had taken me on that wild adventure of Knowings and Suspicions, and now she was doing it again.

(This was in the days before dating apps were mainstream, so there wasn't even any sort of redeeming "cool" factor to this so-called adventure.)

"Hear me out. It's not about the dates or finding Your Person. *It's about getting you out of your comfort zone and meeting the universe halfway.* You're on your own path, and that's great, but I can see that you've gotten into habits that keep you comfortable at the sake of your own growth. I don't want you to wonder what could have been."

She was right. Dammit.

"I'm the same, so I'll join with you!" she added quickly. "Plus, it's free this weekend, and we can meet up after each date and download about how bad it was."

My triggered suspicions wanted to reactively say no, but my intuition knew better. Even though dating, let alone online dating, felt like the last thing I wanted to do—it felt like something society expected from me and yet another way to reinforce the stereotype that a romantic relationship equals success—I couldn't ignore that objective statement from my intuition: *do it.*

Reluctantly, I said yes, downloaded the app, and proceeded to go on a blocking spree so I could pass on men before they even had a chance to get to me. I felt a sense of control and power. If there were no men to contact me, there were no dates to go on! Brilliant! Swipe left, left, left, left . . .

Until I couldn't. A new user profile popped up, and as quickly as it popped into my app's feed, a phrase popped into my head.

I know him.

To be clear, I had never met this person before in my life. I know that for certain because that person is now my husband, Jeremy.

~

Following your intuition doesn't mean you won't have doubts or fears come in and try to sway you. It also doesn't mean you won't question yourself along the way. But it does mean you're on the right track. And you've got to trust that. Fiercely. Even when you don't know why it's the right track or where it's leading.

If Austin Man and I never had our non-love love story, he would have never met his now-wife on that flight home. If I hadn't experienced the objective, intuitive feeling of "that's not him," I would have never known the objective, intuitive feeling of "yep, *that's* him." And if I hadn't experienced two months of believing my triggered suspicions, I wouldn't have known to tell them to take a backseat when Jen suggested something so out of my comfort zone. If I hadn't felt how brave I could be when I felt safe enough to embrace the unknown, I wouldn't be a fraction as brave as I am now, because life is the biggest unknown there is.

"Tapping into your intuition" has only in the last few years become something that's talked about in mainstream culture. Before that, the phrase was mostly reserved for psychics or spiritual leaders or self-help books or people with "special powers." And yes, your intuition is a special power. But it's not special because it's rare—it's special because it's powerful. You have the exact same magic inside of you that any sort of "intuitive" has, whether you identify as one or not. We all do. It's a skill anyone and everyone can hone.

The world will always be a noisy place, but in the corner of your mind, there's a quiet place you can always come back to, where that knowing echoes loud and proud.

Be sure you don't talk yourself out of entering, because there's a lot of gold that's in there waiting for you.

Chapter Thirteen

BECOMING OTHER-PEOPLE-PROOF

A few years ago, I opened up Instagram, and—*surprise!*—I'd been awarded my first Instagram Bully.

Earlier in the day, I'd posted a photo of me sitting in my home on a perfectly-ish made bed. I loved this photo so much: I was wearing my favorite grey jeans and my favorite "Phenomenal Woman" t-shirt, an ode to the Maya Angelou poem. My smile was wide and my eyes were sparkly, and I'd written a caption all about being comfortable in your skin and owning who you are and how that's pretty great and etc., etc., etc. I was proud of this little social media moment. I felt like the person I was online was exactly who I was offline. The alignment felt good.

Of course, that feeling was short-lived.

I turned off my phone and went about my day. When I opened Instagram back up, there he was. The Insta-bully had swooped into the comments section with the one joke I'd been trying to avoid since middle school:

Your last name is Hor Witch? Lol. You live up to it don't you.

This wasn't the first time I'd ever been harassed online (and most certainly not the first time I'd been harassed at all), but it was the first public-facing internet-written comment directly thrown at me with the purpose of knocking me down and dehumanizing me. I'd received disgusting DMs in the past on all platforms, and seen men tag each other in my posts, commenting with wagging tongues or some other crude emoji or outburst. In the early days of social media, I even had two so-called friends write mean messages making fun of me back and forth on their own Facebook walls (that was fun to find). This was just the first time it had happened out in the open, speaking directly *to* me, for everyone to see.

My heart dropped when I saw the comment show up in my notifications.

And almost immediately, I was embarrassed and ashamed that I even cared.

You can define your Through Line, shift your words, dive in and dig deep on all your truest intentions, but sometimes someone will come along with their own baggage and opinions and negative self-talk patterns, and you're back where you began, questioning the Self you've worked so hard to find and be.

Yes, it's an ever-evolving practice to redefine and reinterpret your internal language, but how do you make yourself Other-People-Proof?

Can you?

~

If trust and truth are the cornerstones of self-love and self-actualization, control and manipulation are the cornerstones of self-loathing and self-abandonment. When we try to control ourselves at all costs, we abandon the quest for what is true and replace it with the hunt for approval. There's no place for trust in this manipulative model, because trust requires that you let go of the reins and relinquish the need to micro-manage every single moment.

In my decade-plus of talking with women about shifting their self-talk, the question that has always inevitably come up is this one: "I'm good on my own, and then someone else comes in and criticizes me, or tells me I'm wrong, or interrupts and talks over me, and I leave the situation feeling beaten down. I go into control-mode and become so hard on myself. How do I proactively shift my negative self-talk when my negative self-talk is triggered by *others*?"

Forget about gendered terms like manterrupting or mansplaining. Because it can happen to anyone, from anyone. I prefer the gender-neutral term for what this is: talk-blocking.

Talk-Blocking

Talk-blocking is when you're talked over, talked down to, or talked into being someone you're not. The only "official" description I could find was on the pop-culture website UrbanDictionary.com, where almost every user-entered definition describes some form of hindering a preexisting conversation from continuing. (Yes, exactly like the term you're thinking about that uses a word that sounds very similar to "talk.")[1] I've just taken the liberty of extending the "talk-blocking" umbrella beyond general conversations with other people to cover when someone is intentionally trying to stop you from being YOU.

Talk-blocking doesn't always happen in person. Actually, now that so much of our lives are lived out loud on the internet, I'm guessing you might even experience more talk-blockers online than you do in person. Everyone's a bit bolder on the internet.

After I saw that comment and felt the pang of shame, I gave myself a beat. I closed my eyes and visualized physically removing myself from the situation and the sting. I breathed. I needed to get myself back to a neutral state of mind instead of a triggered one.

I opened my eyes and started laughing.

My first Insta-bully. I guess I've made it, I cheered to myself. *Happy day!*

I proceeded to check out this person's account then block and report them—not before, of course, snapping a screenshot and texting it to my friends. Not because I wanted any sort of validation from his sub-par creative jab, but because I knew sharing this troll's comment would be a little social experiment . . .

I'd come to expect a wide gamut of reactions to harassment, based on the wide gamut of experiences and perspectives each person brings to the conversation. So when it came to my particular Insta-bully, I wondered. How many people would laugh? How many would get angry? How many would sigh that this is sadly expected? How many would tell me not to care? And how many would be agog that this would happen to *me*, "aggressively optimistic" Katie Horwitch, who keeps her posts PG-13 at their raciest and proactive at their most charged?

I got all variations of the above reactions. But what blew me away was the prevalence of one, recurring comment:

This is obviously a very sad person, and we should send them love and light.

Here's why this affected me so much. I was strong and confident the day I received that Insta-bully's comment. I knew that in the grand scheme of internet bullying, it was a pretty tame jab, and I knew I'd be just fine. But some people aren't. Saying things like "Don't let it get to you, they're just sad in real life"—no matter how mild or harsh the talk-blocking—excuses a bully's behavior, writing it off as a supporting example of a greater thesis statement about that person's life. A life that doesn't involve you, but in this moment, actually does. Using excuses like "what a sad human being" normalizes the act of *pushing others down to make yourself feel better.* Even *more* than that—and this is what really gets me—it can make the harassed person feel *guilty* for not showing compassion to the person who hurt them.

I see it happen on a small scale in instances like the one with my wisecracking Insta-bully, and on a more serious scale in instances of homophobia, transphobia, racism, anti-Semitism, sexism, ableism, ageism, and more. And then we're told we should feel sorry for the people who speak hateful, harmful words. That these bullies—to summarize—*are hurt people who hurt people*, and that we should send them—to paraphrase—*love and light.*

There is a place for love and a place for light.

In this case: I call BS on love and light.

I call BS on good-vibes-only, and on the default of "putting yourself in the shoes" of someone or something that is objectively causing harm to someone or something else—whether it's the man catcalling you on the street or the online troll smearing your DMs with racism. And often repeatedly causing that harm, by the way, because if they're doing it to you, you can be sure they're doing it to someone or something else too. Yes, it's true that there are layers, and no one is just one thing. And also, it's true that people are predictable. No one is just one thing *once.*

I call BS on the normalization of the narrative that this is Just The Way Things Are, and that there's nothing we can do.

I call BS on it all.

Passive-Aggressive Talk-Blockers

Not every bully speaks the language of demeaning insults. Some prefer to take a more passive route—one that's consciously meant to cut you down or unconsciously does it anyway.

When others cut you down, you start to watch yourself more—like a commentator giving a play-by-play analysis of each thought, decision, and action you take. And self-censoring is a nice sturdy foundation for negative self-talk patterns to be built upon.

Just for kicks, here's a brief list of things I've been told within the last few years:

> "You're amazing."
>
> "You've got a ways to go."
>
> "You're a breath of fresh air."
>
> "You're a little boring."
>
> "You're so determined and don't miss a beat."
>
> "You need to get more serious."
>
> "Your words are exactly what I need."
>
> "Your words are too narrow and specific."
>
> "You work too hard."

"You don't work hard enough."

"Take care of yourself first."

"You're being selfish."

"Stay true to who you are."

"Play the game if you want to succeed."

All cut and dried. All conflicting. Lined up nicely in a list, it's easy to see how they contradict each other. It doesn't make the jabs any less painful or the praise any less precious. (When we give power to one, we give power to the other.)

But sometimes, talk-blocking comes at you in a different form, and you'll get talk-blocked in the name of your "best interests."

For kicks again, here are some phrases I've heard that have instantly made me feel utterly shitty inside:

"I'm just being honest."

"But you know, it's because I care."

"Don't let it go to your head."

"I'm just watching out for you."

"If I can't tell you, who can?"

Familiar to you too? Yeah. I'm not talking about genuine concern, or about healthy, respectful discourse. I'm talking about those times someone has made you feel guilty, ungrateful, less-than, or just plain childish under the guise of it being "for your own good." It's sneaky yet skillful manipulation.

We're all familiar with these relationship dynamics. So familiar, you can probably think of one or two instances off the top of your head. And I'm guessing they might have involved some of the people you also love the most.

How do you identify, then let go of, what no longer serves you—particularly other people's opinions—when you can't (or don't *want* to) always let go of the people themselves?

A Note on Criticism vs. Feedback

Something to note before we go on: the goal of becoming Other-People-Proof, as the chapter title says, isn't to cut yourself off from other people's opinions entirely. It's to have tools and tactics at the ready so that when you encounter them, you know how to respond proactively. A big part of this is being able to recognize the difference between a flame that brightens your surroundings, and a fire that's likely to spread and burn everything to the ground.

Opinions are important. They help make us who we are. And despite the catchy yet brash idea that we should "give zero fucks" about what other people think, maybe we should be focusing more on giving selective fucks instead of giving all of them or none at all.

Listening to other people's opinions isn't a bad thing to do. But there's a difference between mere opinion, and two of its sub-categories, criticism and feedback:

- **Opinion** is focused on what a person thinks or how a person feels about a thing. It can be favorable, or unfavorable, or somewhere in between. There may or may not be a goal attached, and it may or may not be criticism or feedback. ("I like/don't like your story about archaeology," for example, is an opinion.)

- **Criticism** is an opinion that's focused on the flaws or disapproval of a thing, and usually identifies what the person criticizing the thing doesn't prefer. It usually doesn't offer solutions or suggestions to uplift the thing it's criticizing and doesn't concern itself with helpfulness. And while this isn't always the case, the goal of criticism is often to tear someone/

something down for the criticism-giver's own benefit—whether that's to make them feel more powerful, in control, or just better than others. ("I thought your story about archaeology was really boring, so I stopped listening," for example, is criticism.)

- **Feedback** is different from pure opinion or criticism. Feedback is opinion that's focused on helping create what's desired and improving what's already there. It might be talking about the strengths or weaknesses, but no matter what, it's got the future vision in mind. ("I couldn't understand the technical terminology in your story about archaeology, and found myself tuning out—using more conversational phrases might help people who aren't archaeologists understand it better next time you tell it," for example, is feedback.)

Not everyone is an expert at feedback-giving, and it might read as criticism if they're (and you're!) not aware of the difference. Because sometimes feedback, like the example above, is tricky to give and hard to hear. Some people like to use the phrase *constructive criticism* when it comes to feedback, but I prefer keeping these two concepts separate to help distinguish the two in my head.

Criticism stays stalled. Feedback looks forward.

Where the people-proofing comes into play is when you realize that there's more criticism present than feedback, that the goal of the opinion is to make you less of who you are, and that you've started to care more about what someone else thinks of you than what *you* think of you. Store this distinction in the back of your mind somewhere for when you need it next. If it's not helping anyone move forward, it might not be as constructive as you're being made to believe it is, and it might be worth taking with a grain of salt (or not taken at all).

People-Proofing

I've always had these reoccurring, mostly passive-aggressive bully characters pop up in my life—from friends in the schoolyard who'd ditch me for the cooler girls, to the acquaintances who'd ask me when I was going to get a "real job"—which helped me write a self-talk story that others viewed me as a runner-up, second-best type of girl. I figured I was probably, usually, doing something wrong. Or just not doing it as right as someone else was.

The thing is, I *knew in my heart* I was a leader. Given the opportunity to, I was way more than just capable; I was actually able to, dare I say it, connect and inspire. Go figure!

But—a big "but"—the way I was being pushed around made me wary of *owning* my abilities. I would constantly wrestle with striving to fulfill my own ambition while also checking in with others to see what was "right." I would feel pulled in so many different directions without even knowing what was really going on. *Get back in line.*

When I was an actor, the narrative around the industry was focused on criticism and how "tough" you needed to be to survive it. And so my goal was to skirt the criticism by being as easy to like as possible. This, of course, reinforced my mindset and kept me stuck in a game of follow-the-leader.

It wasn't until I started teaching fitness classes and writing professionally that I learned that if I took everyone's opinions of me into account, I would never get better at my work and would never grow beyond where I was. I would constantly be reinventing myself based on who I thought other people wanted me to be or not be. And I couldn't just turn myself off either—because I wanted to make an impact, and impact isn't made by staying in that neutral zone of likability. If I wanted to become someone whose work deeply resonated with other people, I had to be okay with the fact that some people wouldn't like what I had to give. If I was good enough in the eyes of everyone, I'd be great in the eyes of no one. I had to show up as fully and authentically as I could, in the best way I knew how, and then keep moving forward. I had to learn how to separate the useful feedback from the criticism and mere opinions, and even more so from the talk-blocking criticism aimed at cutting me down and stalling my progress. I had to learn that if I'm going to ask, "What do they think of me?" I then need to follow up that question with: *But what do* I *think of me?*

I used to tell other people, "I'm not a quitter!" and wear it with a badge of pride. But now I know better. Quitting is great when you're a strategic quitter. And the one thing I've quit and never regretted is allowing myself to be sneakily pushed around.

~

If you're being sneakily (or not-so-sneakily) pushed around to the point where your Self is starting to suffer, it's time to take action. Here's how to handle a talk-blocker:

- **Breathe.**
  Do you—like me—hold your breath when you're upset, angry, or nervous?

  If that's you, or even if it isn't—start here. Always start here.

  When Jeremy and I are both working from home, sometimes he'll hear me let out a deep, heavy sigh. "What's wrong!?" He'll auto-panic. Oh, how the tables have turned.

  "Nothing's wrong," I assure him. I've just been holding my breath through writing something that feels particularly vulnerable (like this book!).

  Your breath might not be able to slow down time, but it can most certainly slow down how you move through it. Whether you've honed a formal "breathwork" practice or not, everyone should get into the habit of breathing deeply (myself included, especially when I'm writing). Scientifically, it keeps your blood pressure from skyrocketing and feeds your cells with much-needed oxygen so they can function at their best. Purely subjectively, it feels freaking good. And when you're being pushed around, you need something to calm you down and make you feel freaking good.

- **Mentally download and reprogram your Anchor Words from earlier in this book.**
  Remember, your Anchor Words are three believable words you can remember no matter what or where that will remind you of who You are. When you're thrown off and talk-blocked, it's hard to remember who that person is. I like to stick with three words because three feels well-rounded, and also, three feels easy to remember. You'll need them to be easy to remember, because they're not meant to just use here and there. They're ever-present roots. They're there to ground you—to *anchor* you—in who you are and what you stand for. You can't stay your Self if you're not anchored into who that Self is in the first place.

  My Anchor Words are *worthwhile, visionary,* and *fearless.* When I remind myself of these words when I'm talk-blocked, I'm able to pause, be proactive instead of reactive, and muster up fearlessness (more on fearlessness in the next chapter).

- **Bust your Power Move.**
  Okay. This one's my favorite. And of course, it has a story.

  There's a concept that social psychologist Amy Cuddy talks about called a Power Pose.[2] It's sort of like a physical mantra: you're supposed to stand in a pose that you mentally associate with being powerful. Cuddy says that our body language informs how we think and feel about ourselves. Naturally, then, striking a pose that you associate with power would make you feel powerful, right?

  Well, you'd think so—except that after her TED talk on power posing was released, there was harsh criticism of Cuddy and Power Posing's efficacy. She's since then published a paper passing all the science-research-y tests to support that Power Posing works—although now, it's called "postural feedback."[3]

  I find *so much* interesting about the story of Amy Cuddy and the Power Pose. The fact that she created such a buzz among women by giving them a strategy to feel powerful is telling. The fact that the second time around, the name was changed from something catchy to something more academic is telling. The fact that it was criticized as harshly as it was when, in fact, women were actually feeling more powerful because of Power Posing is very, very telling.

Our world is engineered to keep women small. We're supposed to shrink our bodies, voices, ideas, presence, and yes, our posture until we slowly blend in and fade away.

And a talk-blocker loves nothing more than a woman who shrinks down and gives up.

You don't need someone else to tell you what's beneficial and what's bullshit when it comes to staying your Self. Everybody is different. Power Posing doesn't hurt—it can only help. And so, thank you, Amy Cuddy. I am a big fan of the Power Pose, if only for the reason that if it works for you, it works.

I like to go one step further than the Power Pose, though. I call it busting your Power Move. (And no, I will not change the name to be less catchy, because I like catchy names.) A Power Move can be physical (let's say a shoulders-back, gaze-out stance), or it can be verbal (such as a go-to confrontational phrase that disarms your talk-blocker). The point is to pick a Power Move that makes you feel *expansive*. Not necessarily comfortable or happy, but expansive. Happiness and comfort are fleeting—expansive power *sticks*.

The following are some Power Move phrases I use if my talk-blocker is of the passive-aggressive kind. Feel free to snag any that make you feel expansive when you say them out loud:

"I understand where you're coming from. I need to do what's right for me."

"I appreciate your honesty. Here's how I view it . . ."

"Tell me more about that." (A talk-blocker never sees that one coming.)

"That way makes sense for you. And, this way actually makes sense for me."

"I'm not looking for feedback right now, but I'll let you know if I am in the future!"

"I promise you—I've got this."

And if your talk-blocker is more aggressive-aggressive than passive-aggressive? Move right on to the next strategy.

- **Say something.**
I'm not talking about silencing voices when you merely disagree about something, *especially* if it involves someone else's lived experience. Please don't. Don't do that. It's not good or helpful—to put it mildly.

I'm talking about the old public transportation PSA: "If you see something, say something." I'm talking about if someone's *coming at you or someone else* with toxic, malicious vitriol.

If you're online, take a screenshot for your records and then report it or contact a team member. Social media platforms in particular are preaching that they have zero tolerance for hate speech and harassment. But at the end of the day, they're businesses. They exist because of us. And their claims of working to become an inclusive, tolerant zone, as much as I would love to say they are all about their core values, are most likely *also* a direct result of a shift in user experience and a push for hate speech to be silenced.

It didn't happen online, and instead happened out in the real world? Tell a trusted family member or mentor. Report it to your HR department. Call a hotline that hires experts on the other end of the line who are well versed in the kind of situation you're experiencing. Write a letter to someone who values taking action and standing up for the right thing, and ask them to do exactly that. A friend of mine once had a phone harassment situation—when she came to me feeling frazzled and scared, we devised a game plan to not only protect her in the moment, but file harassment reports to protect both she and others in the future. I'm not an expert on this by any means, but there are so many people and organizations who are, and they're here to help.

This would be an incomplete chapter if I didn't mention the more extreme or scary cases that don't fall under the umbrella of talk-blocking or any quippy term. Because not every situation is solved with a phrase or pose—especially if it's behavior that's been normalized to some extent within a culture or environment. That's why it's so important to, if and when the situation allows it, confide in someone who feels safe and will be an ally to you.

Know that your words have power. It can be complicated, and it can be scary, and there's a difference between an Insta-bully making a rude joke online and a coworker sexually harassing you or a threat being made to your safety. There are so many ways to say something—the details of where or how you say it vary, but the "see = say" equation remains consistent. And, bonus points for you, saying something can help you feel stronger in a moment when someone else has intentionally tried to knock down that strength.

- **Immediately perform an easy yet impactful act of self-care.** No matter what happened, it's important to turn the love and attention back on yourself when you've been the subject of someone else's maliciousness. Performing an easy yet impactful act of self-care is like chugging down a strong dose of anti-meanness medication. After hearing hurtful words, or standing up for yourself if the situation allowed for it, do something that brings you back to your Self. Turn on your favorite music or podcast. Sing. Hug your friends. Compliment your neighbors.

Cook yourself a meal. Read. Text someone you love and tell them how much you love them.

My favorite science-supported self-care method after something tense takes place? MOVE. If you've ever watched a dog after taking a bath, you'll know this to be true: animals instinctively know to shake themselves after a stressful event to release the tension that built up. It doesn't have to be anything fancy. It could be as simple as a couple of jumping jacks, or as structured as a gym session, or as subtle as a walk around the block. It could even be a dance party in your living room. Whatever it is, make like an animal after a stressful situation—or like Taylor Swift herself—and "shake it off" by moving your body. While it won't make the situation go away, you'll likely feel at least 2 percent more like your Self—and 2 percent is better than nothing at all.

I wish I could tell you that talk-blockers fade away, but from what I've observed, they don't. Childhood bullies get replaced by teenage bullies, teenage bullies get replaced by adult bullies, and adult bullies get replaced by senior citizen bullies. Talk-blocking transcends age or life stage, and rarely looks like just one stereotype of a human.

I remember doing a lecture on confidence and talk-blocking a few years back. When we got to the Q+A portion, people were asking things like: What if my talk-blocker is my parent? My partner? What do I do if I get talk-blocked in public?

And then one incredible, insightful, bold woman raised her hand and widened her eyes—if she'd been a cartoon, a big lightbulb would have appeared over her head.

"I just realized: *I'm* the talk-blocker we're talking about!"

The room broke out in laughter that felt like a collective exhale after holding our breaths with our secrets.

We were all sometimes the talk-blockers we were talking about.

None of us are only one thing, good or bad, positive or negative.

None of us are only cheerleaders or only talk-blockers. We hold a dichotomy of it all inside us. Just like negativity is a bonding tactic we learn at a very young age and carry with us throughout our lives, talk-blocking is a habit that we can carry with us into old age if we don't give ourselves an intervention of unrelenting awareness and proactive action.

We all slip and do it every so often, but if you can catch talk-blocking and do something with it when you feel the effects on the receiving end, you'll be way less likely to do the same, not just to others, but to *yourself.* Self-censoring can be helpful, or it can be hurtful. And when it comes to your life, you should be *playing* in the game of your life, not wrapped up in keeping score.

Epilogue to Insta-Bully

There will *always* be people out there who have exactly opposing viewpoints of who you are, what you're doing, and how you're doing it. I get that it's hard to give selective fucks. I'm a recovering people-pleaser and detoxed perfectionist, with a personality that can get addicted to the quest to be the best. It's been a lifelong process to separate what's pure opinion, what's criticism, what's feedback, and what actually has value—then figuring out what I implement and how.

The process will look different for everyone. But the most important thing is that whatever you're doing, you keep your Through Line and integrity intact. That no matter what, you stay committed to trust, truth, and the kind of self-love that's lasting. That you aim to be proactive, not reactive, acknowledging the reality in front of you and choosing to move forward even when the steps are small and don't seem to make much of a difference. They do.

People will say what they will. They'll think you're the best thing since sliced bread, and they'll also think you're undeserving of what you've worked hard for. Neither opinion really matters. I'm all about the results and the proof. My way might not match up with your way, and that's fine by me. And when I can stand by my choices and say, "I did the best I could and stayed true to my Self," I can clearly see the results of my Me-ness and the proof of my power underneath all the other stuff.

Oh, and as for my last name? The one my Insta-bully was so keen to dissect?

I didn't change it when I got married. Katie Tucker is pretty adorbs and could have worked quite nicely. It could have also avoided that eye-roll-inducing Insta-bullying comment. But here's the thing: I've spent years making peace with my last name. I've spent *years* emotionally separating myself from the self-deprecating comments my family members have made about how much it sucks, and my female relatives telling me to make the change as soon as I can. I've learned to make loving jokes about my uncouth last name, and I've learned to find the power and strength in it. I refuse to abandon a part of myself I've learned to love and take pride in, even if the world tells me I shouldn't. It actually makes it more exciting to do so, to be honest.

One crisp and slightly ethereal autumn day last year, I ran into my friend Michael after I'd finished teaching a class. Not unusual because we work at the same place, and we run into each other semi-often—but this time, his face lit up differently when he saw me in the hallway. Like I was a walking epiphany.

"This might sound weird," he said, "but I was thinking about your last name the other day."

"Ha ha ha—tell me more!" I ribbed.

Oh no, I thought. *Here it goes. . . .*

"I broke it down, and I realized your last name is made up of two labels devised by the patriarchy. 'Whore' (or Hor) for a sexually empowered woman, and 'witch' for a socially and politically revolutionary feminist. Your last name is made up of two terms that were created to demean strong and powerful women who were viewed as threats. Your last name is basically the most badass, most powerful, and most on-brand last name you could have. Empowered and revolutionary and a threat to the status quo. That's you, Katie. That's who you're meant to be."

I'll take it.

Chapter Fourteen

FEELING FEAR LESS

I've had this one plant in my home for the last five years. A ZZ plant, named for its genus-species combo *Zamioculcas zamiifolia* (not the classic rock band ZZ Top, a lack of association I was bummed to find). Never in my life was I a "plant person"—so when I moved to New York and began to fill the apartment with greenery, I stuck to what I knew in Southern California. I bought some small succulents. They melted in the summer humidity. Literally melted into mushy goo on my windowsill. A few weeks later I walked into the plant store on Greenwich Avenue and tried to sound nonchalant when I asked which plant was easiest to take care of, when all I wanted to say was *Please tell me I got a lemon of a succulent arrangement and its transmission just blew and there's nothing I could have done.* The florist pointed me the way to some waxy green leaves. I picked out a medium-ish ceramic pot. We (ZZ and I) went home, and I placed her on a small table of her own, and she lived. I don't know whether it was my watering skills or the resilience of the ZZ, but she lived. Not only did she live, she *thrived.*

Until she didn't. A little over a year ago, I started to notice that she'd stopped growing. More than that, though: she was crowding her own space. On the outside, she looked like a fairly healthy plant. But having watched her sprout new stems and leaves year after year, I could tell something wasn't right underneath it all.

I showed my friend Kholi one day over a Zoom call. Kholi is one of those soul-friends who knows how to see the magic in most anything. She's also a gifted gardener—a Taurus who, true to her sign's nature, is passionate about nurturing the earth. I felt safe showing my planty pity party to her. I asked questions like a worried parent. "Does she need more water?" "Do I trim her stems?" "What about fertilizer?" "Will singing to her make her happy?"

Kholi laughed and looked at me with the eyes of someone who knows. "Katie. She's *root-bound.* Her roots have become so dense they're wrapping around each other. She just needs a bigger home to grow into."

And thus began my first repotting adventure. Maybe not an adventure to you, but an adventure to me. With no park close by, much less a backyard, I took all my supplies into the bathtub with me. And when I say supplies, I'm being generous. A bag of soil. Some rocks for drainage. A new pot for potting. A soup spoon for digging. Coaxing the ZZ out of her pot took what felt like forever (partially because soup spoon), and when I finally lifted her up and out, I could see why: her roots were tangled and mangled and HUGE. How long had they been like this?

My sweet little plant. I'd been so concerned with keeping her alive, and so thrilled that she seemed to be staying alive, that I'd failed to realize she'd long outgrown the container I'd put her in. She'd gotten everything she needed, and now had no place else to go.

This plant, this ZZ, was literally tying herself in knots just to keep on existing.

Fear

I don't think I've lived one day of my life not afraid of *something.* Call it high sensitivity, call it empathy on uppers, call it anxiety. Call it what you will, but whatever it is, I cannot remember one day of my multiple decades of existence that wasn't either slightly dappled with or completely drenched in fear.

The kind of fear I live with is less of a momentary jolt and more of a slow, underlying rumbling. My insides are like the tectonic plates I geeked out over as a kid growing up along the fault lines of California: always in motion, always shifting, always swirling in the vast openness of space. The rumbling is always there. Every so often, there's a quake. Just because there's no shaking doesn't mean the rumbling isn't going on underneath the surface.

I'm highly attuned to my rumbling, which often manifests in fear of disappointment. Not a fear of being disappoint*ed*, but a fear of being disappoint*ing*. There's always a residual fear of being in trouble that lingers under my surface. Fear that I'm doing something wrong. That I'm someone's investment, and they aren't seeing any return. And when I say always, I mean *always*.

The fear of being a disappointment is the underlying rumble. And then I'll do something or feel something, and this rush of adrenaline hits my system—the kind of rush you get before the roller-coaster drop. Maybe not the kind you get. But the kind I get. I don't do roller coasters. My body freezes and my limbs go numb. My face heats up. My breathing stops. It's not a fun thing to experience. I'm knocked out by the fear. It's happening. This is the thing. This is when I become a disappointment.

Over the years, my various fears of being various shades of disappointment have congregated and given me a nice little Fear Mission Statement: *I don't want to be left behind.*

The Fear Mission Statement

A Fear Mission Statement is exactly what it sounds like: a mission statement for your fear to lean on. If you had to sum up the main thing you're afraid of in your life, your Fear Mission Statement would be it.

When I dive into what's behind most of my biggest fears, I see that my Fear Mission Statement is usually about being left behind. Like if I don't hit all my marks just so, I'll be a disappointment. Or just uninteresting. That I'll be forgotten and because of that, I'll stay stuck in a story of the past. Being left out and left behind while everyone else moves on and moves forward, and there I am making castles in the sand while the tide just keeps coming up and washing them away over and over again. Me in my little Sisyphean limbo.

(Sisyphus: that guy in Greek mythology who was dealt an eternal punishment of rolling a big, heavy boulder up a hill, and every time he reached the top, it would fall back down. And so on and so forth forever and ever into eternity.)

Whether my Fear Mission Statement developed instantly in that preschool classroom as I stared up at my artwork and the line started moving without me or whether it took shape over time, I know that it's led me into a habit of looking backward, not forward. When I let my Fear Mission Statement take the wheel, there's a whole lot of *do*ing and not a lot of *be*ing going on: because my main motivator is "not wanting to be left behind," I do whatever I need to do for that to not happen, almost always ending up right back where I started, feeling the fear of being left behind and disappointing everyone. Like my ZZ plant twisting her roots over and under upon themselves, I begin to assume this is all the space I have. And so I stall my growth for the sake of fitting in.

~

We all have a Fear Mission Statement we walk through the world with. It's a core phrase and piece of information that's there to help us take the next step. The problem with living life by your Fear Mission Statement is that you end up fighting *against* something instead of *for* something, focusing on what you *don't* want instead of homing in on what you *do* want, and playing catch-up instead of moving forward. When you make decisions based on what you fear, what you loathe, or what you don't want to happen, where does that take you? A whole lot of nowhere. What happens when that thing is no longer an issue or no longer a problem or worry? You've got a whole lot of blank space. Without clarity in what you're fighting *for*, you'll just revert back to whatever it is you're used to doing, saying, or feeling. Not because it's what you want—but because it's what you've been rehearsing.

When I do almost any workshop or speaking gig, I do the Through Line exercise with the people attending. They're mostly women. Women, I've found, are very good at identifying what they *don't* want. I am never surprised. From decades' worth of ads that tell us to "fight acne" and "combat cellulite" to political commentators declaring a female candidate would be more likable if "she didn't sound so angry," we've got a lot of information coming at us every day in every way to make us believe how we look, what we say, what we do, and who we are just aren't good enough. ("Good enough," of course, always being vague and subjective.) We're trained to be convenient—which really means that we're trained to be in a constant state of longing and reaching and rolling our own boulders up the hill, always anticipating the fall.

As I pass out my worksheets (as a kid of the '80s/'90s, I *love* a worksheet) and the participants get to work, I always scan the room and search the faces. It's obvious that this "simple two-step exercise" I've given them isn't all that simple at all.

A brave soul gives me a look. I walk over.

"I've made the lists of everything I love and the goals of everything I do. But I'm having trouble coming up with a phrase that feels like my Through Line."

As I look at her page, I can see things like *travel to new countries, hikes with friends, attending concerts, visiting museums,* even *first dates* written down where she's been asked to make a list of everything she loves and enjoys doing.

And then, under the section where I ask her to list why she loves to do the things she does, I see a roll of phrases like *fear of missing out, life is too short,* and *don't want to regret* scribbled down among a few more general, more sparse phrases like *feels good, is fun,* and *is exciting.*

I don't start by pressing her to go deeper. I start by pressing her to see the other side of the hill.

Let's say you do this thing you say you're doing because you're afraid of missing out on something. What happens after you do it?

How do you feel, and why do you feel it?

What comes next?

Let's say you have all the time in the world. That life is *not* too short. That it's endless.

Would you still do this thing?

If so, why?

Let's say you do this thing you said you'd regret not doing. You did it, so there's no regret, right?

How do you feel on the other side, knowing regret isn't even an option?

Her Fear Mission Statement has been leading the way: *Life is short, and I don't want to feel regret.* But when I keep pressing and asking questions—and probably annoyingly but definitely necessarily suggesting that she define what *feels good, is fun,* and *is exciting* actually mean and feel like too—we finally find the common themes and goals of *adventure* and *connection.*

I see her eyes light up. She sighs. "This feels right."

Fighting *for* something always feels right.

It may not be easy—but it's right.

Redefining Fearless

The word "fearless" has become one of my Anchor Words, and one of the most grounding, actualizing words in my vocabulary.

If you've ever Googled "fear" or "fearless," you've probably come across some of the most self-help-y solutions that the self-help industry has to offer:

Overcome your fear!

Do what scares you!

Feel the fear, and do it anyway!

I personally have some beef with these definitions and directives as blanket-statement definitions. Feel the fear, and *do it anyway?*

What if that's what we told children as they saw a stranger approach them on the playground, promising a new puppy around the corner? What if that's what we told our friend when we were out with her late at night, and a man approached her begging to let him take her home?

Fear is a human emotion. It exists *for a reason.* Fear can show up in many forms—in jittery nervousness before entering onto a stage, in the dull rumble of Knowing and Not Knowing we spoke of earlier, and most notably here, in inexplicable intuitive hits and triggered suspicions working in tandem telling you to *run.*

The kind of fear that's a sign something is *not* right, and you should *not* do it anyway is the kind that, when you get very still, feels like peril; the kind that, when you ask yourself how you'll feel after it's through, you know will make you feel contracted, less You, maybe even more fearful. This kind of fear is useful and valid.

There's another kind of valid fear, though—it's the kind that, when you get very still, feels like possibility; the kind that, when you ask yourself how you'll feel after it's through, you know will make you feel more expansive and more You. There's a level of excitement attached to it—the fear is mostly about it being unknown. It's still fear; it's just telling you something different.

Because fear comes in so many different shapes and scenarios, I don't define *fearless* as the absence of fear or "doing it anyway."

Instead, I subscribe to this kind of fearlessness:

Fearless* is when the *fear* is *less* than the *faith.

To be fearless is when the fear you have of the situation is overpowered by the faith that you have in your Self. The reason this works in so many different kinds of fear-inducing situations is because it's not centered around doing (or not doing) what you fear. Instead, it puts the power back in your own hands and refocuses the lens on what you're fighting *for*, not *against.*

The Fear-To-Faith Ratio

Fear is one of the most universal human emotions. To lower your fear is exponentially tougher than those self-help-y Google searches will make it seem.

But to raise your faith? That's much easier.

"Fearless is when the fear is less than the faith" is a pretty phrase and a cute tweetable. I know. Trust me; I've tweeted it out many a time.

But it's also an equation.

One quick note: the words "fear" and "faith" can be loaded words for some people—especially the latter one, since it can make people think of religion. I'm not religious, but I'm also not here to redefine "faith" entirely if that kind of faith is a kind you hold dear. Rather, I'm hoping to put it in a different context and help you broaden that definition. So if you're someone who thinks of "faith" in the religious sense, let's add on. Can you take that same kind of strong belief you have in something else and extend it to your Self too?

Becoming fearless is about shifting the Fear-To-Faith Ratio from one side to the other. Less fear. More faith. If you're able to tip the scales toward the faith instead of the fear, you're able to trust who you are and what you have to offer and make the not-easy-but-right choice that works for you in any given fear-inducing situation.

Here's how to work the equation:

1. **On a piece of paper, write your fear at the top of the page.** It can be as broad as your Fear Mission Statement (e.g., *I don't want to be left behind*) or as specific as a current circumstance (like *interviewing for that new job*). Then draw a line down the center of the page, just below the statement, creating two columns.

2. **At the top of the left column, write FEAR.**

3. **At the top of the right column, write FAITH.**

4. **Start with the FEAR column.** Underneath this heading, write every single reason you can think of for why you are afraid of that scenario. Number each Fear Point so that you can clearly see how many things you're afraid of in this context by the time you're done.
5. **Then, move over to the FAITH column.** Underneath this word, write every single thing you can think of that you have faith in when it comes to *you* in that scenario. Nothing is too small, and nothing is too insignificant. Case in point: when I did this exercise for myself before a keynote I was giving at a conference, I wrote down the very uninspiring and not-sexy Faith Points of "I know how to hold a microphone" and "I know how to project my voice." Why? Because no matter what happened, I had faith that I'd be heard. And remember, this is about you, not someone or something else—write about the things that start and end with you, not the things that are out of your control.
6. **Now number each Faith Point just like you numbered each Fear Point.** Hopefully, you end up with more Faith Points than Fear Points. Not the case? Keep going. Oftentimes, we dial into the nitty-gritty of all the tiny reasons we're afraid but only focus on the more general reasons we have faith in ourselves. The good news about that is that if we have the ability to spiral in the fear direction, we're also capable of spiraling in the faith direction. It's just that most of us are out of practice.

The goal is to tip the scales toward the faith instead of the fear, with the former outnumbering the latter. It doesn't have to be huge either: even if you only end up with *one* more Faith Point than Fear Point, that's enough to make a difference. One point—just like one person, one voice, one decision—is enough to change everything.

Just like most of the exercises in this book, you can do this Fear-To-Faith exercise in the macro-moments or the micro-moments. You can do it before an event or milestone, or when you start to feel something like self-doubt affecting your ability to stay your Self out there in the world. You can do it whenever you need it, why-ever you need it. It's a tool in your self-talk toolkit that you can pull out at any time.

The Faith Mission Statement

Over the years, my various fears of being various shades of disappointment have given me the Fear Mission Statement of *I don't want to be left behind.*

But what happens once the scales are tipped? I begin to preach the gospel of my Faith Mission Statement instead—a mission statement for my Self-oriented faith to lean on.

A Fear Mission Statement is just information. If you have one, and you've worked through the equation proving that your fear is less than your faith, that information will now make finding your Faith Mission Statement a whole lot easier. And not because you're going to rework your Fear Mission Statement into a mantra that's automatically the exact opposite of whatever you were saying before, but because you now have a solid base of proof for what you have faith in. That faith can now overpower your fear, and morph it into something useful and proactive. You've now got proof, through listing out the things you have faith in when it comes to who you are, that you don't always have to *do*. *Be*ing is more than enough.

Instead of telling myself, *I don't want to be left behind*, I draw on my Faith Points and see that I could never be left behind. Not *really.* I have faith in my intuition, my tenacity, and my capacity to love. I have faith in *so* much more than what I fear. And I know for a fact that because I am *Be*ing first and *Do*ing second—and when I *do* Do, I Do proactively, not reactively—I'm on my own right track.

Instead of telling myself, *I don't want to be left behind*, I say . . .

My spot is saved.

The universe, I believe, is saving my spot. And I'll show up to claim it, because I know I'll take the steps necessary to get there.

I control what I can and let the rest go because I have a solid base of faith in my Self. I know my best-for-me place is inevitably mine for the taking, because I know I won't sit back and rely on someone else to define and deliver it to me. I know that I can do the next-right-thing, over and over, and those next-right-things add up.

~

Staying put is only as comforting as the story you've told about it. Twisting and contorting to fit a container that no longer fits you. But underneath it all, the real fear lies: the fear of what's on the other side of all those unknowns. And when given the choice between two fears—the fear of what could happen if you move forward or the fear of what could happen if you don't—most people will pick what feels the most familiar. Chalking it up to the idea of *standing your ground.* But can it really be called standing your ground if you're root-bound?

The constant rumbling of fear is what makes me check in with my faith so often. Sticking with something because it's what you know is only helpful when it's got a component of faith attached to it, giving you a reason to stay put beyond the reason of merely staying put. There is beauty in letting go of what once was, even if it once served you, in order to be who you are, where you are. And that can be scary. It's a risky choice to leave behind what you know for what's up ahead. Or is it risky either way you spin it?

Feeling my fears is a part of my magic, not a barrier to it. I am a work in progress and a practice in proactivity. I am not just what you see on the outside; I am the whole world underneath. I am a Self-in-Training, honing my ability to stand up for my ideas and stand up for all I love. My roots growing into the open space around them, and my personal reminder on constant repeat: *Fight for it, not against it.*

So I'm training myself to fight for it. To offer my whole Self to the world each day—not in expectation of changing anything or anyone, but in hopes of opening up doors and windows and sunroofs, and letting huge giant sunbeams spill through, and letting my seeds sprout, grow, and blossom so that hopefully someone else feels like shining too.

And if my heart gets broken, it will be because it mattered, and because my place mattered, and because I chose to move forward fearlessly and find my way. Not because I'm not good enough. Not because I've been left behind. And definitely not because I've disappointed the world and become silent.

We're no different than the flowers and the trees. We give so much, just by growing.

Part Five

YOU NEED A SELF
FIND YOUR SELF
BE YOUR SELF
STAY YOUR SELF
WANT YOUR SELF

Chapter Fifteen

ONE DAY

We sometimes think a future version of our Self will know better. Be stronger. Speak louder.

Or that, one day, we'll be successful enough to say what we truly mean instead of saying what we think we should say. One day, we'll be well established enough to live into our life instead of around it.

The stakes are too high right now, we convince ourselves. *The time isn't right yet.*

Like once we achieve a very specific level of success or self-development, it will be our turn.

When that happens, we say, we'll talk about the things that matter. Do the things that hold meaning. We'll embrace it all. *When, when, when.*

Yet each time we say "when," we put our Self on the sidelines.

Here's the thing. You cannot find your Self, and then bury parts of her away. You cannot be your Self, but only selectively and sparsely. You cannot tell parts of your Self to stay, and parts of your Self to run. To want your Self, you must show up fully, with all you've found and all you've been, and stand with your Self through both the sunshine and the storms. Only then will you know how You you truly are.

I Will Do Well

There's this vintage TV clip of Oprah Winfrey that's become somewhat of a North Star for me. It's 1986, and *The Oprah Winfrey Show* is about to go into national syndication. She's not yet the iconic force of nature we know her as today: she's a local morning talk show host out of Chicago, Illinois, about to get her big break, or not.

As you watch this clip—an interview on the show *60 Minutes* with reporter Mike Wallace, who seems skeptical of it all—you see and hear something magical happen. I've transcribed it for you:

> MIKE WALLACE: "So this show that is just getting underway nationally—"
>
> OPRAH WINFREY: "Mmm-hmm. It's going to do well."
>
> MW: "And if it doesn't?"
>
> OW: "If it doesn't, I'll STILL do well."
>
> She gives the slightest smile.
>
> OW: "I'll do well because I'm not defined by a show. I think we're defined by the way we treat ourselves, and the way we treat other people."
>
> And then, the kicker:
>
> OW: *"It would be wonderful to be acclaimed as this talk show host that's 'made it.' But if that doesn't happen? There are other important things in my life."*[1]

When I tell you I've watched this clip hundreds of times, I'm not exaggerating. And each time, I'm struck by how the words themselves are just as powerful as how they're said. The conviction Oprah holds for not only her work but her Self. Practicing trust and truth, on purpose, with purpose. Saying what she means and meaning what she says. Investing in the journey while also investing in the idea that the journey is not defined by what you get on the other side.

I think about this interview from 1986, more than half her lifetime ago, and think about how to some it might seem prophetic. *How did she know?!* Yes, the show—and Oprah herself—became a hit and a cultural phenomenon. But I don't view her words as prophetic as much as I find them pragmatic. This woman, all of thirty-two years old, carrying with her a deep knowledge that her Self is as fluid as it is fixed. A knowing that while she will grow and evolve, the way she spends the small moments—with integrity, trust, and truth, honoring a self-love that's unconditional—is what will ultimately tell her story. Not what she does but who she chooses to be while she does it.

What Oprah helps me know, in this little time capsule of a micro-moment filmed all those decades ago, is that the constant unfolding of the journey is the destination itself. The goal isn't the thing you go after; it's how you go after it and what you find along the way.

The Opt-In

Plot twist: I've started singing again. After over a decade. And I don't mean in the shower or on a car ride somewhere. I mean voice lessons. I mean in front of other people. I mean taking a mic in a karaoke bar and letting some Bonnie Raitt rip with my full voice and full body. I'm singing, and I'm not hesitating or hiding while I do it.

Where it'll take me, I have no clue. But what I do know is that I feel a part of me waking up from a long nap . . . or rather, walking in the front door after an extended vacation. No performance to prepare for, or panel of directors that suddenly appeared waiting to be impressed—just a pull for pure passion that ignited over the last few years, during what's seemed like global existential crisis after global existential crisis. In a way, I feel like it's some part of my Self remembering who she's meant to be. I have no clue where it will take me, if anywhere, and if wherever it takes me will "do well." But I know *I* will do well, because I'm the one who's the architect of that wellness.

Singing was so tied to my professional aspirations for so long that the pull to start up again felt a little confusing when it bubbled to the surface. *Do I want to pivot back into a former life path? Am I about to do yet another big career switch?* But no: I had no interest in pivoting from my life. Only expanding and enhancing it.

It took removing all the external factors vying for my attention—mostly, the expectations of what having this passion in my life would need to mean for me and my identity both professionally and personally—to uncover the love that was there all along. And since starting back up, I feel like a light's been turned on from the inside out. And when that light is on, my head and heart and body and voice won't let me pretend. When I sing, I'm me—all of me. And when I'm not or I'm tentative, my body tenses and my throat closes up. I love the honesty it requires from me and the hell-yes level of commitment. Singing, to me, is a practice in consciously opting into who I am. And not doing it out of obligation. Doing it out of *desire.*

Your passions and loves are there for a reason. Maybe they're there for big life-path-related reasons . . . or maybe they're simply there to light you back up when things get dark. Isn't that reason enough? For me, yes. What a relief it is to no longer feel like I need to "believe in myself" for the sake of anything else but believing in my Self.

I spent so much of my life seeing my Self, then looking to others to check if they saw what I was seeing. If they did, I'd work to live up to their expectations. If they didn't, I'd follow their lead and posture as whatever they told me was right. And that felt like a smart choice. *They're on the outside, after all. They can see me—literally, see me. All I have are mirrors for that kind of seeing, and so I should probably rely on someone else's eyes to tell me where I go.*

But seeing your Self has very little to do with what's on the outside. The moments when you see your Self are like bolts of lightning jolting you awake and alert. There's a sense of recognition that happens—a connection that seems prophetic but also pragmatic. It can happen in a conversation, on a stage, on a page, on a Classroom Art Corkboard.

It's a feeling that feels so sure, so objective, so much like you know and at the same time don't know how you know.

Seeing your Self can happen in any moment of recognition. Maybe it's something you've done, or maybe it's something someone else has brought into your life. Listening to a podcast conversation can help you see your Self just as much as if you were having that conversation in your own words. Your self-recognition doesn't have to be self-generated, and can come in the form of anything that sparks that *I know this and I know them* feeling in you. The role models I developed in childhood and teendom didn't feel like they matched other people's role models, which made me feel like I was doing the whole "role model" thing wrong: I felt like I was supposed to care about fame and success and talent, but I didn't care how famous or successful or talented someone was. I mean, that was nice, but that's not what elevated them to role model status for me. My parameters were different. Did I believe them? Did I trust them? And when I looked at them or heard them speak, could I see a part of myself in what they had to offer to the world? Did I feel a knowing, a premonition almost, like I was looking into the future at some part of myself? Did my confidence in them inspire confidence in me? Did I feel seen by them? By me?

The best role models, I now believe, are like the best books or pieces of art. They don't show us the path we must emulate—they unlock the door to the path we were meant to create. And what's even more important is that those moments of feeling like you really *see your Self* are what help you build a personalized, evergreen toolkit of You-ness that transcends age or life stage. Life will still get to you, because life will always get to you, but in a way, you become situation-proof. Not that you become immune to the world—rather, you open up fully to it. You get to be You wherever you go, regardless of where exactly that ends up being.

~

Yes, we sometimes think a future version of our Self will know better. Be stronger. Speak louder. But what we usually fail to realize is that our future Self is here right now. Now is the later you dreamed about yesterday. Later is the now you'll experience tomorrow. Holding back in hopes of "one day" only ensures one thing: that a bunch of One Days will inevitably pass you by.

What Oprah knew back in 1986, that I hope we all come to know, is that waiting for a thing, a person, or an event to spark something in you is putting your Self on hold indefinitely. One thing cannot be your everything, and one moment you look to in the future cannot be the thing you bank on making or breaking you. Because you *just don't know.* You don't know what's around the corner, and you don't know how that moment will land. But you can take a lesson from here and a story from there, and cultivate a unique set of mental and emotional habits that you can apply anywhere in your life, for your entire life. You can pay attention to the details now, as jumbled as they might seem, instead of hoping for the details that will arrive in the future all lined up neat and tidy. In the future, you might even look back and see they weren't all so jumbled at all—but you'll never know if you never notice.

It might not do well. But *you* will do well.

You can't micro-manage your future. But you *can* notice the micro-moments of your Now.

You can't control who or what wants you. But you *can* dive into your deepest ends and want your Self.

This is who I am.

This is what I have.

This is who I choose to stand for.

One Day is today.

One Day starts now.

Chapter Sixteen

(BE)COMING HOME

I was born into a sea of nostalgia: a family of trinket collectors and long-standing traditions and story upon story, told over and over like flowers in a sprawling garden. Continuity, my comfort. Sameness, my security blanket. My family and traditions and gardens of stories, they were all birthed in Los Angeles, where they almost all still reside amidst its familiar streets.

It's 2016. I'm on the brink of my thirties, and for the first time in my entire life, I'm preparing for a move away from LA. Jeremy has been offered a job opportunity in New York City, and being someone who always dreamed of moving to NYC after college but never did, I say yes even before he does. WANT is gaining momentum, and I can do my work from anywhere. The gym chain I work for in LA also has multiple locations in Manhattan, and I can transfer easily. Some of my closest friends live in NYC already. I ask myself if it's the right choice for me, and my insides feel expansive.

And so, we're moving.

But moving away from the place you've always been is complicated.

People ask *how I'm feeling* and *if I'm excited,* and all my answers to their questions seem to fall short. It's so much more complicated than that. The City of Angels is my safe haven in a way I struggle to express with accuracy. Sure, the space is familiar, but it's more of the energy within that space that keeps me feeling safe. LA feels less like a city and more like an extension of myself. The twisted freeways I learned to drive on, the blue and green signs, and the busy off-ramps puncturing the road ahead like ticks on a timeline. There's the off-ramp for my preschool. There's the sign that signals I'm on my way to art class. The spaces LA holds are like snow globes for my memories. The movie theater where I had my first kiss. The beach where my mom took me each summer. The boyfriends, the best friends, the strip mall parking lots where I first practiced parking, and the high rises I still look up at with awe. The adventures with my brother, my cousins, and all the people who have made me Me. Those boulevards have been like talismans to me my entire life, signifying good luck in a dandelion popping up from the concrete or a safety net around the corner in my Gammy's house. This city tells the story that made me . . . well, my Self.

The Dreams We Wake Up From

You know those dreams you have where you're in a place, but it seems slightly *off*? Maybe it's supposed to be your middle school homeroom, but your family is there, and the blackboard is green. Or you're walking down the grocery aisle, then suddenly it morphs into a pet shop where the Fuji apples used to be.

When you live in the city you grew up in for your entire existence, that's what life can feel like sometimes. The place morphs without warning. Shifts without reason. Enough remains for it to feel familiar and personal, but enough has changed for it to feel *just off-kilter* in a way you can't quite pinpoint. With the transience of time comes a city that naturally shifts to suit its people: You see it in the strip malls that change tenants over the years and the housing developments that pop up in the old fields, the playgrounds catering to a new generation before you stop and realize you've way outgrown the swing set. Two decades ago feels like two days ago. Or was it two years ago? Have the condominiums to your right always been there, or did they take the place of an old orange grove? Your heart caves at the For Lease signs and expands with the familiar neon lights. Each block holds a memory, each zip code a sense of déjà vu. The nostalgia eats you alive.

Or, at least, that's what it often felt like to me. Living in Los Angeles for three decades brought three decades' worth of both sameness and shifts. I would hear people talk of coming and going from the city in terms of *escape*—an escape to the sun, from the cold, to the mountains, from the traffic—and yet the city seemed to follow me wherever I'd go, however I'd grow. I could feel both held and detached at the same time. I saw crumbs of my story sprinkled down the boulevards lest I forget. The past felt more like last night's dream than it did a distant memory. My life was all where I left it, yet things just seemed . . . *different.*

Kind of like me.

We all have a place we call home, or at least a vision of a place we've once called home. We decorate our walls and furnish our houses. Some of us create a safe place to land. Some of us learn to make do with what we have.

But life happens, and time happens, and sometimes we must stray from the place we've called home for so very long.

What happens then? we wonder.

Will I wake from my dream and fade into the darkness too?

If I am not my surroundings, and I am not my talismans, who am I?

And as you venture down the road and turn the pages of your own story, you start to realize you were never merely a sum of your places and spaces. Your home was never around you, already built and ready for you to move in.

It was in you, being constructed and strengthened in each moment.

Home

Your Self is not the easy choice. But it's the right one. Because your Self is your home. The only home, in fact, that you'll carry with you everywhere no matter where you go.

That's not to say the places and spaces don't matter. Each setting in which you find, be, and stay your Self holds clues to the You you know you're meant to be, and each place unlocks doors that would have otherwise remained closed.

But the places and spaces you inhabit are only one part of the equation. *You* are the constant. No matter where you go or who you meet or who impacts your worldview, your sense of home begins and ends with you finding, being, and staying your Self. Only when we commit to owning our story and our Self-ness can we feel safe enough in the skin we're in to take a big exhale.

And that is what home feels like to me—a big, long *exhale.*

~

As the days grow closer to my cross-country move, I wonder why it is that I—someone so very highly sensitive, so very sentimental, and so intertwined with her community—am not freaking out or melting down in the midst of this major life transition. I wonder out loud one day to my mom too. And I hear myself say something I've never said out loud before: "I will always love LA. And, I'm also ready for what's next."

People come and go from LA and talk about it as an escape.

My move is not an escape.

My move is an unfolding.

A *becoming.*

It's so easy to blur your story with those of your community. It all seems the same, sometimes. And there's a certain beauty in that collective story and sense of togetherness. That is, until the lines become so blurred that there's no way of knowing where you stand within it all.

In the past, I've felt an obligation to turn the pages for others and modify my story to fit the narrative that surrounds me. *My legacy is easiest to understand when others get it*, I've thought. *It's where I derive my importance and my worth. In the ease of the known and being known. In the fact that I can live this dream of past moments without ever fully waking. I can know each step of the way. If someone else understands my steps, and can see where they came from, then they're the right steps to be taking.*

But now I know that to be untrue. My worth, my importance, and my legacy all stem from my Self. When I work to find my Self, and then I work to be my Self, and then I work to stay my Self, over and over and over again, I start to develop a sort of internal infrastructure that supports me on my highest days, in my lowest moments, and during all the times in between. I claim ownership of everything that makes me ME, and I live those things out loud daily. My high sensitivity. My Professional-Noticer abilities. My childlike spirit that feels like it's still seven. My intuitive soul that feels like it's already seventy-two.

I have not always been an easy person to be, but the more I have been her, the more convinced I've become that there's no other Me to be. Owning the full spectrum of my Self has led me not just to having a Self, but to wanting the Self I have.

I want to be home. And home is in me.

To Myself, I Belong—Still

The secret to navigating transitions, I've found, is to notice the micro-moments before you realize they were moments at all. To be acutely aware of your unfolding and becoming, so that you can always trust the next steps in your journey. Like them? Maybe not. Be excited for them? Sometimes. But trust them? Always.

Moving day is a day away. I look around at Los Angeles, wondering what the future holds for our relationship. Will she still feel like an extension of myself when I come back to visit? Will my memory of her be something I can't quite pinpoint when trying to describe her to others decades in the future? Will she become the stereotype I've heard about on the outside but rarely seen myself from my insider point of view?

Will I only remember the good?

The bad?

Will I forget that none of it was all good or all bad to begin with—just chapters in a story unfolding?

I sit in the soon-to-be-morning darkness on my soon-to-be-sold couch in my soon-to-be-old home and wonder if my present will soon be that "dream I woke up from." If I'll forget the details as they fade away into the daylight of my future life. If only I could save my city's charm or trap it in a snow globe. LA has not always been an easy place to be, but she has always been my place to be. A city that can take my breath away no matter how shitty the day has been. Comfort me with a familiar sight or sound. She is my friend. My partner. My teacher. My mentor. She is the family member I don't always agree with but love to the core. My love for her is the unconditional kind. If I can just keep my eyes closed long enough, I think, maybe I'll never lose that magic.

But maybe that's the true beauty of it all. The magic isn't in the places or spaces we inhabit; it's in us as we inhabit them. We get to decide where we belong. We get to decide where to bring our magic. We can choose whether our transitions mean hard stops and wake-ups, or if they just mean we're in the midst of our story, an ever-morphing dream we've never needed to wake up from.

I belong to me.

To me, I belong.

In my opinion, I belong.

I get to belong anywhere I choose because I belong to Me before anywhere else.

Addendum to Los Angeles: The Exhale

Seven years ago, I moved to New York City.

I moved with my then-boyfriend, future fiancé, now-husband. I moved with my then-purpose, future career, now-calling. I moved with no expectations, some trepidations, and an enormity of determinations.

Seven years ago, I fulfilled the choice to choose my Self and choose my story. I could have said *no*; I could have said *wait*. But it's easy to say no when you should say yes, just like it's easy to say yes when you should say no.

Seven years ago, my heart started beating a little faster, and my mind started to go a little slower. The pace around me started to move quicker, but the pace inside me started to calm. Seven years have brought so much to the forefront, sunk so much into the background noise. The things I thought mattered some, matter less. The things I thought mattered most, matter way more than I realized.

I can *feel* the shift that seven years has brought. I know now that I had wrung all the lessons, all the love, all the heartache, and all the heart-aid out of my West Coast surroundings, and in order to grow, I needed to shift my perspective. Through a turn of a kaleidoscope or a cross-country move, it's amazing how the same-old can become completely new all over again. Through a different lens or a different time zone, it's amazing how many things become brighter than you knew them to be. Or dimmer. Or maybe both at once.

But I also know that you don't need to change your physical surroundings to see a shift in your life. The shift comes from becoming the You you know you're meant to be—from coming home to your Self. And while a big thing like a move can certainly help facilitate that, it's usually the smallest things that make the biggest differences. The conversation you overhear. The book you pick up. The question you ask. The nod you give. The seconds of silence that hold an eternity of meaning. All these small moments add up. Your interpretation and choices write the chapters of your story. The plot can take a twist at any moment.

In my plans and dreams, I always lived in New York City. A thriving Broadway career, an apartment in I Don't Even Know Where. In my dreams, I didn't know how anything fit together. I just knew whatever it was that made me a "success" led the way.

In my reality, I am here. I don't visit Broadway stages nearly as often as I'd like and certainly haven't acted on one, but I've found the stages that suit me best. I've lived in four different apartments now in opposite parts of the city. My lows are super low. My highs feel like I'm flying. And what I relish most is that glorious in-between where I feel the *exhale* and *becoming* happening.

I've learned how to be malleable but true to my heart.

I've learned how to bend but not break.

And most of all, I've learned that challenge begets change, but also begets truth. In my life thus far, I've probed for truth and learned how to see it as my ally. Even the truths I would rather not see. Even the truths that hurt. I ask more proactive questions instead of reactively fighting against the answers that pain me. I have fought for a life that rings true each day, and in seven years, I now see it before me. It's not something I take lightly or take for granted. Only when I trust my truth can I be who I am. Only when my fear of the world is less than my faith in my Self can I move forward fearlessly.

What's even more poignant to me is the fact that as of a year ago, I am now a homeowner. A reflection of where I am in my Self journey as well.

And so here I am, seven years after packing the boxes and shipping the bins—seven years after that feeling of readiness but also of complete surrender. I have kept many traditions and also created new ones. I have let go of what no longer serves me, and I have embraced what maybe always will. It hasn't been easy, and it hasn't always been fun, but it has been soul-stirring and soul-lifting and brought me in touch with a deeper layer of my Self that I didn't even know was there. And anyway, I don't want easy. I want right.

~

To grow, we must stay aware. And to stay aware, we must stay awake. And to stay awake, we must challenge ourselves to displace our gaze and notice what arises. And then do it again. And again. We must sponge up the world, and instead of letting it define who we are, we must metamorphosize and reinterpret it. We must not shy away from the darkness and not cling to the light. If we always ride the same waves, we'll never truly see the spectrum.

Once you learn the thing, once you master the now, once you have become home, where do you go from there?

Seven years later, I'm living the answer:

You exhale fully. And shift the kaleidoscope.

Chapter Seventeen

THE DECLARATION

Not good enough.

Not smart enough.

Not talented enough.

Not attractive enough.

Too sensitive.

Too awkward.

Too **much**.

Too much of **everything**.

To be kind, to be humble, to be gracious, to be boisterous, but not too much. To be soft, to be resilient, to be a leader, but not too much. To be heard, but not absorbed; to be astounding, but blend in.

This is the dichotomy of being human.

Just human.

And should you dare to be daring in the midst of your humanity —oh, jeez! That is a task in and of itself, a dance more precise and more sweat-inducing than walking through eggshells:

You must be bold.

You must be brave.

You must be a mind-reader and truth-teller . . .

. . . but always know when and where your place is to read such minds and tell such truths. One misstep and the craaaaaaaaack of everything delicate below you rings loud in your ear.

The system you've been born into is rigged; you're not imagining it. It's the system that favors sameness, stoicism, subordination, and fake superiority. It's the system that's made you believe false truths that nothing you do will ever be enough. Success, you must learn, is relative. And success, you must say, is nothing but smoke and mirrors. For success, you must think, is something you're supposed to want and not want all at the same time.

But success, you must learn, is both the pinnacle of acceptance and the beginnings of lifelong critique:

> You're not kind enough.
>
> Humble enough.
>
> Gracious enough.
>
> Or you're . . .
>
> Boisterous, but way too much.
>
> No softness.
>
> Too pushy.
>
> Too flashy.
>
> Too forceful.
>
> *Get back in line.*

Because when you dare to be You, you're your Self lived out loud. And everyone will have something to say.

I believe in you. I believe in your grandness and your solitude, your quietness and your noise. I believe in the way you walk through the world, step by forceful step; the way you trip sometimes but always keep going. There are pebbles lodged in the soles of your shoes and dirt encrusted on the laces, relics from the places you've been, and the things you have seen. Resist the urge to scrape them off. They belong there. They complete you. Shoes were never meant to stay crisp and clean.

Your sensitivity is your greatest strength, and your gut is your navigation system that never fails. Your eyes, wide open, are direct portholes from your heart peering into the world. Because of this, you will see things others don't and feel things others won't. Your inner sense of knowing will be on high alert. There is a very specific type of hurt that comes with knowing, and most people push it away.

I sometimes wonder if that's why there's so much lingering hurt in the world. Most people don't let life rip them open, and the hurt has no way out.

But you are not most people.

Let life rip you open. Tell it, "Come and get me! Take your best shot!"

Because, what if not? What if it passes you by and leaves you exactly as you were, and you walk away with a numb apathy and a forgotten moment? Is that how to live a life?

You might be wary to love hard, because loving hard could mean hurting hard. Do it anyway. Let yourself be moved and softened and changed for the better. Because what's even more scary than a broken heart is one that could never be broken at all.

Surround yourself with people who matter. Do things that could very well leave you tear-stained. Sit with life's music. Lean into each note. Let it pour out your doors and windows and sunroofs, flooding your senses and driving your dance. Life will break your heart if you let it, and believe me, you should let it.

The difference between self-sabotage and self-love? Trusting you've got the power to turn your heartbreak into hope. The world depends on your wide-open heart—because after the breaking comes the making. We sculpt and we score and we fuse up our edges. In pieces, we finally become whole.

You have the answers you're looking for, deep down. Whether they've made their way to the surface yet, I can't tell for sure. You're not supposed to wake up one day and know it all. Anyone who says they do or assumes the opposite is a liar. Surprise, surprise, the hallmark of being human is knowing that you will never know it all.

You are grappling with the Knowing and the Not Knowing. To that, I say, you're doing it right. The world wants you to believe it expects you to know, but all that is is a desperate plea to fill in the blanks. Blanks that aren't yours to fill; blanks that aren't meant to be filled in the first place. Without blank spaces, all our moments would meld together into an incoherent mish-mosh. The blank spaces allow us to inhale deeply and exhale fully and soak in the story of it all.

Nothing you do will ever be enough?

Everything you do is already enough, by the very nature that you're doing it.

Nothing you are will ever be enough?

Everything you are is already enough, because you already *are* You.

The world is reactive, so you must be proactive.

The world takes cues, so you must make your own.

I don't want you to look down at the quicksand and moan through tears, "How Dare They?"

I want you to stand in the center of the storm and proudly declare, "How Dare I!"

Epilogue

MOVING FORWARD FEARLESSLY

My maternal grandmother Dione was part of the river that flowed before me, molding me like clay. My paternal grandmother, Myra, my Nana, is still doing it.

Myra, I suspect, is the kind of woman she would have been in any lifetime. Herself in an evergreen way—except for one. The way I notice that she is, and has been, most affected by the world around her has nothing and everything to do with the time she was born and the body she was born in.

My Nana has been a lifelong activist in politics and social justice. She was initially inspired by the Civil Rights movement, the Women's Liberation movement, and the words of JFK—which all compelled her to take action that continued well into her eighties. I once asked if there was someone else in her family who modeled this for her—the clay that came before her in this aspect of her life. Nope, she told me. In stark contrast, actually: not only were her family members not involved in activism, but her friends weren't either. She was told her pursuits were "cute," or that she must be interested because of the attractive men she worked alongside.

But she drew upon pragmatic, proactive positivity, had faith in herself, and kept on going. The talk-blocking of her peers didn't stop her. She felt that she was young, had lots of energy, and was driven to do something about the things that broke her heart. If *she* didn't, she thought, how could she expect anyone else to?

I once asked her what she suspected made some people take action and some people withdraw. What drew some people toward the kind of work she'd done throughout her life, and what made some people feel that even if things are bad, unjust, and cruel, there's "nothing they can do about it"?

She paused to contemplate my question.

"You know, Katie . . . I believe it's about where your focus is to begin with."

Treat Your Self

If you've been telling yourself a story that your actions don't make a difference, or that you go where you're told, or that you should gladly give up your voice to blend in with the crowd, or you've got to smooth your edges to be Just So, it makes sense that you would tell yourself there's nothing you can do about the things that break your heart. It makes sense that you might even block your Self off from pain altogether. Because it's all about where your focus is to begin with. The story you've been telling all along.

You can't do something to change the world around you if you haven't explored the ways in which you fit into it, and the ways it's affecting you minute by minute by micro-moment. Just like you can't shift your self-talk (and make shifts that last) by starting with the talk part, you can't "treat others the way you'd want to be treated" (and do it not only consistently but when it's hardest to do so) if you're not treating your Self that way in the first place.

Yes, of course it's possible to be kind to others without offering that same kindness toward your Self—or to degrade others while pumping your Self up. But kindness is only half the story. The bare minimum. In order to shift your self-talk, champion others, and not only find, be, and stay but truly *want* the Self you are, the intention and impact have to work in multiple directions simultaneously. There has to be respect and courage in the mix too. Respect for others and your Self, and courage to stand true in who you are as you stand up for the community around you. Without these things, our kindness runs the risk of becoming a one-way street full of potholes—moving in a single direction over and over, so much that the road has eroded and cracks begin to develop. The focus must be two-fold: we've got to not only treat others the way we'd want to be treated—which is ultimately as the unique individuals we are, with needs and preferences and desires all our own—but also *treat ourselves* the way we aim to *treat others*. In other words, we must treat others the way they'd want to be treated—and treat ourselves with that same level of care and consideration. And not just one part of ourselves, but the whole spectrum of our experience. Because just like anyone else, we're nuanced and we're varied, and that's what makes us more than a body but a *soul*.

When we put this into practice, we're ultimately training ourselves to speak in a way that's proactive and kind both internally and externally—which, of course, is how we become fluent in the language we were looking to learn all along.

Radical Shift

We are not just our highs or lows. We are the whole spectrum in between. And not just me or you, but all of us. It's not just our own light or darkness that matters, but the way our beams bounce off one another.

When we feel shaky in who we are, we typically do one of three things: we search inside, we submit to others, or we steal away power. But we live in a society that tries to steer us far from who we are, and then rarely models what it looks like to search inside to get back on course. So some of us shrink down until our bodies are weak, and our voices barely exist, craving validation from others and calling it "living." And some of us lash out, using hateful words and violence to assert the power we wish we had. This can have deep, devastating repercussions.

To change this and build a New Normal (that's *not* just For-Now), we need radical policy shifts. We need systems protecting the safety of those who have not only historically been marginalized and dehumanized but are very much currently under daily threat simply for existing. We need to examine what's working, what's not, and what needs to be completely reimagined because it's never existed before. We need to make space for everyone to be able to flourish and re-envision what's possible.

And.

We need radical personal shifts.

We need to use our voice so that when the chance comes to make a change, we speak up and out instead of shying away. We need to trust our truth so that when new opportunities are open to us, we jump in instead of shrinking with doubt. We need to sit with our darkness as it comes and goes so that we don't try to offload it onto someone else via hateful words or violent acts. We need to celebrate our lightness as it comes and goes so that we don't cling to it and become fearful when it goes away. We need to find, be, stay, and want our Self not just for us but for our families, communities, children, and all the people who are around us and will come after us.

And why do we need to do this, while simultaneously addressing such a dire need of a New Normal that's more than just For-Now? Because we cannot get complacent or take our Selves for granted, not for one second. Once systems and structures are in place, we need to have people who believe in themselves enough to move forward fearlessly with and into them. Or else, just like negative self-talk, whatever was once normal, however harmful, will come back around—simply because it was the practiced habit. The fluent language. The habit that never really changed in the first place, because we thought if we replaced one word with another, what's underneath would just fade away on its own. It's about where your focus is to begin with. The fight for the world we want to live in begins with shifting our self-told story.

Your Story, Unfolding

I have learned that what I have to say matters.

What I have to give matters.

And what you have to say and give does too.

Some people are told to get back in line and end up staying there, following rules made by others and speaking a language they never intended to become fluent in. The world will constantly try to steal your voice and reclaim it as its own, but your impact is yours to make. Your legacy isn't in the things you birth or the structures you build, but the knowledge you pass on and the impact you make. And on the toughest days, leaning into that profound knowing can be what brings you back to center and reminds you of who you are.

Your Self is a story unfolding, an ever-evolving journey, and one the world needs you to continue. There is no small shift, really, because every single micro-moment adds up to make a big difference.

Be intentional with those small shifts. Because they're not small at all. Those small shifts are about something *so much bigger* than the here and now. Those small shifts are the key to creating the big change you wish to see, and the key to being the You you know you're meant to be.

Notice each micro-moment.

Each wave.

Smudge.

Shiny piece of glitter and scrap of tissue paper.

Together, they make an ocean.

Notice the continuous unfolding of your story.

And keep writing its pages.

The End

ACKNOWLEDGMENTS

This book has been years in the making—and these acknowledgments, just as many. This book might have my name on the cover, but it is truly a collective effort. My deepest gratitude goes out to so many incredible souls who've not only helped bring *Want Your Self* to life, but me as well.

To Nicole T., a hope and wish come to life, for the way you've championed this book and me, for your vision, for your honesty, and for the way your fierce commitment to what-might-not-be-easy-but-is-certainly-right inspires me to be bolder in pursuit of what I know to be true. Your unique combination of empathy and badassery is a gift.

To Diana, the editor of my dreams: the universe was high-fiving itself when it brought us together. For your enthusiasm, your empathy, your expertise, your transparency, your joy, your attention to detail, your belief in this work, and your hand to hold, I thank you profusely. You made this book so much better. You make everything better, really.

To Alan, Rebecca, Penny, Mike, Tami, and the entire Sounds True team, for making this book a reality in a way that still astounds me. A first-time author could only dream of feeling so aligned and taken care of. Thank-you beyond thank-you for the way you've brought these words into the world.

To Lily, for the generous connection that started it all, and the belief in me when I needed it deeply. I'm so glad you called when you thought I was maybe a spam text.

To Annick and Kris, the first eyes, minds, and hearts to read this book. Your insight, expertise, cheerleading, and passion are embedded in these pages forever.

To Richelle, for being an actual superhero. You swooped into my life right on time.

To Phoebe, for being the first to hold my hand. And even though you downplay it, I will never forget it. Your friendship is a treasure.

To Jacki, who helped clarify the vision all those years ago. All goals are possible when you are a part of their formation.

To Jessica M., for the nudge into the unknown, over and over again. I am stronger and braver because of you.

To Talia, for being in the moment, every moment. You are the kind of cheerleader everyone should be so lucky to have in their corner. You make it easy to believe that all things are possible.

To the people who so generously read *Want Your Self* in advance and offered up such glowing endorsements, there are not enough words to express my gratitude. Every single "I'd love to read it" felt like a vote of confidence and infused this book with love as it made its way out into the world.

To every person who has contributed to, shared, and supported WANT since its initial inception in 2007. From *The WANTcast* guests and blog interviewees, to the event hosts and collaborators, to the editors, strategists, and web developers, to the people who've attended talks and workshops over the years, to the readers and listeners and members of The WANT Community—your belief in and dedication to this mission has created a ripple effect. Thank you for diving into this work alongside me. You have made a difference in so many lives, including mine.

To the entire team at The Maker: without your hospitality, this book might have looked very different (or at the very least, not been turned in on time!). Thank you for making sure I felt at home as I finished these pages.

To the friendships I hold so dear from so many stages of my life, my cup runneth over. Thank you for your deep well of love and support. How blessed I am that there are too many people to name—I've got so much anxiety thinking I might miss someone, so I will keep this general for now. From CA to NY to in-between and worldwide, I never imagined I could/would have such robust, authentic community in my life. You will all be getting personalized love notes and thank-yous.

To my fellow author friends, especially those who were working on their own books at the same time I was working on *Want Your Self,* this process felt so much less solitary because I knew we were all in it together. It is an honor to support your work, and you all.

To Kholi and Holley, my forever soul/gut-checks and reminders that home is in me. For seeing me so fully, sharing so deeply, and blessing the world with exactly who you are, over and over again. Satiating or bust.

To Jen S., for your deep listening and even deeper reflections. Thank you for leaning in, thank you for being the bubbles in the champagne, thank you for the adventure.

To the friends who have literally and figuratively held my hand through the many years of launching WANT and writing this book, for listening deeply, offering feedback, asking questions, wearing merch (remember the merch?!), giving pep talks, clinking glasses, and making me feel so seen—including, in no particular order, Lynn C., Sasha W., Nicole S., Jen T., Sarah G., Carly S., Ashlee P., LBD, Sarra M., Loi J., Emily S., Diane M., Jess T., Paul P., Pat B., Roy G., Michael K., Marquis J., John T., Chris H., Ben M., Jeremy R., Gerren L., thank you for believing in this, and me, for over a decade.

To Rachel, for always knowing how to ask the right questions, and teaching me how to find my own answers.

To Myrona, for sticking with me and seeing the magic in me when I couldn't. You changed my life in the very literal sense. And to the Claire Trevor School of the Arts, for giving me a sandbox to explore myself as an artist and a stage to feel safe upon (even and especially in my darkest moments).

To all of my teachers from K–12, whose influence is all over these pages. Bill Garrett, Josh Barroll, Kristi Reed, Elaine Tunick, and Delia Grigorian, who taught me some of my most valuable and unforgettable lessons way beyond their yearly curriculum. And to everyone at Castlemont, a place I held dear, who witnessed and supported my growing up and becoming.

To Shelley and The Female Quotient team, for giving me my first WANT-related opportunity by generously and enthusiastically inviting me into your world, and trailblazing on behalf of so many around the globe. And to Robyn, for being a forever-champion of your people, and of me.

To Angela, the kind of person everyone wishes to have in their corner, I'll never get over my gratitude that you're in mine. For your commitment to showing up fully as who you are, for your legendary ability to give the most stellar and robust feedback, for making this process more meaningful, for being my person. To quote one of the lines you underlined, you give so much just by growing. WDBH.

To Caroline, for your constant encouragement, enthusiasm, and ability to dive in and dive deep on the turn of a dime. Your keen eye, spot-on insight, and huge heart made this book a bajillion-and-one times better. Thank you for consistently giving your all to the things you care deeply about and allowing me to tag along.

To Kara, for being down for the last-minute feedback and support that I now know I couldn't have published this without. Your creativity helps me be more creative, and your courage helps me be more bold. Thank you for setting the example, over and over again.

To the authors, artists, and activists that have served as a constant North Star for me, in particular: Glennon Doyle, Karen Walrond, Sutton Foster, Jess Weiner, Gloria Steinem, Brené Brown, Natalia Mehlman Petrzela, Oprah Winfrey, Cheryl Strayed, Marie Forleo, Christen Brandt, Tammy Tibbets, Jen Pastiloff, and Melissa "Lizzo" Jefferson. Thank you for helping me work and live with an unwavering commitment to integrity—I'm in deep gratitude for the way you lead the way.

To Keith for believing in me from our first meeting. I'll never forget it. And to my Equinox colleagues and class members on both coasts for giving me a sense of community I hold so dear. A special shout-out to my Soho Saturday crew, who welcomed me into NYC with open arms and have seen me through every stage of writing this book.

To Team Aaptiv, for embracing the way fitness is about so much more than fitness. So many of you have found me and WANT because of Aaptiv. It's an honor to cheer you on in so many aspects of your life.

To the Barnetts, the Kimballs, the Kristensens, the Leffs, the Schlazers. The love you've showered me with through every stage of my life is profound and a part of who I am. And to my mom's childhood friends whom I've been fortunate enough to build relationships with, especially Lisa Gatsby, Judy, and Kim. I love that my story gets to be intertwined with yours.

To Yvette, who I'm always thinking of, for being a vital part of the fabric of who I am.

To my extended family: not everyone is as lucky as I am to have such deep and sprawling roots. The fact that I get to thank second cousins, great aunts and uncles, and beyond here is a tremendous blessing. To the Horwitch, Scult, Feder, and Myers sides of my family, thank you for your constant support and love that is felt no matter how much time passes.

To my aunts and uncles on both sides of my family, who make me feel so loved and have seen me through so many versions of the Katie in this book. I am so proud to be your niece.

To Lisa Cassel, you are a constant ear and hand to hold. Thank you for seeing me.

To my cousins, for walking alongside me through thick and thin. Not everyone who has cousins even knows their cousins, let alone has a meaningful relationship with each one. We are all being shaped and sculpted like clay together. I wrote this for us.

To Becky Dahling, for the example of goodness and passion you set for us all. To Ashley, for your deep empathy and altruistic spirit. To Erin, for your grounded sincerity and genuine enthusiasm. To Jenny, the younger sister granted to me by the universe, for your fearlessness in navigating this life alongside me.

To the Tucker and DeReimer families, for embracing me from the get-go and extending so much love my way. To Victoria, for your belief in me and nurturing spirit. To Josh and Marlo for always being there with open arms, and Owen, Lockwood, and Westin for inspiring me with your curiosity and creativity (and for officially inducting me into auntie-dom).

To Ron, Papa Ronny, for your deep insight, brilliant talents, and advocacy for the arts not only in my life and your family's life, but in your community at large. Being the recipient of your admiration is an honor. Thank you for empowering me to dig deeper, feel stronger, and aim as high as I ever want to go. And, of course, thank you for being the first one to introduce me to all the good that can happen when you turn on a computer.

To Myra, my Nana, for being the ultimate cheerleader and shining example of what it means to stand true in who you are. For not only reading, listening, and watching everything I've ever put out there, but constantly letting me know you are in my corner always. Your ability to find meaning in life's micro-moments is astounding, and your passion for standing up for the kind of world you want to live in is something I'll carry with me my whole life.

To Dione, for inspiring so many of these words. Thank you for always insisting I "make sure I put it in my journal." I wish I could reach through time and give this to you.

To Burt and Bill, Papa and Poppy, who are not here physically, but always with me. Papa, you'd love all the ins and outs of the business of book creation. Poppy, you'd be endlessly fascinated by this journey and crack up at so many of the steps along the way. You'd also probably joke it needed more chapters about you, containing words you made up and stories that may or may not be true. I am sharing this with you in my heart. I know you'd love it.

To Kelsey, for your grounded presence, your whip-smart humor, your bravery to do hard things, your sense of Self that continues to shine as you stand strong in her, and most of all, for adding all these things and more to our family—and my life.

To Ford, for letting me in on how you see the world. The level of empathy you possess is more than many experience in their lifetime, let alone at the age of three. And to your sibling, who will be born by the time this book comes out, who I cannot wait to meet. Thank you both for inspiring me to be intentional with every word. I can't wait for you to read this one day knowing I wrote it with you in my head and heart.

To Alex, for, well, everything. You are my conscience, my speed-dial, my connection to who I am. Being your sister will forever be the role I'm most proud of. Thank you for keeping me true to myself, for being my forever champion, and making me feel like no matter what, I am never alone. We're in this together.

To Dad, for constantly being in my corner, and I mean constantly. Your eagerness to help, guide, support, and cheer has made a world of difference in my path both personally and professionally. Thank you for modeling how to live with integrity and go after what it is you want with both complete conviction and zero ego. You have the biggest heart and I hit the lottery that you just happen to be my dad.

To Mom, for being my rock, my heart, my first call, my double-checker, my confidante, my comic relief (even when we're the only ones who think we're funny). Thank you for showing up fully for yourself, for others, and especially for me. Thank you for being the leader of your own life, because it helps me be the leader of mine. And thank you for the last-minute power-read, the answers to my weird questions with no context, the celebratory FaceTimes, the venting sessions. Your story is my story, and I would have it no other way. I am me because you are you.

To Frankie, your dad told me you "can't read," and so I "don't need to include you in the acknowledgments," but he is wrong. Thank you for your endless love, your welcome levity, and for literally staying by my side as I finished this whole thing. I am so grateful you're my soul-pup.

To Jeremy, for bringing me home to my Self, for enhancing me in every way, for challenging me, for experiencing life fully alongside me and always working toward what makes us strongest as individuals and as a team. Your commitment to trying hard things, enjoying life, and feeling deep gratitude allows me to do the same. Your belief in me buoys me up, and your proactive support through the tough stuff makes it all seem manageable. Thank you for being all-in through every micro-moment and for loving the full spectrum of who I am. Look at this beautiful life we live. Can you freaking believe it?!

And to you, the person who is reading this book—for taking a chance on something new, for trusting me with your time and your heart, and for continuing this journey to find, be, stay, and want your Self long after you finish reading these pages. Thank you for taking who you are out into the world, moving forward fearlessly, and being the you You know you're meant to be. The world needs us all being exactly who we are. Together, we make an ocean.

APPENDIX OF EXERCISES

Positivity Proof Points (pg 75)

- I am___________ (a characteristic you're proud of, like: kind, hilarious, generous, a good friend, loving, true to my word, compassionate, analytical, perceptive, a great listener, driven, etc.)
- I have__________ (a quality that helps you through tough times, like: resilience, perspective, humor, stellar gut instincts, non-attachment, etc.)
- I know__________ (a belief that makes you feel expansive, like I am doing the best I can, I can find community anywhere, I'm not alone, I can face any challenge, my life will be an adventure, etc.)

Through Line (pg 84)

Step 1: Make a list of everything you love to do or experience.

Step 2: Find a common theme and goal within your answers.

Step 3: Formalize your Through Line Statement.

Try using this formula: I [common theme in everything you love] to [common goal in everything you do].

Truth Maintenance (Four Questions) (pg 97)

1. Is my self-talk really about what I say it is?
2. Do I really want the reality (and result) of making a change, or do I want whatever the process of trying to figure it out gets me?
3. Am I using negative talk to distract or *convince* myself that I'm doing something to activate change in my life?
4. What's my priority? Is this one of them?

Pre-Paving Your Self (pg 113)

1. How do I want to look?
2. How do I want to act?
3. How do I want to sound?
4. What are the one to three points I want people to hear?
5. How do I want people to feel after they've left me?
6. How do I want to feel after leaving a situation, completing a task, or finishing a day of life?
7. What three Anchor Words (that I will remember no matter what or where) can I use to ground me and remind me of the Me I'm meant to be?

Planned Freak-Out (PFO) (pg 153)

Part One:

1. Grab a notebook and open up a spread of two pages. At the top of one side, write THINGS I HATE. On the other side, make the heading THINGS I DISLIKE.
2. Set a timer for twenty minutes and list everything that's on your mind right now that's causing you Overwhelm.

Part Two:

1. Once you have your two lists, write another heading on a new page: SO WHAT THE FUCK AM I GONNA DO ABOUT IT?
2. Set the timer again, and write down as many specifics as possible, getting as granular as possible.

Parts Three and Four:

1. When you're ready, open your notebook to a new spread of pages. At the top of one side, write THINGS I LOVE. On the other side, write the heading THINGS I LIKE.
2. Set your timer for twenty minutes and go. Write down all the things and feelings you love and like.
3. Once you've got your two lists, write in bold letters: SO WHAT THE FUCK AM I GONNA DO ABOUT IT?

Fear-Less Equation (Fear-To-Faith Ratio) (pg 212)

1. On a piece of paper, write your fear at the top of the page. Draw a line down the center of the page, just below the statement, creating two columns.
2. At the top of the left column, write FEAR.
3. At the top of the right column, write FAITH.
4. In the FEAR column, write every single reason you can think of for why you are afraid of that scenario. Number each Fear Point so that you can clearly see how many things you're afraid of in this context by the time you're done.
5. In the FAITH column, write every single thing you can think of that you have faith in when it comes to *you* in that scenario. Write about the things that start and end with you, not the things that are out of your control.
6. Number each Faith Point just like you numbered each Fear Point. Keep repeating Step Five until you have tipped the scales toward the faith instead of the fear, with the former outnumbering the latter.

NOTES

Prologue: The Navigation

1. Julie Tseng and Jordan Poppenk, "Brain meta-state transitions demarcate thoughts across task contexts exposing the mental noise of trait neuroticism," *Nature Communications* 11, no. 3480 (2020), doi.org/10.1038/s41467-020-17255-9.

2. John Simpson, "Finding Brand Success In The Digital World," *Forbes*, August 25, 2017, forbes.com/sites/forbesagencycouncil/2017/08/25/finding-brand-success-in-the-digital-world/?sh=.

3. Joanne V. Wood, W. Q. Elaine Perunovic, and John W. Lee, "Positive Self-Statements: Power for Some, Peril for Others," *Psychological Science* 20, no. 7 (July 2009): 860–6, doi.org/10.1111/j.1467-9280.2009.02370.x.

Chapter One: The Misinterpretation

1. Elaine Aron, *The Highly Sensitive Person* (New York: Broadway Books, 1997).

2. Brené Brown, *Daring Greatly* (New York: Avery, 2015), 58.

Chapter Two: Frozen in Time

1. Judy Wilkins-Smith, "Relationship DNA" workshop, accessed December 29, 2022, judywilkins-smith.com/product/relationship-dna-2023/.

2. Jennifer K. Bosson et al., "Interpersonal chemistry through negativity: Bonding by sharing negative attitudes about others," *Personal Relationships* 13, no. 2 (June 2006): 135–50, labs.la .utexas.edu/swann/files/2016/03/bosson_etal06_chemistry.pdf.

3. Suzanne McGee and Heidi Moore, "Women's rights and their money: a timeline from Cleopatra to Lilly Ledbetter," *The Guardian*, August 11, 2014, theguardian.com/money/us-money -blog/2014/aug/11/women-rights-money-timeline-history.

4. Cheryl Strayed, "The Ghost Ship That Didn't Carry Us," *Tiny Beautiful Things* (New York: Vintage Books, 2012), 248. Also posted on The Rumpus, April 21, 2011, therumpus.net/2011/04 /21/dear-sugar-the-rumpus-advice-column-71-the-ghost-ship-that -didnt-carry-us/.

Chapter Three: Lonely Is Love with Nowhere to Go

1. Nausicaa Renner, "How Social Media Shapes Our Identity," *New Yorker*, August 8, 2019, newyorker.com/books/under-review/how -social-media-shapes-our-identity.

2. Carrie Kholi-Murchison and Katie Horwitch, "Valuing Your Agency & Inclusive Actualization with khoLi," February 22, 2019, in *The WANTcast*, podcast, MP3 audio, 69:51, podcasts.apple .com/us/podcast/068-valuing-your-agency-inclusive-actualization -with/id1031793292?i=1000430404757.

Chapter Four: The Reimagination

1. Carl Rogers, "A theory of therapy, personality relationships as developed in the client-centered framework," in S. Koch, ed., *Psychology: A Study of a Science, Vol. 3: Formulations of the person and the social context* (New York: McGraw Hill, 2017).

2. Wendell Berry, "Do Not Be Ashamed," *New Collected Poems* (New York: Counterpoint, 2013), 82.

Chapter Six: Loosening the Grip

1. Gill Corkindale, "Overcoming Imposter Syndrome," *Harvard Business Review*, May 7, 2008, hbr.org/2008/05/overcoming-imposter-syndrome.

Chapter Seven: Internal GPS

1. Shaunacy Ferro, "The Science Behind Why People Hate the Word Moist," Mental Floss, June 11, 2015, mentalfloss.com/article/64984/science-behind-why-people-hate-word-moist.
2. Inge Bretherton, "The Origins of Attachment Theory: John Bowlby and Mary Ainsworth," *Developmental Psychology* 28, no. 5 (1992): 759–75, psychology.sunysb.edu/attachment/online/inge_origins.pdf.

Chapter Eight: Building Your Trust Fund

1. Merriam-Webster, s.v. "integrity," accessed April 14, 2023, merriam-webster.com/dictionary/integrity.
2. Abraham Hicks, "Prepaving Your Future Manifestations—Abraham Hicks," The Joy Within (website), January 21, 2020, thejoywithin.org/authors/abraham-hicks/prepaving-your-future-manifestations.

Chapter Nine: Emotionally Heavy Words

1. Lucy Maude Montgomery, *Anne of Green Gables* (Boston: L.C. Page & Co., 1908), chap. five, accessed December 31, 2022, cs.cmu.edu/~rgs/anneV.html#:~:text=%22Well%2C%20I%20don't,thistle%20or%20a%20skunk%20cabbage.

2. Carl Jung, "The Association Method," *American Journal of Psychology* 21, no. 2 (April 1910): 219–69, pure.mpg.de/pubman/item/item_2350960_4/component/file_2350959/Jung_1910_Association_Method.pdf.

3. *Merriam-Webster*, s.v. "hate," accessed December 31, 2022, merriam-webster.com/dictionary/hate.

4. Elie Wiesel, "One Must Not Forget," interview by Alvin P. Sanoff, *US News & World Report*, October 27, 1986.

5. Online Etymology Dictionary, s.v. "ugly," accessed December 31, 2022, etymonline.com/word/ugly.

Chapter Eleven: Overwhelm and the Art of the PFO

1. Online Etymology Dictionary, s.v. "overwhelm," accessed December 31, 2002, etymonline.com/word/overwhelm.

2. Gay Hendricks, *The Big Leap* (New York: HarperOne, 2010).

3. Benjamin Gardner, Phillippa Lally, and Jane Wardle, "Making health habitual: the psychology of 'habit-formation' and general practice," *British Journal of General Practice* 62, no. 605 (December 2012): 664–66, doi.org/10.3399/bjgp12X659466.

Chapter Thirteen: Becoming Other-People-Proof

1. Urban Dictionary, s.v. "talk blocking," accessed December 31, 2022, urbandictionary.com/define.php?term=Talk%20Blocking.
2. Amy Cuddy, "Your body language may shape who you are," TEDGlobal 2012, July 2012, video, 20:46, ted.com/talks/amy_cuddy_your_body_language_may_shape_who_you_are?language=en.
3. Amy J.C. Cuddy, S. Jack Schultz, and Nathan E. Fosse, "P-Curving a More Comprehensive Body of Research on Postural Feedback Reveals Clear Evidential Value for Power-Posing Effects: Reply to Simmons and Simonsohn (2017)," *Psychological Science* 29, no. 4 (2018): 656–66, doi.org/10.1177/0956797617746749.

Chapter Fifteen: One Day

1. Oprah Winfrey, "Oprah's Breakout Interview on 60 Minutes," interview by Mike Wallace, *60 Minutes*, December 14, 1986, video, 12:56, youtube.com/watch?v=n1NftcOkgic.

ABOUT THE AUTHOR

Katie Horwitch is a nationally recognized writer, speaker, mindset coach, and activist who has spent over a decade working to shift the cultural self-talk paradigm. She has spoken across the country about self-confidence, living fearlessly, and shifting the stories and habits that help shape our negative self-talk patterns. Praised by CNN as a "woman empowering others around the world," Katie is the founder of the multimedia platform WANT: Women Against Negative Talk and the host of *The WANTcast: The Women Against Negative Talk Podcast*. She's spoken at SXSW, and has been featured on media outlets like The Cut, Romper, mindbodygreen, and Livestrong. As a leadership and mindset coach, she has worked with Fortune 500 companies on reshaping their internal culture and coached executives on how to lead with integrity and purpose. She believes that shifting your self-talk is an essential part of shaping the world you actually want to live in—and is more important now than ever before. She lives in New York City with her husband and their dog-daughter, Frankie.

To learn more about Katie and her work, visit katiehorwitch.com and womenagainstnegativetalk.com. You can also find her on social media at @katiehorwitch.

ABOUT SOUNDS TRUE

Sounds True was founded in 1985 by Tami Simon with a clear mission: to disseminate spiritual wisdom. Since starting out as a project with one woman and her tape recorder, we have grown into a multimedia publishing company with a catalog of more than 3,000 titles by some of the leading teachers and visionaries of our time, and an ever-expanding family of beloved customers from across the world.

In more than three decades of evolution, Sounds True has maintained our focus on our overriding purpose and mission: to wake up the world. We offer books, audio programs, online learning experiences, and in-person events to support your personal growth and awakening, and to unlock our greatest human capacities to love and serve.

At SoundsTrue.com you'll find a wealth of resources to enrich your journey, including our weekly *Insights at the Edge* podcast, free downloads, and information about our nonprofit Sounds True Foundation, where we strive to remove financial barriers to the materials we publish through scholarships and donations worldwide.

To learn more, please visit SoundsTrue.com/freegifts or call us toll-free at 800.333.9185.

Together, we can wake up the world.